SO-AAD-038

everything's an argument

Second Edition

EVERYTHING'S AN argument

Andrea A. Lunsford
Stanford University

John J. Ruszkiewicz
University of Texas at Austin

BEDFORD/ST. MARTIN'S
BOSTON ■ NEW YORK

For Bedford/St. Martin's

Executive Editor: Marilyn Moller
Editorial Assistant: Priya Ratneshwar
Senior Production Editor: Michael Weber
Senior Production Supervisor: Joe Ford
Marketing Manager: Brian Wheel
Art Direction and Cover Design: Lucy Krikorian
Text Design: Anna George
Photo Research: Alice Lundoff
Cover Photos: Dilbert and Ruby slippers: Photofest; Breast Cancer Ribbon: Joel
   Gordon; Red Rose: Superstock
Composition: Monotype Composition Company, Inc.
Printing and Binding: R.R. Donnelley & Sons Company

President: Charles H. Christensen
Editorial Director: Joan E. Feinberg
Editor in Chief: Nancy Perry
Director of Marketing: Karen R. Melton
Director of Editing, Design, and Production: Marcia Cohen
Managing Editor: Erica T. Appel

Library of Congress Control Number: 00-103339

Copyright © 2001 by Bedford/St. Martin's

All rights reserved. No part of this book may be reproduced, stored in a retrieval
system, or transmitted in any form or by any means, electronic, mechanical, photo-
copying, recording, or otherwise, except as may be expressly permitted by the
applicable copyright statutes or in writing by the Publisher.

Manufactured in the United States of America.
6 5 4 3 2 1
f e d c b a

For information, write:
Bedford/St. Martin's
75 Arlington Street
Boston, MA 02116   (617-399-4000)

ISBN: 0-312-25039-8

ACKNOWLEDGMENTS

*Acknowledgments and copyrights are at the back of the book on page 379, which constitutes an
extension of the copyright page. It is a violation of the law to reproduce these selections by any
means whatsoever without the written permission of the copyright holder.*

PREFACE

The first edition of *Everything's an Argument* was a labor of love, an introduction to rhetoric drawn directly from our experiences teaching persuasive writing. Clearly, the book struck a chord with many students and instructors, and it immediately became the most widely taught brief guide to argument. So we are pleased now to offer a second edition, updated to address important new concerns in composition classrooms today.

The title of this text sums up two key assumptions we share. First, language provides the most powerful means we have of understanding the world and of using that understanding to help shape our lives. Second, all language—including the language of visual images or of symbol systems other than writing—is persuasive, pointing in a direction and asking for response. From the cover of *Newsweek* to the pink ribbon commemorating those who have died of breast cancer, from the Nike swoosh to James Bond's BMW, we are surrounded by texts that beckon, that aim to persuade. In short, we walk, talk, and breathe persuasion very much as we breathe the air: ***everything* is an argument.**

For twenty-some years now, we have spent much time illustrating for our students the ways argument pervades our lives and thinking about how best to teach the arts and crafts of persuasion. We have also examined various argument textbooks carefully and have asked our students to work with many of them. As the influence of visual and electronic media has become everywhere more pervasive, we've looked for a text that would show students, directly and briefly, that "everything is an argument." We wanted a book that would focus less on complicated terminology and structures and more on concrete examples and that would engage students in understanding, criticizing, and—most important—participating in arguments. These wishes crystallized for us during some intense discussions with students who told us, frankly, that they were unhappy with the textbooks we had been asking them to use—and in particular, that they disliked books that have more detail than they need and that focus on topics that are too broad or distant from students' own lives.

With their words ringing in our ears, we began work on *Everything's an Argument*. We've aimed to present argument as something that's as natural and everyday as an old pair of Levi's, as something we do almost from the moment we are born (in fact, an infant's first cry is as poignant a claim as we can imagine), and thus as something worthy of careful attention and practice. In pursuing this goal, **we've tried to use ordinary language whenever possible and to keep our use of specialized terminology to a minimum.** But we also see argument—and want students to see it—as a craft both delicate and powerful. So we have written *Everything's an Argument* to be itself an argument for argument, with a voice that aims to appeal to readers cordially but that doesn't hesitate to make demands on them when appropriate.

We've tried to pay attention to the critical *reading* of arguments (analysis) and the actual *writing* of arguments (production). And we have tried to demonstrate both with lively—and realistic—examples, on the principle that the best way to appreciate an argument may be to see it in action.

We have tried as well to broaden the context of argument to include not only visual media but also the public spaces and electronic environments that students now inhabit so much of the time.

Most of all, we have tried to be brief. Long-winded discussions and explanations can do more to confuse than clarify, more to *dis*suade than *per*suade. Students have told us they want basic information about argument, concrete examples of how persuasion works, and then lots of space to maneuver in as they try producing arguments of their own. We hope that this book, like most effective arguments, gets to the heart of the matter quickly enough to sustain interest and provoke dialogue.

Highlights

- A new approach, going beyond pro/con and showing that argument is everywhere—in essays, poems, advertisements, cartoons, posters, prayers, Web sites, and other electronic environments.

- Student-friendly, with explanations in simple, everyday language, many brief examples, and a minimum of technical terminology.

- Full chapters on visual argument, argument in electronic environments, spoken argument, and humor in argument.

- Ten sample essays, including five by student writers, annotated to show rhetorical features.
- Extensive coverage of using sources in argument, with full chapters on assessing and using sources, documenting sources in MLA and APA styles, and intellectual property.

What's New

- A new chapter on oral arguments, since students now are routinely asked to present their ideas to live audiences, often with the aid of presentation software.
- A significantly expanded chapter on visual argument to give students much more specific advice about how they can use images and design elements in their own writing.
- Boxes offering advice about argument across cultures.
- A new design. Taking our own principles of visual argument to heart, we have redesigned *Everything's an Argument* to make its key features more accessible—and, we think, more appealing visually.

Please note: For instructors wanting more readings, we now offer *Everything's an Argument, with Readings,* a version of this book with a full anthology.

Acknowledgments

We owe a debt of gratitude to many people for making possible *Everything's an Argument* possible. Our first thanks must go to the students we have taught in our writing courses for more than two decades, particularly the first-year students at Ohio State University and the University of Texas at Austin. Almost every chapter in this book has been informed by a classroom encounter with a student whose shrewd observation or piercing question sent an ambitious lesson plan spiraling to the ground. (Anyone who has tried to teach claims and warrants on the fly to skeptical first-year students will surely appreciate why we have qualified our claims in the Toulmin chapter so carefully.) But students have also provided the motive for writing this book. More than ever, tudents need to know how to read and write arguments effectively if they are to secure a place in a world growing ever smaller and more rhetorically demanding.

After our students, our editor at Bedford/St. Martin's, Marilyn Moller, deserves the most sustained applause for bringing *Everything's an Argument* into a second edition. We're still not entirely sure how she persuaded us to do the book in the first place, but we know it was Marilyn who nurtured and sustained the project and recognized, earlier and perhaps more clearly than we did, its full potential. Her creativity knows no bounds, and we are grateful for her intelligence, good will, and common sense. *Everything's an Argument* would not exist without her.

We are similarly grateful to others at Bedford/St. Martin's who contributed their talents to our book, especially Michael Weber, Priya Ratneshwar, Lucy Krikorian, Joe Ford, and especially Anna George, whose design contributes so much to the book's appeal and accessibility. Thanks also to Karen Melton and Brian Wheel for their superb marketing. And of course we thank Joan Feinberg and Chuck Christensen — for welcoming us into their lives and for their support for this book.

And we thank those colleagues who reviewed *Everything's an Argument* for their astute comments and suggestions: Jo-Anne Andre, University of Calgary; Diane Belcher, Ohio State University; Stuart C. Brown, New Mexico State University; Lauren Sewell Coulter, University of Tennessee at Chattanooga; Jane Mathison Fife, East Central University; Elizabeth Anne Hull, William Rainey Harper College; Amy Muse, University of Minnesota; Julie Price, University of Illinois at Urbana-Champaign; Tammy Price, University of Minnesota; Andrea Sanders, Walters State Community College; Kathy Overhulse Smith, Indiana University Bloomington; Lolly Smith, Everett Community College; and Josephine Koster Tarvers, Winthrop University.

Thanks, too, to Ben Feigert who prepared most of the exercises for *Everything's an Argument*. Ben is the most enthusiastic teacher of Toulmin argument we know. He rocks. So do the students whose fine argumentative essays appear in our chapters.

We hope that *Everything's an Argument* continues to respond to what students and instructors have told us they want and need. And we hope readers of this text will let us know how we've done: please share your opinions and suggestions with us at <www.bedfordstmartins.com/everythingsanargument>.

Andrea A. Lunsford
John J. Ruszkiewicz

CONTENTS

PART 3   WRITING ARGUMENTS   89

everything's an argument

PART 1

INTRODUCING argument

chapter one

Everything Is an Argument

"Best Ribs in Texas!" a sign in front of a restaurant promises.

A professor interrupts a lecture to urge her students to spend less time on the Internet and more in the company of thick, old books.

Claiming to have been a good boy for most of the year, a youngster asks Santa Claus for a bicycle with lots of gears.

A senator argues with a C-SPAN caller that members of Congress need a raise because most political perks have disappeared and it is expensive to maintain a home in Washington, D.C.

A nurse assures a patient eyeing an approaching needle, "This won't hurt one bit."

A sports columnist blasts a football coach for passing on fourth down and two in a close game—even though the play produces a touchdown.

A traffic sign orders drivers to 🛑.

"Please let me make it through exams!" a student silently prays.

■ ■ ■

An argument can be any text—whether written, spoken, or visual—that expresses a point of view. When you write an argument, you try to influence the opinions of readers—or of yourself. Sometimes arguments can be aggressive, composed deliberately to change what readers believe, think, or do. At other times your goals may be more subtle, and your writing may be designed to convince yourself or others that specific facts are reliable or that certain views should be considered or at least tolerated.

In fact, some theorists claim that *every* text is an argument, designed to influence readers. For example, a poem that observes what little girls do in church may indirectly critique the role religion plays in women's lives, for good or ill:

> **I worry for the girls.**
> **I once had braids,**
> **and wore lace that made me suffer.**
> **I had not yet done the things**
> **that would need forgiving.**
> **   –Kathleen Norris, "Little Girls in Church"**

To take another example, observations about family life among the poor in India may suddenly illuminate the writer's life and the reader's experience, forcing comparisons that quietly argue for change:

> **I have learned from Jagat and his family a kind of commitment, a form of friendship that is not always available in the West, where we have become cynical and instrumental in so many of our relationships to others.**
> **   –Jeremy Seabrook, "Family Values"**

Even humor makes an argument when it causes readers to become aware—through bursts of laughter or just a faint smile—of the way things are and how they might be different:

There is a serious question in my mind about whether guys actually *have* deep innermost feelings, unless you count, for example, loyalty to the Detroit Tigers, or fear of bridal showers.

–Dave Barry, "Guys vs. Men"

More obvious as arguments are pieces that make a claim and present evidence to support it. Such writing often moves readers to recognize problems and to consider solutions. Suasion of this kind is usually easy to recognize:

Discrimination against Hispanics, or any other group, should be fought and there are laws and a massive apparatus to do so. But the way to eliminate such discrimination is not to classify all Hispanics as victims.

–Linda Chavez, "Towards a New Politics of Hispanic Assimilation"

The real cultural fear is not that women are becoming too Victorian but that they are becoming too damn aggressive—in and out of bed.

–Susan Faludi, "Whose Hype?"

Resistance to science is born of fear. Fear, in turn, is bred by ignorance. And it is ignorance that is our deepest malady.

–J. Michael Bishop, "Enemies of Promise"

ARGUMENT ISN'T JUST ABOUT WINNING

If in some ways all language has an "argumentative edge" that aims to make a point (after all, even saying "good morning" acknowledges that someone deserves a greeting and asks that you be acknowledged in return), not all language use aims to win out over others. In contrast to the traditional concept of "agonistic" or combative argument, communication theorists such as Sonja Foss and Josina Makau describe an invitational argument, which aims not to win over another person or group but to invite others to enter a space of mutual regard and exploration. In fact, as you'll see, writers and speakers have as many purposes for arguing as for using language, including—in addition to winning—to inform, to convince, to explore, to make decisions, even to meditate or pray.

Of course, many arguments *are* aimed at winning. Such is the traditional purpose of much writing and speaking in the political arena, in the business world, and in the law courts. Two candidates for office, for example, try to win out over each other in appealing for votes; the makers of one soft drink try to outsell their competitors by appealing to public tastes; and two lawyers try to defeat each other in pleading to a judge and jury. In your college writing, you may be also called on to make an argument that appeals to a "judge" and/or "jury" (your teacher and classmates). You might, for instance, argue that doctor-assisted suicide is a moral and legal right. In doing so, you may need to defeat your unseen opponents—those who oppose doctor-assisted suicide.

At this point, it may be helpful to acknowledge a common academic distinction between argument and persuasion. In this view, the point of argument is to discover some version of the truth, using evidence and reasons. Argument of this sort leads audiences toward conviction, an agreement that a claim is true or reasonable, or that a course of action is desirable. The aim of persuasion is to change a point of view, or to move others from conviction to action. In other words, writers or speakers argue to find some truth; they persuade when they think they already know it.

Argument (discover a truth) ⟶ conviction

Persuasion (know a truth) ⟶ action

In practice, this distinction between argument and persuasion can be hard to sustain. It is unnatural for writers or readers to imagine their minds divided between a part that pursues truth and a part that seeks to persuade. It is not surprising that people tend to admire those public figures whose lives embody the very principles they reasonably advocate; for example, Gandhi, Eleanor Roosevelt, Martin Luther King Jr., Margaret Thatcher. They move others to pursue the truths they have arrived at themselves.

And yet, you may want to reserve the term *persuasion* for writing that is aggressively designed to change opinions through the use of both reason and other appropriate techniques. For writing that sets out to persuade at all costs, abandoning reason, fairness, and truth altogether, the term *propaganda,* with all its negative connotations, seems to fit. Some would suggest that *advertising* often works just as well.

But, as we have already suggested, arguing isn't always about winning or even about changing others' views. In addition to invitational argument, another school of argument—called Rogerian argument, after the psychotherapist Carl Rogers—is based on finding common ground and establishing trust among those who disagree about issues, and on approaching audiences in nonthreatening ways. Writers who follow Rogerian approaches seek to understand the perspectives of those with whom they disagree, looking for "both/and" or "win/win" solutions (rather than "either/or" or "win/lose" ones) whenever possible. Much successful argument today follows such principles, consciously or not.

Some other purposes or goals of argument are worth considering in more detail.

Arguments to Inform

You may want or need to argue with friends or colleagues over the merits of different academic majors. But your purpose in doing so may well be to inform and to be informed, for only in such detailed arguments can you come to the best choice. Consider how Joan Didion uses argument to inform readers about the artist Georgia O'Keeffe:

> This is a woman who in 1939 could advise her admirers that they were missing her point, that their appreciation of her famous flowers was merely sentimental. "When I paint a red hill," she observed coolly in the catalogue for an exhibition that year, "you say it is too bad that I don't always paint flowers. A flower touches almost everyone's heart. A red hill doesn't touch everyone's heart."
>
> –Joan Didion, "Georgia O'Keeffe"

By giving specific information about O'Keeffe and her own ideas about her art, this passage argues that readers should pay close attention to the work of this artist.

Less subtle and more common as informative arguments are political posters featuring the smiling faces of candidates and the offices they are seeking: "Paretti 2000; Slattery for County Judge." Of course, these visual texts are usually also aimed at winning out over an unmentioned opponent. But on the surface at least, they announce who is running for a specific office.

Arguments to Convince

If you are writing a report that attempts to identify the causes of changes in global temperatures, you would likely be trying not to conquer opponents but to satisfy readers that you've thoroughly examined those causes and that they merit serious attention. As a form of writing, reports typically aim to persuade readers rather than win out over opponents. Yet the presence of those who might disagree is always implied, and it shapes a writer's strategies. In the following passage, for example, Paul Osterman argues to convince readers of the urgency surrounding jobs for all citizens:

> Among employed 29- to 31-year-old high school graduates who did not go to college, more than 30 percent had not been in their position for even a year. Another 12 percent had only one year of tenure. The pattern was much the same for women who had remained in the labor force for the four years prior to the survey. These are adults who, for a variety of reasons—a lack of skills, training, or disposition— have not managed to secure "adult" jobs.
>
> —Paul Osterman, "Getting Started"

Osterman uses facts to report a seemingly objective conclusion about the stability of employment among certain groups, but he is also arguing against those who find that the current job situation is tolerable and not worthy of concern or action.

Arguments to Explore

Many important subjects call for arguments that take the form of exploration, either on your own or with others. If there's an "opponent" in such a situation at all (often there is *not*), it is likely the status quo or a current trend that—for one reason or another—is puzzling. Exploratory arguments may be deeply personal, such as E. B. White's often-reprinted essay "Once More to the Lake." Or the exploration may be aimed at solving serious problems in society. William F. Buckley Jr. opens just such an argument with a frank description of a situation he finds troubling:

> This is an exploratory column, its purpose to encourage thought on a question that badly needs thinking about.
>
> *The Problem:* The birth every year of one million babies to unwed mothers.
>
> *The Consequence:* One million children who, on reaching the age of 13, tend to run into difficulties. The statistics tell us that a child raised by a single parent is likelier by a factor of 600 per cent to commit crimes, consume drugs, quit school, and bear, or sire, children out of wedlock. Assume—if only to be hopeful—that the problems diminish after age 19; we are still left with six million teenagers who are a heavy social burden, as also, of course, a burden to themselves.
>
> —William F. Buckley Jr., "Should There Be a Law?"

Perhaps the essential argument in any such piece is the writer's assertion that a problem exists and that the writer or reader needs to solve it. Some exploratory pieces present and defend solutions. Others remain open-ended, as is the case with Buckley's column, which concludes with an unusually direct appeal to readers:

> All these are designed as open questions, to flush out thought. Although commentary can't be acknowledged, I'd welcome having it, directed to me at *National Review.*

Arguments to Make Decisions

Closely allied to argument that explores is that which aims at making good, sound decisions. In fact, the result of your exploratory arguments may be to argue for a particular decision, whether that decision relates to the best computer for you to buy or to the "right" person for you to choose as your life partner. In the following paragraph from a novel, a minister's young daughter uses argument as a way to make her own personal decision not to undergo baptism:

> I bit my fingernails whenever I thought about baptism; the subject brought out a deep-rooted balkiness in me. Ever since I could remember, Matthew and I had made a game of dispelling the mysteries of worship with a gleeful secular eye: we knew how the bread and wine were prepared for Communion, and where Daddy bought his robes (Ekhardt Brothers, in North Philadelphia, makers also of robes for choirs, academicians, and judges). Yet there was an unassailable magic about an act as public and dramatic as baptism. I felt toward it the slightly exasperated awe a stagehand might feel on realizing that although he can identify with professional exactitude the minutest components of a show, there is still something indefinable in the power that makes it a cohesive whole. Though I could not have put it into words, I believed that the decision to make a frightening and embarrassing backward plunge into a pool of sanctified water meant that one had received a summons to Christianity as unmistakable as the blare of an automobile horn. I believed this with the same fervor with which, already, I believed in the power of romance, especially in the miraculous efficacy of a lover's first kiss. I had never been kissed by a lover, nor had I heard the call to baptism.
>
> —Andrea Lee, *Sarah Phillips*

Arguments to Meditate or Pray

Sometimes arguments can take the form of intense meditations on a theme, or of prayer. In such cases, the writer or speaker is most often hoping to transform something in him- or herself or to reach a state of equilibrium or peace of mind. If you know a familiar prayer or mantra, think for a moment of what it "argues" for and of how it uses quiet meditation to accomplish that goal. However, such meditations do not have to be formal prayers. Look, for example, at the ways in which Michael Lassell's poetry uses a kind of meditative language to reach understanding for himself and to evoke meditative thought in others:

> Feel how it feels to
> hold a man in your arms
> whose arms are used to holding men.
> Offer God anything to bring your brother back.
> Know you have nothing God could possibly want.
> Curse God, but do not
> abandon Him.
> —Michael Lassell, "How to Watch Your Brother Die"

Another sort of meditative argument can be found in the stained-glass windows of churches and other public buildings. Dazzled by a spectacle of light, people pause to consider a window's message longer than they might were the same idea conveyed on paper. The window engages viewers with a power not unlike that of poetry.

As all these examples suggest, the effectiveness of argument depends not only on the purposes of the writer but also on the context surrounding the plea and the people it seeks most directly to reach. Though we'll examine arguments of all types in this book, we'll focus chiefly on the kinds made in professional and academic situations.

OCCASIONS FOR ARGUMENT

Another way of thinking about arguments is to consider the public occasions that call for them. In an ancient textbook of rhetoric, or the art of persuasion, the philosopher Aristotle provides an elegant scheme for classifying the purposes of arguments, one based on issues of time—past, future, and present. His formula is easy to remember and helpful in suggesting strategies for making convincing cases. But since all classifications overlap with others to a certain extent, don't be surprised to encounter many arguments that span more than one category—arguments about the past with implications for the future, arguments about the future with bearings on the present, and so on.

Arguments about the Past

Debates about what has happened in the past are called forensic arguments; such controversies are common in business, government, and academia. For example, in many criminal and civil cases, lawyers interrogate witnesses to establish exactly what happened at an earlier time: *Did the defendant sexually harass her employee? Did the company deliberately ignore evidence that its product was deficient? Was the contract properly enforced?*

The contentious nature of some forensic arguments is evident in this brief exchange between a defender of modern technology (Kevin Kelly) and an opponent (Kirkpatrick Sale):

> **KK: OK, then you tell me. What was the effect of printing technology? Did the invention of printing just allow us to make more books? Or did it allow new and different kinds of books to be written? What did it do? It did both.**
>
> **KS: That wasn't mass society back then, but what it eventually achieved was a vast increase in the number of books produced; and it vastly decreased forests in Europe so as to produce them.**
>
> **KK: I don't think so. The forests of Europe were not cut down to create books for Europe.**
>
> —Kevin Kelly, "Interview with the Luddite"

You can probably imagine how these claims and counterclaims will blossom, each speaker looking for evidence in the past to justify his conclusion. Obviously, then, forensic arguments rely on evidence and testimony to re-create what can be known about events that have already occurred.

Forensic arguments also rely heavily on precedents—actions or decisions in the past that influence policies or decisions in the present—and on analyses of cause and effect. Consider the ongoing controversy over Christopher Columbus: Are his expeditions to the Americas events worth celebrating, or are they unhappy chapters in human history? No simple exchange of evidence will suffice to still this debate; the effects of Columbus's actions beginning in 1492 may be studied and debated for the next five hundred years. As you might suspect from this case, arguments about history are typically forensic.

Forensic cases may also be arguments about character, such as when someone's reputation is studied in a historical context to enrich current perspectives on the person. Allusions to the past can make present arguments more vivid, as in the following text about Ward Connerly, head of an organization that aims to dismantle affirmative action programs:

> Despite the fact that Connerly's message seems clearly opposed to the Civil Rights Movement, some people are fond of pointing out that the man is black. But as far as politics goes, that is irrelevant. Before black suffrage, there were African Americans who publicly argued against their own right to vote.
> —Carl Villarreal, "Connerly Is an Enemy of Civil Rights"

Such writing can be exploratory and open-ended, the point of argument being to enhance and sharpen knowledge, not just to generate heat or score points.

Arguments about the Future

Debates about the future are a form of deliberative argument. Legislatures, congresses, and parliaments are called deliberative bodies because they establish policies for the future: *Should Social Security be privatized? Should the United States build a defense against ballistic missiles?*

Because what has happened in the past influences the future, deliberative judgments often rely on prior forensic arguments. Thus, deliberative arguments often draw on evidence and testimony, as in this passage:

> The labor market is sending a clear signal. While the American way of moving youngsters from high school to the labor market may be imperfect, the chief problem is that, for many, even getting a job no longer guarantees a decent standard of living. More than ever, getting ahead, or even keeping up, means staying in school longer.
> —Paul Osterman, "Getting Started"

But since no one has a blueprint for what is to come, deliberative arguments also advance by means of projections, extrapolations, and reasoned guesses — *if X is true, Y may be true; if X happens, so may Y; if X continues, then Y may occur:*

> If we liberate entrepreneurs and make it relatively easy for them to discover and invent our new world, we will be rearing a generation that increases our wealth and improves our lives to a degree that we can now barely imagine.
> —Newt Gingrich, "America and the Third Wave Information Age"

Arguments about the Present

Arguments about the present are often arguments about contemporary values—the ethical premises and assumptions that are widely held (or contested) within a society. Sometimes called epideictic arguments or ceremonial arguments because they tend to be heard at public occasions, they include inaugural addresses, sermons, eulogies, graduation speeches, and civic remarks of all kinds. Ceremonial arguments can be passionate and eloquent, rich in anecdotes and examples. Martin Luther King Jr. was a master of ceremonial discourse, and he was particularly adept at finding affirmation in the depths of despair:

> Three nights later, our home was bombed. Strangely enough, I accepted the word of the bombing calmly. My experience with God had given me a new strength and trust. I know now that God is able to give us the interior resources to face the storms and problems of life.
> —Martin Luther King Jr., "Our God Is Able"

King argues here that the arbiter of good and evil in society is, ultimately, God. But not all ceremonial arguments reach quite so far.

More typical are values arguments that explore contemporary culture, praising what is admirable and blaming what is not. Sven Birkerts, for example, indirectly frames an argument against the current fascination with computers by posing some questions about contemporary values:

> [W]e may choose to become the technicians of our auxiliary brains, mastering not the information but the retrieval and referencing functions. At a certain point, then, we could become the evolutionary opposites of our forebears, who, lacking external technology, committed everything to memory. If this were to happen, what would be the status of knowing, of being educated? The leader of the electronic tribe would not be the person who knew the most, but the one who could exercise the widest range of technological functions. What, I hesitate to ask, would become of the already antiquated notion of wisdom?
> –Sven Birkerts, "Perseus Unbound"

By establishing and reinforcing common values in this way, ceremonial arguments can even be the means by which groups and coalitions form.

KINDS OF ARGUMENT

Yet another way of categorizing arguments is to consider their status or stasis—that is, the kinds of issues they address. This categorization system is called stasis theory. In ancient Greek and Roman civilizations, rhetoricians defined a series of questions by which to examine legal cases. The questions would be posed in sequence, since each depended on the question(s) preceding it. Together, the questions helped determine the point of contention in an argument, the place where disputants could focus their energy. A modern version of those questions might look like the following:

- Did something happen?
- What is its nature?
- What is its quality?
- What actions should be taken?

Here's how the questions might be used to explore a "crime."

Did Something Happen?

Yes. A young man kissed a young woman against her will. The act was witnessed by a teacher and friends and acquaintances of both parties. The facts suggest clearly that something happened.

What Is Its Nature?

The act might be construed as "sexual harassment," defined as the imposition of unwanted or unsolicited sexual attention or activity on a person. The young man kissed the young woman on the lips. Kissing people who aren't relatives on the lips is generally considered a sexual activity. The young woman did not want to be kissed and complained to her teacher. The young man's act meets the definition of "sexual harassment."

What Is Its Quality?

Both the young man and young woman involved in the action are six years old. They were playing in a schoolyard. The boy didn't realize that kissing girls against their will was a violation of school policy; school sexual harassment policies had not in the past been enforced against first-graders. Most people don't regard six-year-olds as sexually culpable. Moreover, the girl wants to play with the boy again and apparently doesn't resent his action.

What Actions Should Be Taken?

> The case has raised a ruckus among parents, the general public, and some feminists and anti-feminists. The consensus seems to be that the school overreached in seeking to brand the boy a sexual harasser. Yet it is important that the issue of sexual harassment not be dismissed as trivial. Consequently, the boy should probably be warned not to kiss little girls against their will. The teachers should be warned not to make federal cases out of schoolyard spats.

As you can see, each of the stasis questions explores different aspects of a problem and uses different evidence or techniques to reach conclusions. Stasis theory can be used to understand some common types of arguments.

Arguments of Fact — Did Something Happen?

An argument of fact usually involves a statement that can be proved or disproved with specific evidence or testimony. Although relatively simple to define, such arguments are often quite subtle, involving layers of complexity not apparent when the question is initially posed.

For example, the question of global warming—*Is it really occurring?*—would seem relatively easy to settle. Either scientific data prove that global temperatures are increasing as a result of human activity, or they don't. But to settle the matter, writers and readers would first have to agree on a number of points, each of which would have to be examined and debated: *What constitutes warming? How will global warming be measured? Over what period of time? Are any current temperature deviations unprecedented? How can one be certain that deviations are attributable to human action?*

Nevertheless, questions of this sort can be disputed primarily on the facts, complicated and contentious as they may be. (For more on arguments based on facts, see Chapter 7.)

Arguments of Definition — What Is the Nature of the Thing?

Just as contentious as arguments based on facts are questions of definition. An argument of definition often involves determining whether one known object or action belongs in a second—and more highly contested—category. One of the most hotly debated issues in American life today involves a question of definition: *Is a human fetus a human being?* If one argues that it is, then a second issue of definition arises: *Is abortion murder?*

As you can see, issues of definition can have mighty consequences—and decades of debate may leave the matter unresolved.

Consider Hector St. Jean de Crèvecoeur's famous response to the definitional question he posed to himself: *What is an American?* Today, his extended, idealized, and noticeably gendered reply would likely prompt disputes and objections among the many groups that bristle at the prospect of their assimilation into an American mainstream:

> He becomes an American by being received in the broad lap of our great *Alma Mater.* Here individuals of all nations are melted into a new race of men, whose labors and posterity will one day cause great changes in the world.
>
> —Hector St. Jean de Crèvecoeur, "What Is an American?"

Bob Costas, eulogizing Mickey Mantle, a great baseball player who had many human faults, advances his assessment by means of an important definitional distinction:

> In the last year, Mickey Mantle, always so hard upon himself, finally came to accept and appreciate the distinction between a role model and a hero. The first he often was not, the second he always will be.
>
> —Bob Costas, "Eulogy for Mickey Mantle"

But arguments of definition can be less weighty than these, though still hotly contested: *Is bowling a sport? Is Madonna an artist? Is ketchup a vegetable?* To argue such cases, one would first have to put forth definitions, and then those definitions would have to become the foci of debates themselves. (For more about arguments of definition, see Chapter 9.)

Arguments of Evaluation—What Is the Quality of the Thing?

Arguments of definition lead naturally into arguments of quality—that is, to questions about quality. Most auto enthusiasts, for example, would not be content merely to inquire whether the Corvette is a sports car. They'd prefer to argue whether it is a *good* sports car or a *better* sports car than, say, the Viper. Or they might wish to assert that it is the *best* sports car in the world, perhaps qualifying their claim with the caveat *for the price.* Arguments of evaluation are so common that writers sometimes take them for granted, ignoring their complexity and importance in establishing people's values and priorities.

Consider how Rosa Parks assesses Martin Luther King Jr. in the following passage. Though she seems to be defining the concept of "leader," she is measuring King against criteria she has set for "*true* leader," an important distinction:

> Dr. King was a true leader. I never sensed fear in him. I just felt he knew what had to be done and took the leading role without regard to consequences. I knew he was destined to do great things. He had an elegance about him and a speaking style that let you know where you stood and inspired you to do the best you could. He truly is a role model for us all. The sacrifice of his life should never be forgotten, and his dream must live on.
>
> —Rosa Parks, "Role Models"

Parks's comments represent a type of informal evaluation that is common in ceremonial arguments; because King is so well known, she doesn't have to burnish every claim with specific evidence. (See p. 13 for more on ceremonial arguments.) In contrast, Peggy Noonan in praising Ronald Reagan makes quite explicit the connections between her claim and the evidence:

> *He was right.* He said the Soviet Union was an evil empire, and it was; he said history would consign it to the ash heap, and it did. Thirty-one years ago . . . he said: high taxes are bad, heavy regulation is bad, bureaucracies cause more ills than they cure and government is not necessarily your friend. It could have been said by half the congressional candidates of 1994—and was.

An argument of evaluation advances by presenting criteria and then measuring individual people, ideas, or things against those standards. Both the standards and the measurement can be explored argumentatively. And that's an important way to think of arguments—as ways to expand what is known, not just to settle differences. (For more about arguments of evaluation, see Chapter 10.)

Proposal Arguments — What Actions Should Be Taken?

Arguments may lead to proposals for action when writers have succeeded in presenting problems in such a compelling way that readers ask: *What can we do?* A proposal argument often begins with the presentation of research to document existing conditions. Knowing and explaining the status quo enable writers to explore appropriate and viable alternatives and then to recommend one preferable course of action. David Thomas, for example, in arguing that reform is needed in the education of young boys, cites evidence that leads him to diagnose what he regards as a significant problem:

> Do we, however, make the best of what nature has provided when the time comes to educate our young? Over the last few years, nationwide exam results have shown an increasing gap between the performances of girls and boys, in the girls' favor. Many more boys than girls leave school without any form of qualification.
>
> —David Thomas, "The Mind of Man"

CULTURAL CONTEXTS FOR ARGUMENT

If you want to communicate effectively with people across cultures, then you need to try to learn something about the norms in those cultures—and to be aware of the norms guiding your own behavior.

- Be aware of the assumptions that guide your own customary ways of arguing a point. Remember that most of us tend to see our own way as the "normal" or "right" way to do things. Such assumptions guide your thinking and your judgments about what counts—and what "works"—in an argument.

- Keep in mind that if your own ways seem inherently right, then even without thinking about it you may assume that other ways are somehow less than right. Such thinking makes it hard to communicate effectively across cultures.

- Remember that ways of arguing are influenced by cultural contexts and that they differ widely across cultures. Pay attention to the ways people from cultures other than your own argue, and be flexible and open to the many ways of thinking you will no doubt encounter.

- Respect the differences among individuals within a given culture; don't expect that every member of a community behaves—or argues—in just the same way.

The best advice, then, might be *don't assume*. Just because you think a navy blazer and a knee-length skirt "argues" that you should be taken seriously as a job candidate at a multinational corporation, such dress may be perceived differently in other settings. And if in an interview a candidate does not look you in the eye, don't assume that this reflects any lack of confidence or respect; he or she may intend it as a sign of politeness.

Where a need for change is already obvious, writers may spend most of their energies describing and defending the solution. John Henry Newman, for example, in proposing a new form of liberal education in the nineteenth century, enumerates the benefits it will bring to society:

> [A] university education is the great ordinary means to a great but ordinary end; it aims at raising the intellectual tone of society, at cultivating the public mind, at purifying the national taste, at supplying true principles to popular enthusiasm and fixed aims to popular aspiration, at giving enlargement and sobriety to the ideas of the age, at facilitating the exercise of political power, and refining the intercourse of private life.
>
> –John Henry Newman, *The Idea of a University*

Americans in particular tend to see the world in terms of problems and solutions; indeed, Americans expect that any difficulty can be overcome by the proper infusion of technology and money. So proposal arguments seem especially appealing, even when quick-fix attitudes may themselves constitute a problem. (For more about proposal arguments, see Chapter 12.)

IS EVERYTHING AN ARGUMENT?

In a world where argument is as abundant as fast food, everyone has a role to play in shaping and responding to arguments. Debate and discussion are, after all, key components of the never-ending conversation about our lives and the world that is sometimes called academic inquiry. Its standards are rigorous: take no claim at face value, examine all evidence thoroughly, and study the implications of your own and others' beliefs. Developing an inquiring turn of mind like this can serve you well now and into the future. It might even lead you to wonder, with healthy suspicion, whether *everything* really is an argument.

RESPOND●

1. Can an argument really be any text that expresses a point of view? What kinds of arguments—if any—might be made about the following items?

   the embossed leather cover of a prayer book

   a newspaper masthead

a New York Yankees hat

the label on a best-selling rap CD

the health warning on a bag of no-fat potato chips

a belated birthday card

the nutrition label on a tub of margarine

the cover of a romance novel

a peace emblem worn on a chain

a Rolex watch

2. Decide whether each of the following items is an example of *argument, persuasion,* or *propaganda.* Be prepared to explain your categorization. Some of the items might be difficult to classify.

a proof in a geometry textbook

a flag burned at a protest rally

a U.S. president's State of the Union address

a sermon on the biblical Book of Job

a lawyer's opening statement at a jury trial

a movie by American film director Oliver Stone

the ABC television show *Politically Incorrect*

a lecture on race in an anthropology class

a marriage proposal

an environmental ad by a chemical company

3. Write short paragraphs describing times in the recent past when you've used language to inform, to convince, to explore, to make decisions, and to meditate or pray (write a paragraph for each of these purposes). Then decide whether each paragraph describes an act of argument, persuasion, or both, and offer some reasons in defense of your decisions.

In class, trade paragraphs with a partner, and decide whether his or her descriptions accurately fit the categories to which they've been assigned. If they do not, work with your partner to figure out why. Is the problem with the descriptions? The categories? Both? Neither?

4. In a recent newspaper or periodical, find three editorials—one that makes a ceremonial argument, one a deliberative argument, and one a forensic argument. Analyze the arguments by asking these questions: Who is arguing? What purposes are the writers trying to achieve? To whom are they directing their arguments?

Then consider whether the arguments' purposes have been achieved in each case. If they have, offer some reasons for the arguments' success.

5. If everything really is an argument, then one should be able to read poetry through the same lens, and with the same methods, as one reads more obviously argumentative writing. This means considering the occasions, purposes, and stasis of the poem—a process that may seem odd but that might reveal some interesting results.

   Find a poem that you like and that seems completely *nonargumentative* (you might even pick one that you have written). Then read it as a rhetorician, paying attention to the issues in this chapter, searching for claims, thinking about audience, and imagining occasions and purposes. Write a few paragraphs explaining why the poem is an argument.

   Next, for balance (and to make this a good argument), write a paragraph or two explaining why the poem is *not* an argument. Make sure you give good reasons for your position. Which of the two positions is more persuasive? Is there a middle ground—that is, a way of thinking about the poem that enables it both to be an argument and *not to be* an argument?

chapter two

Reading and Writing Arguments

"And ain't I a woman?" former slave Sojourner Truth is reported to have asked over and over again in a short speech arguing for women's rights. Her refrain punctuates descriptions of the difficult life she has endured, making it clear that women can do anything men can—and likely more:

Look at me! Look at my arm! I have ploughed and planted, and gathered into barns, and no man could head me. And ain't I a woman? . . . I have borne thirteen children, and seen most all sold off to slavery, and when I cried out with my mother's grief, none but Jesus heard me. And ain't I a woman?

— Sojourner Truth,
"Ain't I a Woman?"

To attribute the power of this passage to some particular method of argumentation would be extremely simplistic. Great arguments often arise from situations that no one can predict or control. Sojourner Truth's rhetoric soars because of her vivid images, her command of biblical cadences, and the authority she has earned sweating behind a plow.

Yet it still makes sense to try to examine arguments systematically, because one can, in fact, judge the scope of writers' claims, assess the reliability of their evidence, and react to the nuances of their language. Everyone evaluates arguments routinely, whenever they read editorials or listen to political speeches: *I don't see her point. Are those statistics up to date? Why did he have to resort to name-calling?* Most people know when a case is convincing or weak.

When people write arguments themselves, they are also aware of options and choices. Typically, they begin an argument knowing approximately where they stand. But they also realize they'll need evidence strong enough to convince both themselves and others more completely that their position makes sense. And often they surprise themselves by changing their views when they learn more about their subject.

Given the variety of arguments (see Chapter 1) and all the different readers and occasions they serve, we can't outline a simple process for writing a convincing argument. Moreover, no serious forms of writing can be reduced to formulas. But we can at least draw your attention to six key issues that readers and writers routinely face when dealing with arguments:

- connecting as reader or writer (Chapter 3)
- understanding lines of argument (Chapters 4–7)
- making a claim (Chapter 8)
- giving an argument shape (Chapters 9–13)
- giving an argument style (Chapters 14–17)
- managing the conventions of argument (Chapters 18–22)

As this list indicates, each of these matters is discussed in one or more chapters in this book.

CONNECTING AS READER OR WRITER

Just as "know thyself" is the philosopher's touchstone, "know thy *audience*" has long been the watchword among people who are interested in persuasion. You've probably heard of the demographic studies that advertisers and TV producers use to target their consumers—detailed surveys of consumers' likely ages, preferences, and habits. But understanding audiences isn't just a matter of figuring out the age, income level, reading preferences, and hair color of those for whom you expect to write. Connecting entails far more, whether you are a reader or a writer.

It should come as no surprise to you to learn that American society is riven by markers of race, gender, ethnicity, class, intelligence, religion, age, sexuality, ability, and so on. To some extent, *who* Americans are shapes what and how they write. And how readers imagine the writer affects how they receive what has been written. Neither writers nor readers are neutral parties handling information impassively. Life would be much less interesting if they were.

These complex relationships between readers and writers are always shifting. Sometimes as you read, you may be highly conscious of your gender and that of the writer; sometimes you may compose while thinking of yourself in terms of ethnicity or religion or economic class, alone or in combination with other factors. In the passage cited earlier, Sojourner Truth connects with many readers (particularly contemporary ones) in part because she is a former slave pleading for justice. But one can just as easily imagine other listeners turning deaf ears to her, precisely because of who she is.

In short, as you read or write arguments, you must be aware of points of contact between readers and writers—some friendly, others more troubled. And, of course, any writer or reader exploring a subject should come to it willing to learn that territory. Readers should ask what motivates writers to argue a case—what experiences they bring to the table. And writers, as they begin working with a subject, must consider how (and whether) they ought to convey to readers who they are. Consider how Shelby Steele, an African American who is worried about the voluntary resegregation of college campuses, positions himself within his argument to suggest what he knows about it:

> When I went to college in the mid-sixties, colleges were oases of calm and understanding in a racially tense society. . . . If I met whites who were not anxious to be friends with blacks, most were at least vaguely friendly to the cause of our freedom.
>
> —Shelby Steele, "The Recoloring of Campus Life"

Connecting means learning to identify with a writer or a reader, imagining yourself in someone else's shoes. Writers who fail to move beyond their own worlds or routines—who haven't considered alternative views—can be easily faulted. If you're reading an argument that strikes you as narrow, you might ask yourself: *What is the writer missing? Who is he or she excluding from the audience, deliberately or not?*

As a writer, you may want to connect with readers who share your own concerns. For example, Anthony Brandt, an author who wonders whether nonreligious parents owe their children religious training, aims his deliberative argument directly at parents in his situation, addressing them familiarly as *us* and *we*:

> **For those of us without faith it's not so easy. Do we send our kids to Sunday school when we ourselves never go to church? Do we have them baptized even though we have no intention of raising them as religious?**
> –Anthony Brandt, "Do Kids Need Religion?"

Brandt's technique illustrated here is just one of many ways to build an author-reader relationship. Yet some readers might find his appeal too overt, or aimed more at self-justification than at connecting with an audience. Argument is never easy.

Another bond between readers and writers involves building trust. In reading arguments, you should look for signals that writers are conveying accurate, honest information. You may find such reassurance in careful documentation of facts, in relevant statistics, or in a style that is moderate, balanced, and civil. Also look for indications of a writer's experience with the subject. You'd probably trust a student writing an essay about teaching who gave you the following reassurance:

> **I write this essay to offer a student perspective on the issues of power in the classroom. And although it is only one perspective, I've done a lot of thinking about teaching styles, about writing, and about conducting classes in my first year of college.**
> –Christian Zawodniak, "Teacher Power, Student Pedagogy"

After all, before you agree with an argument, you want to be sure it is presented by someone who knows what he or she is talking about. Needless to say, as a writer of arguments you have to pay attention to the very same issues—and do it right from the start of the writing process.

In short, connecting to an audience also means gaining authority over your subject matter—earning the right to write. (For more about connecting, see Chapter 3.)

UNDERSTANDING LINES OF ARGUMENT

When you encounter an argument, your instinct as a reader should be to explore its premises, the statements or positions the writer assumes as true, and the evidence that supports it. Likewise, when you write an argument, you must decide on strategies to use to build your case. That case can usually be constructed by considering four types of appeals, or lines of argument:

- arguments from the heart
- arguments based on values
- arguments based on character
- arguments based on facts and reason

In considering these opportunities, you become involved in an important process of discovery and invention, finding what Aristotle described as "all the available means of persuasion."

Arguments from the Heart

Arguments from the heart are designed to appeal to readers' emotions and feelings. Readers are often told to be wary of such manipulation because emotions can lead them to make unwise judgments. And some emotional appeals are, in fact, just ploys to win readers' attention or consent.

But emotions can also direct readers in powerful ways to think more carefully about what they do. For example, persuading people not to drink and drive by making them fear death, injury, or arrest seems like a fair use of an emotional appeal. So writers need to consider what emotional appeals might be available when making an argument and whether these appeals are legitimate or appropriate. In arguing that wealthier Americans undervalue the academic abilities and achievements of those who are less well-off, Mike Rose evokes feelings of sympathy by describing an immigrant woman seeking to improve her life through education —an aspiration most native-born Americans will admire:

> There is another person in the sparse waiting room. She is thin, her gray hair pulled back in a tight bun, her black dress buttoned to her neck. She will tell you, if you ask her in Spanish, that she is waiting for her English class to begin. She might also tell you that the people here are helping her locate her son—lost in Salvadoran resettlement

camps—and she thinks if she learns a little English, it will help her bring him to America.

—Mike Rose, *Lives on the Boundary*

In reading an argument that is heavy on emotional appeals, you'll always want to question exactly how the emotions generated support the claims a writer makes. Is there even a connection between the claim and the emotional appeal? Sometimes there isn't. Most readers have seen advertisements that promise an exciting life and attractive friends if only they drink the right beer. Few are fooled when they think about such ads. But sometimes emotional appeals move people away from thinking just long enough to make a bad choice—and that's precisely the danger.

Finally, though people may not always realize it, humor, satire, and parody are potent forms of emotional argument that can make ideas or individuals seem foolish or laughable. (For more about emotional arguments, see Chapter 4.)

Arguments Based on Values

Arguments that appeal to core values are closely related to emotional appeals, but they work chiefly within specific groups of people—groups as small as families or as large as nations. In such appeals, writers typically either (1) ask others to live up to higher principles, respected traditions, or even new values, or (2) complain that they have not done so. Henry Scanlon, an entrepreneur who believes that President Clinton unfairly branded owners of small businesses as an "economic elite," makes precisely such an appeal to core American principles:

> I expect that after I have spent decades creating jobs, never cheating anyone, constantly trying to make a positive contribution to the society in which I live, doing everything I can to treat employees, customers and suppliers fairly, honestly, and even generously, not only adhering to the founding principles of this country but actively trying to make an ongoing, positive contribution—that I would not be spoken of by the president of the country as if I were a reptile.
>
> —Henry Scanlon, "Suddenly, I'm the Bad Guy"

Scanlon's argument will succeed or fail depending on how readers react to his catalog of values: hard work, honesty, fairness, generosity in business. Do they admire those virtues, or do they regard them as expressions of an outdated and self-serving individualism?

Appeals based on values take many forms—from the Nike swoosh on a pair of basketball shoes to the peal of a trumpet playing taps at a military funeral. Such appeals can support many kinds of argument, especially ceremonial arguments, which, in fact, define or celebrate the ideals of a society. Any writer hoping to argue effectively needs a keen sense of the values operating within the community he or she is addressing. (For more on arguments based on values, see Chapter 5.)

Arguments Based on Character

Character matters when you read arguments, even when you don't know who the authors are. Readers tend to believe writers who seem honest, wise, and trustworthy. In examining an argument, you should look for evidence of these traits. *Does the writer have authority to write on this subject? Are all claims qualified reasonably? Is evidence presented in full, not tailored to the writer's agenda? Are important objections to the author's position acknowledged and addressed? Are sources documented?*

As a writer of arguments, you must anticipate the very same questions. And you must realize that everything you do in an argument sends signals to readers. Language that is hot and extreme can mark you as either passionate *or* intemperate. Organization that is tight can suggest that you are in control. Confusing or imprecise language can make you seem incompetent; technical terms and abstract phrases can characterize you as either knowledgeable *or* pompous.

Yet arguments based on character reach well beyond the shape and structure of a piece itself. Readers respond powerfully to the people behind arguments, to the experience and power they bring to their work. You can sense that authority in the sweep of the claims offered here by Pope John Paul II:

> The Gospel contains a *fundamental paradox*: to find life, one must lose life; to be born, one must die; to save oneself, one must take up the cross. This is the essential truth of the Gospel, which always and everywhere is bound to meet with man's protest.
> —Pope John Paul II, *Crossing the Threshold of Hope*

A different but equally compelling appeal from character is evident in these sentences in which Terry Tempest Williams affirms a principle of resistance to officials who she believes concealed the dangers of nuclear testing in Utah:

> The officials thought it was a cruel joke to leave us stranded in the desert with no way to get home. What they didn't realize was that we were home, soul-centered and strong, women who recognized the sweet smell of sage as fuel for our spirits.
>
> –Terry Tempest Williams, "The Clan of One-Breasted Women"

Of course, not everyone can write with Williams's power (or from the papal throne). But neither can writers ignore the power their own voices may have within an argument. (For more about arguments based on character, see Chapter 6.)

Where an argument appears also has a bearing on how seriously it is received. Not every such judgment will be fair, but it is hard to deny that a writer who is published in the *New Yorker* or *Commentary* or even *Newsweek* will be more respected than one who writes for a local paper or a supermarket tabloid. An argument that appears in a scholarly book thick with footnotes and appendices may seem more estimable than one that is offered in a photocopied newsletter handed out on the street corner. Likewise, facts and figures borrowed from the congressional Web site *Thomas* will carry more weight than statistics from *Jason's Gonzo Home Page.*

Arguments Based on Facts and Reason

In assessing most arguments, you'll have to judge first whether the linkages between claims and supporting reasons make sense.

Claim	Federal income taxes should be cut . . .
Reason	because the economy is growing too slowly.
Links	Tax cuts will stimulate the economy.
	A slow-growing economy is unhealthy.

Then you'll have to judge whether the writer provides enough evidence to support each part of the argument, in this case both the reason offered to support the claim (proof that the economy is growing too slowly for the good of the country) and the connections between the claim and the reason (evidence that tax cuts stimulate beneficial growth). In other words, when you assess an argument you should read skeptically, testing every assumption, claim, and linkage *between* assumption and claim as well as questioning the merit of every source and authority cited. (For more on arguments based on facts and reason, see Chapter 7.)

When you compose an argument you should write with this skeptical reader in mind. Offer logical arguments backed with the best evidence, testimony, and authority you can find. (For more about logical arguments, see Chapter 8.)

Logical appeals rely heavily on data and information from reliable sources. Knowing how to assess the quality of sources is more important now than ever because developments in information technology provide writers with access to more information than they have ever enjoyed before. The computer terminal is rapidly becoming the equivalent of a library reference room—except that the sources available on-screen vary much more widely in quality. As a consequence, both readers and writers of arguments these days must know the difference between reliable, first-hand, or fully documented sources and those that don't meet these standards. (For more on using and documenting sources, see Chapters 21 and 22.)

MAKING A CLAIM

Not every argument you read will package its claim in a neat sentence or thesis. A writer may tell a story from which you have to infer the claim or assemble it from various incidents. For instance, a much-admired passage in a novel by Maxine Hong Kingston describes how a girl's aunt who bears a child out of wedlock is compelled by a tradition-bound society to destroy herself and the infant because they have no means of support. The incident, starkly horrible, makes many indirect argumentative claims without the narrator having to state any one specifically, though she does comment on the fact that her family forbade anyone to speak of the aunt who had disgraced them:

> But there is more to this silence: they want me to participate in her punishment. And I have.
>
> In the twenty years since I heard this story I have not asked for details nor said my aunt's name; I do not know it.
>
> —Maxine Hong Kingston, *The Woman Warrior*

Readers cannot help being moved by the story of the aunt and the social conventions that made her a nonperson. An argument for justice is spoken even if the story itself is not designed as an argument.

In more traditional arguments, claims are liable to be more explicit. In such cases, writers stake out what they believe is true and what they expect to prove through reason and evidence. Here are three examples of explicit claims. The first comes near the beginning of an argument and previews the contents of an entire book; the second and third occur nearer the conclusion of articles and draw inferences from evidence already presented in great detail:

> **Multiculturalism, in short, has reached the point of *dérapage*. It is a universe of ambitious good intentions that has veered off the high road of respect for difference and plunged into a foggy chasm of dogmatic assertions, wishful thinking, and pseudoscientific pronouncements about race and sex.**
>
> > –Richard Bernstein, *Dictatorship of Virtue*

> **[F]or the most part, the media coverage of the immune system operates largely in terms of the image of the body at war.**
>
> > –Emily Martin, *Flexible Bodies*

> **What I do know, however, is that as a Mormon woman of the fifth generation of Latter-day Saints, I must question everything, even if it means losing my faith, even if it means becoming a member of a border tribe among my own people.**
>
> > –Terry Tempest Williams, "The Clan of One-Breasted Women"

Wherever they are located, claims are, in some sense, focal points of energy in an argument—where writers decide to take their stands. Making a claim is an important early step in writing an argument, with the remainder of the process being involved in testing and refining that claim or thesis.

A lengthy essay may contain a series of related claims, each developed to support an even larger point. Indeed, every paragraph in an argument may develop a specific claim. Thus, in reading arguments you need to keep track of all these separate claims and the relationships among them. Likewise, in drafting an argument you must be sure that readers always understand the connections among individual claims you might make.

Yet a claim itself is not really an argument until it is attached to the reasons that support it and the premises that uphold it. Consider this claim from an article by Lynne Cheney, former head of the National Endowment for the Arts, who is writing about undergraduate education:

> **There are many reasons to be silent rather than to speak out on campuses today.**
>
> > –Lynne Cheney, *Telling the Truth*

The sentence makes a point, but it doesn't offer an argument yet. The argument comes when the claim is backed by reasons that the author will then have to prove. To show the connection, we've inserted a "because" between the two sentences Cheney actually wrote:

> **There are many reasons to be silent rather than to speak out on campuses today. [because] Undergraduates have to worry not only about the power of professors to determine grades, but also about faculty members' ability to make the classroom a miserable place for the dissenting student.**

Now the author has a case she can set out to prove and a reader can test. When you read an argument, you'll always want to look for such claims and reasons, perhaps underlining them in the text you are reading or marking them in some other appropriate way. Then you can measure the argument against its claims—*Is the argument based on reasonable premises? Does the writer provide sufficient evidence to prove the claim?*

When you write an argument, you've got to be open to making changes in your claim, refining it from draft to draft. You'll want to be sure your core claim is clear, reasonable, disputable, and focused. (For more on making and developing claims, see Chapter 8.)

GIVING AN ARGUMENT SHAPE

Most arguments have a logical structure, even when they also rely on appeals to emotions, values, or character. Aristotle reduced the structure of argument to bare bones when he observed that an argument had only two parts:

- statement
- proof

You could do worse, in reading an argument, than just to make sure that every claim a writer makes is backed by sufficient evidence. When you can do so, underline every major statement in an article and then look for the evidence offered to support it. Weigh those individual claims, too, against the conclusion of the essay to determine whether the entire essay is coherent.

Most arguments you read and write will, however, be more than mere statements followed by proofs. Arguments typically require some background to clarify claims for readers who may not know every issue in contention. Arguments need qualifiers to limit claims to questions that writers can prove within the time and space available. They often need to acknowledge alternative views and to offer rebuttals to contrary claims and evidence.

Arguments may also contain various kinds of evidence. Some may open with anecdotes or incorporate whole narratives that, in fact, constitute the argument itself. Or the claim may be buttressed through charts, tables of statistics, diagrams, or photographs. Even sounds and short movies can now be incorporated into arguments when they appear on the World Wide Web, thanks to the capacity of computers to handle multiple types of media.

In any argument you write, all these elements must be connected in ways readers find logical and compelling. Just as a claim may be revised throughout the process of writing, so may the structure of an argument. (For more about structuring arguments, see Chapters 8–13.)

GIVING AN ARGUMENT STYLE

Even a well-shaped and coherent argument flush with evidence may not connect with readers if it is written in a dull, inappropriate, or offensive style. Indeed, as a reader, you probably judge the credibility of writers in part by how well they state their cases. Consider how these simple, blunt sentences from the opening of an argument shape your image of the author and probably determine whether you are willing to continue on and read the whole piece:

> **We are young, urban and professional. We are literate, respectable, intelligent and charming. But foremost and above all, we know what it's like to be unemployed.**
> —Julia Carlisle, "Young, Privileged and Unemployed"

Now consider how you would approach an argument that begins like the following:

> **This is a book about guys. It's *not* a book about men. There are already way too many books about men, and most of them are *way* too serious.**
> —Dave Barry, "Guys vs. Men"

Both styles probably work, but they signal that the writers are about to make very different kinds of cases. Style alone tells you what to expect.

Manipulating style also enables writers to shape readers' responses to their ideas. Devices as simple as repetition and parallelism can give sentences remarkable power. Consider this selection from Andrew Sullivan, who argues for greater tolerance of homosexuals in American culture:

> Homosexuals in contemporary America tend to die young; they sometimes die estranged from their families; they die among friends who have become their new families; they die surrounded by young death and by the arch symbols of cultural otherness. Growing up homosexual was to grow up normally but displaced; to experience romantic love, but with the wrong person; to entertain grand ambitions, but of the unacceptable sort; to seek a gradual self-awakening, but in secret, not in public.
>
> —Andrew Sullivan, "What Are Homosexuals For?"

The style of this passage asks readers to pay attention and perhaps to sympathize. But the entire argument can't be presented in this key without exhausting readers—and it isn't. Style has to be modulated almost like music to move readers appropriately.

Many writers prefer to edit for style after they've composed full drafts of their arguments. That makes sense, especially if you're a writer who likes to get lots of ideas on the page first. But the tone and spirit of an argument are also intimately related to subject matter, so style should not be a last-minute consideration. Often, how you express a thought can be as important as the thought itself. (For more about the style of arguments, see Chapters 14–17.)

MANAGING THE CONVENTIONS OF ARGUMENT

Because arguments rely on sources, many conventions of the genre involve proper presentation of borrowed material. You need to know how to present tables or graphs, how to document borrowed material, how to select and introduce quotations, how to tailor quotations to the grammar of surrounding sentences, how to shorten quoted passages, and so on. (For more about the conventions of argument, see Chapters 18–22.)

New conventions for argument are evolving in electronic environments. That's not surprising because computer forums such as email, Web pages, and MOOs certainly encourage the active sharing of ideas. Inevitably, you will discover that arguments themselves are changed by these environments, and you will have to learn new ways to connect ideas and to merge visual arguments with verbal ones. The prospects are quite exciting. (For more about visual and electronic arguments, see Chapters 15 and 16.)

RESPOND •

1. The opening paragraph of this chapter describes the argumentative power of Sojourner Truth's "Ain't I a Woman?" Describe a similarly persuasive moment you can recall from a speech, an article, an editorial, an advertisement, or your personal experience. Or research one of the following famous moments of persuasion and then describe the circumstances of the appeal: what the historical situation was, what issues were at stake, and what made the address memorable.

    Abraham Lincoln's "Gettysburg Address" (1863)

    Elizabeth Cady Stanton's draft of the "Declaration of Sentiments" for the Seneca Falls Convention (1848)

    Franklin Roosevelt's inaugural address (1933)

    Winston Churchill's addresses to the British people during the early stages of World War II (1940)

    Martin Luther King Jr.'s "Letter from Birmingham Jail" (1963)

    Ronald Reagan's tribute to the *Challenger* astronauts (1986)

    Toni Morrison's speech accepting the Nobel Prize (1993)

2. Before class, find an editorial argument in a recent newspaper or periodical. Analyze this argument with regard to the six components summarized in this chapter: write a few sentences describing and evaluating the author's success at

    connecting to his or her readers

    arguing from the heart, values, character, and facts

    making a claim

    giving the argument shape

    giving the argument style

    managing the conventions of argument

In class, exchange editorials with a partner and analyze the one you've just been given along the same lines. Compare your analysis with your partner's: have you responded similarly to the editorials? If not, how do you account for the differences?

3. As suggested in Chapter 1, there are many ways of thinking about argument. Review the distinctions among purposes, occasions, and stases that were made in that chapter. Using these categories, how would you analyze the editorials you and your partner brought to class? Identify, if possible, the purposes, occasions, and stases of these arguments.

4. Find a paper you wrote for a previous class—it doesn't matter what kind of class or when you wrote the paper. Analyze this paper in the same way you did the editorials in exercises 1 and 2. You might find this assignment very easy, or it might be difficult—many academic papers make arguments that are hard to find. How do the editorials differ from the arguments you offered in your paper?

chapter three

Readers and Contexts Count

All argument calls for response, for the voices of others. Even in thinking through a choice you have to make—for example, one in which you create a kind of argument in your own mind—you will give response to yourself. And because argument is (at least) a two-way street, thinking hard about those people your argument will engage is crucial to effective communication. This kind of thinking is complicated, however, because those in a position to respond to your arguments or to join you in the argument —even if their number is very limited—are always individually complex and varied. In fact, if you can count on any one thing about people, it may be that they are infinitely varied, so varied that it is dangerous to make quick assumptions about what they do or do not think, or to generalize about what will or will not appeal to them.

MAPPING THE TERRITORY OF READERS

Readers or audiences for argument exist across a range of possibilities—from the flesh-and-blood person sitting right across the table from you, to the "virtual" participants in an online conversation, to the imagined ideal readers a written text invites. The sketch in Figure 3.1 may help you think about this wide range of possible readers or audiences.

As you consider your argument and begin to write, you will almost always be addressing an intended reader, one who exists in your own mind. As we write this textbook, we are certainly thinking of those who will read it: you are our intended reader, and ideally you know something about and are interested in the subject of this book. Though we don't know you personally, a version of you exists very much in us as writers, for we are *intending* to write for you. In the same way, the writer bell hooks indicates in an essay that she carries intended readers within her:

> **The most powerful resource any of us can have as we study and teach in university settings is full understanding and appreciation of the richness, beauty, and primacy of our familial and community backgrounds.**
>
> —bell hooks, "Keeping Close to Home: Class and Education"

This sentence reflects hooks's intention of talking to a certain "us"—those who "study and teach in university settings."

But if texts—including visual texts—have intended readers (those the writer consciously intends to address), they also have invoked readers (those who can be seen represented in the text). Later in this chapter, "you" are invoked as one who recognizes the importance of respecting readers. For another example, look at the first paragraph of Chapter 1; it invokes readers who are interested in the goals of argument, whether

FIGURE **3.1** READERS AND WRITERS IN CONTEXT

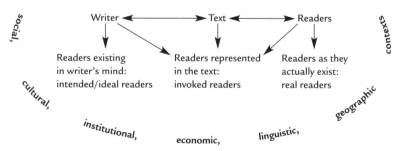

those goals are aggressive or subtle. And bell hooks's text also invokes or inscribes a particular reader within its lines: an open, honest person who regards education as what hooks calls the "practice of freedom" and is willing to build bridges to others without losing "critical consciousness." As she says, "It is important that we know who we are speaking to, who we most want to hear us, who we most long to move, motivate, and touch with our words." To invoke the readers hooks wants, her text uses the pronouns *us* and *we* throughout.

But this device can be dangerous: those who read hooks's text (or any text) and do not fit the mold of the reader invoked there can feel excluded from the text—left out and thus disaffected. Such is the risk that Susan Faludi takes when she opens an essay with this sentence:

> **Did you get the same irksome feeling of *déjà vu* as I did reading about Katie Roiphe's book, "The Morning After," that much ballyhooed attack on so-called victim feminism?**
>
> **–Susan Faludi, "Whose Hype?"**

The words *irksome* and *ballyhooed,* in particular, invoke readers who will agree with those terms. Those who do not agree are not invited into this piece of writing; there is little space made for them there.

In addition to intended readers and the readers invoked by the text of the argument, any argument will have "real" readers—and these real people may not be the ones intended or even the ones that the text calls forth. You may pick up a letter written to someone else, for instance, and read it even though it is not intended for you. Even more likely, you will read email not sent to you but rather forwarded (sometimes unwittingly) from someone else. Or you may read a legal brief prepared for a lawyer and struggle to understand it, since you are neither the intended reader nor the knowledgeable legal expert invoked in the text. As these examples suggest, writers can't always (or even usually) control who the real readers of any argument will be. Nevertheless, as a writer yourself, you would do well to think carefully about these real readers and to summon up what you do know about them.

When, in 1991, Julia Carlisle wrote an op-ed article for the *New York Times* about being "young, urban, professional, and unemployed," she intended to address readers who would sympathize with her plight; her piece invokes such readers through the use of the pronoun *we* and examples meant to suggest that she and those like her want very much to work at jobs that are not "absurd." But Carlisle ran into many readers who felt not only excluded from her text but highly offended by it. One reader,

Florence Hoff, made clear in a letter to the editor that she did not sympathize with Carlisle at all. In fact, she saw Carlisle as self-indulgent and as asking for entitlement to one kind of job while rejecting others—the jobs that Hoff and others like her are only too glad to hold. In this instance, Carlisle needed to think not only of her intended readers or of the readers her text invited in, but of all the various "real" readers who were likely to encounter her article in the *Times*.

No consideration of readers can be complete without setting those readers in context. In fact, reading always takes place in what one might think of as a series of contexts—concentric circles that move outward from the most immediate context (the specific place and time in which the reading occurs) to broader and broader contexts, including local and community contexts, institutional contexts (such as school, church, or business), and cultural and linguistic contexts. Julia Carlisle's article, for instance, was written at a specific time and place (in New York City in 1991), in certain economic conditions (during a recession), and from the point of view of white, college-educated, and fairly privileged people. As we have seen, such broader contexts always affect both you as a writer of arguments and those who will read and respond to your arguments. As such, they deserve your careful investigation.

ESTABLISHING CREDIBILITY

Because readers are so variable and varied, and because the contexts in which arguments are made are so complex, it's almost impossible to guarantee credibility. Nevertheless, careful writers can work toward establishing their credibility by listening closely to those they want to reach, by demonstrating to readers that they are knowledgeable, by highlighting shared values, by referring to common experiences related to the subject at hand, by using language to build common ground, by respecting readers—and by showing that they are trying hard to understand them. (See also Chapter 6, "Arguments Based on Character.")

Demonstrate Knowledge

One good way to connect with readers is by demonstrating that you know what you are talking about—that you have the necessary knowledge to make your case. Notice how Karen Lindsey uses examples and statistics to demonstrate her claims to knowledge and to bolster her argument:

CULTURAL CONTEXTS FOR ARGUMENT

Listening well is an essential element of effective argument. When you are arguing a point with people from cultures other than your own, make a special effort to listen for meaning: what is it that they're really saying? Misunderstandings sometimes occur when people hear only the words, and not the meaning.

- Ask people to explain or even repeat a point if you're not absolutely sure you understand what they're saying.
- Take care yourself to be explicit about what you mean.
- Invite response—ask if you're making yourself clear. This kind of back-and-forth is particularly easy (and necessary) in email.

A recent misunderstanding among a professor and two students helps to make these points. The issue was originality: the professor told the students to be more "original." One student (who was from the Philippines) thought this meant going back to the original and then relating her understanding of it in her own essay. The other student (who was from Massachusetts) thought it meant coming up with something on her own. The professor (who was French) had another definition altogether: he wanted students to read multiple sources and then come up with a point of their own about those sources. Once the students understood what he *meant*, they knew what they were supposed to do.

The traditional family isn't working. This should not come as a startling revelation to anyone who picks up this book: it may be the single fact on which every American, from the Moral Majority member through the radical feminist, agrees. Statistics abound: 50 percent of couples married since 1970 and 33 percent of those married since 1950 are divorced. One out of every six children under eighteen lives with only one parent. The number of children living in families headed by women more than doubled between 1954 and 1975.

–Karen Lindsey, *Friends as Family*

Highlight Shared Values

Even though all your readers will be somewhat different from you, they will not all be completely different. As a result, you can benefit from thinking about what values you hold and what values you may share with your readers. Jack Solomon is very clear about one value he hopes readers will share with him—the value of "straight talk":

> There are some signs in the advertising world that Americans are getting fed up with fantasy advertisements and want to hear some straight talk. Weary of extravagant product claims and irrelevant associations, consumers trained by years of advertising to distrust what they hear seem to be developing an immunity to commercials.
> –Jack Solomon, "Masters of Desire: The Culture of American Advertising"

Anthony Brandt faces a different kind of challenge in "Do Kids Need Religion?" for he assumes that his real readers will include those who would answer that question in very different ways. Since he wants to be attended to by readers on all sides of this issue, he highlights a widely shared value: the love for one's children and the wish for a good life for them. "I hope my children find a straighter road than I've found," he says near the end of the essay, concluding, "The longing for meaning is something we all share." To the extent that readers do share such a longing, they may be more receptive to Brandt's argument. (For more about arguments based on values, see Chapter 5.)

Refer to Common Experiences

In her article "The Signs of Shopping," Anne Norton draws on an experience common to many in her analysis of the ways symbolic messages are marketed to consumers: "A display window of Polo provides an embarrassment of semiotic riches. Everyone, from the architecture critic at the *New York Times* to kids in the hall of a Montana high school, knows what *Ralph Lauren* means." In a very different kind of essay, Susan Griffin draws on a common experience among men to build credibility with readers: "Most men can remember a time in their lives when they were not so different from girls, and they also remember when that time ended." Such references assume that readers have enough in common with the writer to read on and to accept—at least temporarily—the writer's credibility.

Build Common Ground

We've already mentioned the ways in which the use of pronouns can include or exclude readers and define the intended audience. Writers who want to build credibility need to be careful with pronouns and, in particular, to make sure that *we* and *our* are used accurately and deliberately. In her essay entitled "In Search of Our Mothers' Gardens," Alice Walker's use of pronouns reveals her intended audience. She uses first-person singular and plural pronouns in sharing recollections of her mother and demonstrating the way her heritage led her to imagine generations of black women and the "creative spark" they pass down. When she refers to "our mothers and grandmothers," she is primarily addressing other black women. This intended audience is even more directly invoked when she shifts to the second person: "Did you have a genius of a great-great-grandmother who died under some ignorant and depraved white overseer's lash?" Through this rhetorical direct address, Walker seeks solidarity and identification with her audience and builds her own credibility with them.

Respect Readers

Another very effective means of building credibility and of reaching readers comes through a little seven-letter word: *respect*. Especially when you wish to speak to those who may disagree with you, or who may not have thought carefully about the issues you wish to raise, such respect is crucial. In writing to a largely sighted audience, for example, Georgina Kleege, who is legally blind, wants to raise readers' consciousness about their dependence on and valuing of sight, but to do so without being accusatory or disrespectful of others' experiences. She accomplishes this goal through the extensive use of examples, through humor, and through a quiet and respectful challenge to her readers:

> **So go ahead. Close your eyes. It is not an unfamiliar condition for you. You experience it every time you blink. You are the same person with your eyes closed. You can still think, remember, feel. See? It's not so bad.**
> —Georgina Kleege, "Call It Blindness"

Of course, writers can also be deliberately *dis*respectful, particularly if they wish to be funny. P. J. O'Rourke uses this technique in his review of the book *Guidelines for Bias-Free Writing,* which was, he says, the product of "the pointy-headed wowsers at the Association of American University Presses, who in 1987 established a 'Task Force on Bias-Free Language' filled with cranks, pokenoses, blow-hards, four-flushers, and pettifogs." Thus, O'Rourke uses exaggerated and accusatory language to build up his credibility with an intended audience of readers he presumes are equally irritated by such guidelines.

THINKING ABOUT READERS

The following questions may help you craft an argument that will be compelling to your readers:

- How could (or do) you describe your intended readers? What characterizes the group of people you most want to reach? What assumptions do you make about your readers—about their values, goals, and aspirations?

- How does your draft represent or invoke readers? Who are the readers that it invites into the text, and who are those that it may exclude? What words and phrases convey this information?

- What range of "real" readers might you expect to read your text? What can you know about them? In what ways might such readers differ from you? From one another? What might they have in common with you? With one another?

- Whether readers are intended, invoked, or "real," what is their stance or attitude toward your subject? What are they likely to know about it? Who will be most interested in your subject, and why?

- What is your own stance or attitude toward your subject? Are you a critic, an advocate, an activist, a detached observer, a concerned consumer or citizen? Something else? In what ways may your stance be similar to or different from that of your readers?

- What is your stance or attitude toward your readers? That of an expert giving advice? A subordinate offering recommendations? A colleague asking for support? Something else?

- What kinds of responses from readers do you want to evoke?

- Within what contexts are you operating as you write this text? College course? Workplace? Community group? Local or state or national citizenry? Religious or spiritual group? Something else?

- What might be the contexts of your readers? How might those contexts affect their reading of your text?

- How do you attempt to establish your credibility with readers? Give specifics.

Considering and connecting with readers inevitably draws you into understanding what appeals—and what does not appeal—to them, whether they are imagined, invoked, or "real." Even though appeals are as varied as readers themselves, it is possible to categorize those that have been traditionally and most effectively used in Western discourse. These appeals are the subject of Part 2, "Lines of Argument."

RESPOND●

1. Find an example of one of the following items. Explain the argument made by the piece and then describe, as fully as you can, the audience the text is designed to address or invoke.

   a request for a donation by a charitable or political group

   a film poster

   an editorial in a newspaper or magazine

   the cover of a political magazine or journal (such as the *New Republic*, *Weekly Standard*, *Nation*, or *National Review*)

   a bumper sticker

2. What common experiences—if any—do the following objects, brand names, and symbols evoke, and for what audiences in particular?

   the Nike swoosh

   golden arches

   a dollar bill

   a Tommy Hilfiger label

   a can of Coca-Cola

   Sleeping Beauty's castle on the Disney logo

   the Democrat donkey; the Republican elephant

   Martha Stewart

   the Lincoln Memorial

   the UN flag

3. Carry out an informal demographic study of the readership of a local newspaper. Who reads the paper? What is its circulation? What levels of education and income does the average reader have? Are readers politically conservative, moderate, or liberal? How old is the average reader? You'll likely have to do some research—phone calls, letters, follow-ups—to get this information, and some of it might be unavailable.

   Then select an article written by one of the paper's own reporters (not a wire-service story), and analyze it in terms of audience. Who seem to be its intended readers? How does it invoke or "hail" these readers? Does it seem addressed to the average reader you have identified?

PART 2

LINES OF
argument

chapter four

Arguments from the Heart

Emotional appeals (sometimes called pathetic appeals) are powerful tools for influencing what people think and believe. Although it is sometimes taught that formal or academic arguments should rely chiefly on facts and logic, good ideas can be very powerful when they are supported by strong emotions. The civil rights struggle of the 1960s is a good example of a movement sustained equally by the reasonableness and the passionate justice of its claims.

But one doesn't have to look hard for less noble campaigns propelled by emotions such as hatred, envy, and greed. Untempered by reason, emotional arguments (and related fallacies such as personal attacks and name-calling) can wreak havoc in democratic societies divided by economic, racial, religious, and philosophical differences.

For that reason, writers who appeal to emotions must use care and restraint. (For more about emotional fallacies, see Chapter 19.)

UNDERSTANDING HOW EMOTIONAL ARGUMENTS WORK

No one doubts that words can generate emotions. Who hasn't been moved by a eulogy or stirred by a song? Such changes in disposition are critical to understanding how emotional arguments work. If writers can use words to rouse readers to specific feelings, they might also move them to sympathize with ideas associated with those feelings, and even to act on them. Make people hate an enemy, and they'll rally against him; help people to imagine suffering, and they'll strive to relieve it; make people feel secure or happy, and they'll buy products that promise such good feelings.

Emotional arguments probably count more when you are persuading than when you are arguing. Arguments make use of reasons and evidence to convince readers of some kind of truth. The aim of persuasion, however, is to move readers to action.

Argument (discover a truth) ⟶ conviction

Persuasion (know a truth)   ⟶ action

The practical difference between being convinced and acting on a conviction can be enormous. Your readers may logically believe that contributing to charity is a noble act, but that conviction may not be enough to persuade them to part with their spare change. You need a spur sharper than logic, and that's when emotion might kick in. You can embarrass readers into contributing to a good cause ("Change a child's life for the price of a pizza") or make them feel the impact of their gift ("Imagine the smile on that little child's face"). Doubtless, you've seen such techniques work.

USING EMOTIONS TO BUILD BRIDGES

You may sometimes want to use emotions to establish a bond between yourself and readers. Such a bridge is especially important when your argument draws on personal experiences or when you are arguing about matters that readers might regard as sensitive. They'll want assurance that you understand the issues in depth. If you strike the right emotional note, raising feelings in readers they can share with you, you've established an important connection.

That's what bell hooks does in an essay that argues that working-class people shouldn't lose sight of their roots even as education changes their lives. To reinforce her point, hooks lets us peer into her strained relationship with her mother:

> She wants to know, "What hurts, what hurts are you talking about?" "Mom, I can't answer that. I can't speak for all of us, the hurts are different for everybody. But the point is you try to make the hurt better, to heal it, by understanding how it came to be. . . . You know that. And sometimes folk feel hurt about stuff and you just don't know or didn't realize it, and they need to talk about it. Surely you understand the need to talk about it."
>
> –bell hooks, "Keeping Close to Home: Class and Education"

In no obvious way is hooks's recollection an actual argument. But it prepares readers to accept the case she will make, knowing that hooks has experienced conflicts with her mother—as most readers have with their own.

A more obvious way to build an emotional tie is simply to help readers identify with your experiences. If, like Georgina Kleege, you were blind and wanted to argue for more sensible attitudes toward blind people, you might ask readers in the very first paragraph of your argument to confront their prejudices. Here is Kleege:

> I tell the class, "I am legally blind." There is a pause, a collective intake of breath. I feel them look away uncertainly and then look back. After all, I just said I couldn't see. Or did I? I had managed to get there on my own—no cane, no dog, none of the usual trappings of blindness. Eyeing me askance now, they might detect that my gaze is not quite focused. . . . They watch me glance down, or towards the door where someone's coming in late. I'm just like anyone else.
>
> –Georgina Kleege, "Call It Blindness"

Notice that although Kleege seems to be describing the reactions of a class she will be teaching, many readers are likely to feel the same uneasiness, imagining themselves sitting in that classroom and facing a sightless instructor.

Let's consider another rhetorical situation: How do you win over an audience when you regard a subject as more threatening than most readers realize, but you don't want to seem like Chicken Little either? Once again, a sensibly managed appeal to emotions on a personal level may work. That's the tack Richard Bernstein takes to confront what he regards as the dangers of multiculturalism, an intellectual perspective that many readers probably regard as harmless:

> I don't want to be melodramatic here. We are not reexperiencing the French Revolution, and we are not in danger of the guillotine or rule by a national-level Committee of Public Safety (though I think subsequent pages show the existence of rather smaller versions of the same committee). But we are threatened by a narrow orthodoxy—and the occasional outright atrocity—imposed, or committed, in the name of the very values that are supposed to define a pluralistic society.
> —Richard Bernstein, *Dictatorship of Virtue*

Look carefully at the passage and you'll find words designed to ratchet up your concerns (*guillotine, Committee of Public Safety, outright atrocity*) even while worst-case scenarios are dismissed. The bottom line according to Bernstein is that readers should feel threatened by multiculturalism. If they are, they'll want to know what they should do and will read on.

USING EMOTIONS TO SUSTAIN AN ARGUMENT

Emotional appeals can also work as a way of supporting actual claims made in an argument. Quite often the emotion is laid atop logical propositions to make them stronger or more memorable. The technique is tricky, however. Lay on too much anger or pity, and you offend the very readers you'd hoped to convince. But sometimes anger adds energy to a passage, as it does when feminist Susan Faludi accuses writer Katie Roiphe of minimizing the significance of date rape:

> Roiphe and others "prove" their case by recycling the same anecdotes of false accusations; they all quote the same "expert" who disparages reports of high rape rates. And they never interview any real rape victims. They advise us that a feeling of victimization is no longer a reasonable response to sexual violence; it's a hallucinatory state of mind induced by witchy feminists who cast a spell on impressionable co-eds. These date-rape revisionists claim to be liberating young women from the victim mind-set. But is women's sexual victimization just a mind trip—or a reality?
> —Susan Faludi, "Whose Hype?"

Here, the threat in Faludi's sarcasm becomes part of the argument: if you make the kind of suggestion Roiphe has, expect this sort of powerful response.

In the same way, emotions can be generated by presenting logical arguments in their starkest terms, stripped of qualifications or subtleties. Readers or listeners are confronted either with core issues (which may move them a great deal) or with a reduction of the matter to absurdity (which may anger them). Kevin Kelly (KK) takes this risk in the course of a debate he has with Kirkpatrick Sale (KS) over the benefits of technology:

> KK: Do you see civilization as a catastrophe?
>
> KS: Yes.
>
> KK: All civilizations?
>
> KS: Yes. There are some presumed benefits, but civilizations as such are all catastrophic, which is why they all end by destroying themselves and the natural environment around them.
>
> KK: You are quick to talk about the downsides of technological civilizations and the upsides of tribal life. But you pay zero attention to the downsides of tribal life or the upsides of civilizations. For instance, the downsides of tribal life are infanticide, tribal warfare, intertribal rape, slavery, sexism. Not to mention a very short lifespan, perpetual head lice, and diseases that are easily cured by five cents' worth of medicine now. This is what you get when you have tribal life with no civilization. This is what you want?
>
> —Kevin Kelly, "Interview with the Luddite"

You might imagine how you'd respond to Kelly at this point: would a more reasoned approach work, or would the reply have to be just as pointed as Kelly's barb?

It is possible, of course, for feelings to be an argument in themselves when they are powerfully portrayed. Here, for example, is Georgina Kleege again, describing the feelings of the blind in order to change the attitudes of the sighted:

> Face it. What you fear is not your inability to adapt to the loss of sight, it is the inability of people around you to see you the same way. It's not you, it's them. And it's not because you have an unduly malevolent view of human nature. Nor are you guiltily acknowledging this prejudice in yourself. You may not see it as prejudice. Pity and solicitude are not the same as prejudice, you assert. The disabled should be a little more gracious. But the words stick in your throat. You know that's not the only response people have to the disabled.
>
> —Georgina Kleege, "Call It Blindness"

As you can see, it is difficult to gauge how much emotion will work in a given argument. Some issues—such as date rape, abortion, gun control— provoke strong feelings and, as a result, are often argued on emotional terms. But even issues that seem deadly dull—such as funding for

Medicare and Social Security — can be argued in emotional terms when proposed changes in these programs are set in human terms: cut benefits and Grandma will have to eat cat food; don't cut benefits and the whole system will collapse. Both alternatives evoke feelings strong enough to lead toward political action.

In exploring social and political matters, it is easy to get wrapped up in technical issues that are of interest chiefly to experts or insiders. If you want to make a case to a broad audience, you may sometimes want to "step outside the Beltway" and respond to the concerns of ordinary people. In other words, always consider how you can give presence to the human dimension of any problem in your arguments.

USING HUMOR

Just days after he lost the presidential election in 1996, Republican candidate Bob Dole appeared on the *Late Show with David Letterman,* grinning like a youngster and amusing the audience with self-deprecating humor. Some pundits commented that this was the real Bob Dole, who had been sadly absent from the campaign trail. Had more voters seen this easygoing, wry side of the candidate, the outcome of the election might have been different. That's highly speculative, of course. But, as the Dole case may suggest, you can't afford to ignore the persuasive power of humor.

You can certainly slip humor into an argument to put readers at ease, thereby making them well disposed toward a particular claim or proposal you offer. It is hard to say "no" when you're laughing. (Try it sometime.) Humor also has the effect of suspending sober judgment, perhaps because the surprise and naughtiness of wit are combustive: they provoke laughter or smiles, not reflection. Thus, it is possible to make a point through humor that might not work at all in more sober writing. Consider the gross stereotypes about men and women that Dave Barry presents with a decided chuckle:

> Other results of the guy need to have stuff are Star Wars, the recreational boat industry, monorails, nuclear weapons, and wristwatches that indicate the phase of the moon. I am not saying that women haven't been involved in the development or use of this stuff. I'm saying that, without guys, this stuff would probably not exist; just as, without women, virtually every piece of furniture in the world would still be in its original position.
>
> –Dave Barry, "Guys vs. Men"

Our laughter testifies to a kernel of truth in Barry's observations.

The power of laughter to cut to the bone can work in serious contexts as well, enabling the careful writer to deal with a sensitive issue that might otherwise have to be ignored. For example, sports commentator Bob Costas, given the honor of eulogizing the great baseball player Mickey Mantle, couldn't ignore well-known flaws in Mantle's character. So he argues for Mantle's greatness by confronting the man's weaknesses indirectly through humor:

> It brings to mind a story Mickey liked to tell on himself and maybe some of you have heard it. He pictured himself at the pearly gates, met by St. Peter who shook his head and said "Mick, we checked the record. We know some of what went on. Sorry, we can't let you in. But before you go, God wants to know if you'd sign these six dozen baseballs."
> —Bob Costas, "Eulogy for Mickey Mantle"

Not all humor is so well intentioned. In fact, among the most powerful forms of emotional argument is ridicule—humor aimed at a particular target. Lord Shaftesbury, an eighteenth-century philosopher, regarded humor as a serious test for ideas, believing that sound ideas would survive humorous broadsides. In our own time, comedians poke fun at politicians and their ideas almost nightly, providing an odd barometer of public opinion. Even bumper stickers can be vehicles for succinct arguments:

Vote Republican: It's easier than thinking.

Vote Democrat: It's easier than working.

But ridicule is a two-edged sword that requires a deft hand to wield it. Humor that reflects bad taste discredits a writer completely, as does ridicule that misses its mark. Unless your target deserves assault and you can be very funny, it's usually better to steer clear of humor. (For more on humorous arguments, see Chapter 13.)

RESPOND•

1. To what specific emotions do the following slogans, sales pitches, and maxims appeal?

    "Just do it." (ad for Nike)

    "Think different." (ad for Apple Computers)

    "Reach out and touch someone." (ad for a long-distance phone company)

"In your heart, you know he's right." (1964 campaign slogan for U.S. presidential candidate Barry Goldwater, a conservative)

"It's the economy, stupid!" (1992 campaign theme for U.S. presidential candidate Bill Clinton)

"By any means necessary." (a rallying cry from Malcolm X)

"When the going gets tough, the tough get going." (a maxim of many coaches)

"You can trust your car to the man who wears the star." (slogan for Texaco)

"We bring good things to life." (slogan for a large manufacturer)

"Know what comes between me and my Calvins? Nothing!" (tag line for Calvin Klein jeans)

"Don't mess with Texas!" (antilitter campaign slogan)

2. It's important to remember that argument — properly carried out — can be a form of *inquiry*: rather than a simple back-and-forth between established positions, good argument helps people *discover* their positions and modify them. Arguments from the heart can help in this process, as long as they are well tempered with reason.

   With this goal of inquiry in mind, as well as an awareness of the problems associated with emotional arguments, continue the argument between Kevin Kelly and Kirkpatrick Sale, writing their (imagined) responses and using reasonable arguments from the heart. Feel free to imagine Kelly or Sale discovering positions in the other man's statements that help him modify his own.

   You might also do this as a group exercise. Over several days, one group could work together to come up with lines of argument Kelly might use, while another group works to decide on Sale's lines. Then the groups could meet together to write the text of the argument itself. We hope you will find yourself modifying your preplanned statements as you hear what the other group has to say.

3. The Internet is a source of many arguments on the benefits of technology and its relationship to civilization. Using any search engine you feel comfortable with, find as many sites as you can that carry on the debate between Kelly and Sale. Divide the sites into three groups: those that make reasonable arguments from the heart, those that make emotional arguments with little or no rational support, and those that are hard to categorize.

   Make a list of the key words that each site uses to make its argument. Which words are logical? Which ones are emotional? What is the relative balance between logical and emotional words in each site?

chapter five

Arguments Based on Values

Arguments based on values usually occur among members of different groups. Whether they be clubs, sports teams, political parties, religious organizations, ethnic groups, or entire nations, groups come together because of values that individual members share. Lines of argument based on such values are related to both logical and emotional appeals, but they can be powerful enough in their own right to merit careful examination. To make a strong appeal to any group, you need to understand its core values as much as you possibly can since, in most cases, values themselves become the subject of debate. You also need to be critically aware of your own values — what they are as well as how they influence your understanding of the world.

UNDERSTANDING HOW VALUES ARGUMENTS WORK

Values are the principles shared by members of a group. Sometimes such principles are clearly spelled out in a creed or a document such as the Declaration of Independence. At other times, they evolve as part of the history and traditions of a club or movement or political party; for example, what it means to be a loyal Republican, a committed feminist, or an environmentalist may never be entirely clear, but it is always somehow understood. Moreover, the values to which groups and their members aspire are usually ideals all the more powerful for being neither fully attainable nor easily specified.

Such appeals to values are simple but powerful. They typically involve a comparison between what is and what ought to be:

- A person or group does not live up to current values.

- Past values were better or nobler than current ones.

- Future values can be better or worse than current ones.

USING VALUES TO DEFINE

You will likely find appeals to values whenever members of a society or group talk about that group. *What does it mean to be an American? An ecologist? A good Christian? A true Texan? A law-abiding citizen? A concerned liberal?* Everyone who belongs to such a group likely has an answer—as do people who stand outside—and their judgments are apt to be different enough to provoke interesting disagreement.

How would you define an American? Here is Hector St. Jean de Crèvecoeur, a Frenchman, trying in 1782 to do exactly that, speaking in the imagined voice of an American:

> **We are a people of cultivators, scattered over an immense territory, communicating with each other by means of good roads and navigable rivers, united by the silken bands of mild government, all respecting the laws without dreading their power, because they are equitable. We are all animated with the spirit of industry which is unfettered and unrestrained, because each person works for himself.**
>
> –Hector St. Jean de Crèvecoeur, "What Is an American?"

Crèvecoeur's themes are dated (few Americans are farmers now), but one still finds concepts that would resonate in arguments made to Americans today: limited government, fair laws, hard work, self-reliance. Appeals to such shared (and flattering) values are so common that even advertisers exploit them. In Texas, for example, one truck manufacturer advertises its products as "Texas tough," making a safe assumption that Texans like to think of themselves as rugged.

But let's consider an entirely different way of imagining American values, one far less idealistic. This time the commentator is Stanley Crouch, an African American social critic exploring the implications of the O. J. Simpson murder case:

> So we end up in a big, fat, peculiarly American mess, the kind that allows us to understand why one writer said she would choose a good case of murder if her intent was to ascertain the broadest identity of a culture. In this case of blonde on black, omnipresent media magnification, wife-beating, sudden wealth, workout partners, golf courses, the disco life, Bentleys rolling into McDonald's, rumors of drug-spiced promiscuity, and the ugly punctuation marks of two bloody victims in a high rent district, we are forced to examine almost everything that crosses the T's of our American lives.
> —Stanley Crouch, "Another Long Drink of the Blues"

Are hard work and personal responsibility compatible with "sudden wealth" and "the disco life"? Which of these "values" represent the real America? As a writer, you may find that the real America exists in the turbulence between such conflicting views—in the arguments about values that you, like Crèvecoeur and Crouch, will help to shape.

In writing an argument, you may find yourself defining the values you intend to champion and then presenting your claims in terms of those values. This process sounds complex, but it isn't. Consider the "Texas tough" truck mentioned earlier. In the ad, a cowboy slams the pickup down gullies and over cacti, trailing clouds of dust. If toughness is good, so is the truck. Case closed.

EMBRACING OR REJECTING VALUES

A straightforward form of arguments based on values involves identifying one's own beliefs or practices with well-accepted values. So when Terry Tempest Williams is arrested for protesting nuclear testing, she places her activity within an American custom as old and honorable as the Boston Tea Party:

> I crossed the line at the Nevada Test Site and was arrested with nine other Utahns for trespassing on military lands. They are still conducting nuclear tests in the desert. Ours was an act of *civil disobedience.* (emphasis added)
> —Terry Tempest Williams, "The Clan of One-Breasted Women"

By linking her own arrest to the tradition of civil disobedience, she makes an argument in defense of her entire cause. Likewise, Meridel LeSueur justifies feminist political action by embracing the universality of women's struggles as almost a natural force:

> I feel we must be deeply rooted in the tribal family and in the social community. This is becoming a strong and universal force now in our society. Women speaking out boldly, going to jail for peace and sanctuary, defending the children against hunger. We still get half of what men get. But as I saw in Nairobi the struggle of women is now global. My Gramma and mother are not any more silenced and alone. Writing has become with women not a concealment, but an illumination. We are not alone.
> —Meridel LeSueur, "Women and Work"

As you might guess, it is also possible to spin arguments based on values in the opposite direction, associating one's opponents with values that most readers reject. For instance, in a paragraph arguing for greater change in society, Newt Gingrich strategically associates government with the concept of monopoly, an idea unpalatable to most Americans:

> Why are governments so painfully slow at adjusting to change? Why are their agencies almost always obsolete? The basic reason is that governments aren't consumer driven. Governments almost always grant monopoly status to their own operations so they won't have to compete. Look at public education. Look at the post office. It's the same story everywhere. Consumers are too often stuck with inefficient service and poor products because they're not allowed to go anywhere else.
> —Newt Gingrich, "America and the Third Wave Information Age"

COMPARING VALUES

Many arguments based on values involve comparisons. Something is faulted for not living up to an ideal, or the ideal is faulted for not reaching far enough, or one value is presented as preferable to another or in need of redefinition. It would be hard to find an argument based on values more clearly stated than the following example from a book by Stephen Carter that explores what Carter sees as a trend toward intolerance of religion among America's legal and political elites:

> **The First Amendment guarantees the "free exercise" of religion but also prohibits its "establishment" by the government. There may have been times in our history when we as a nation have tilted too far in one direction, allowing too much religious sway over politics. But in late-twentieth-century America, despite some loud fears about the weak and divided Christian right, we are upsetting the balance afresh by tilting too far in the other direction—and the courts are assisting in the effort.**
>
> **–Stephen Carter, *The Culture of Disbelief***

In this case, a First Amendment balance between "free exercise" and "establishment" of religion is the value Carter uses to ground his argument. If readers share his interpretation of the First Amendment, they are also likely to agree with his inference that any deviation from this equilibrium is undesirable. Because of the high regard most Americans have for the First Amendment, Carter's argument is relatively easy to make. No extended defense of the basis for it is required. But consider how much more difficult it would be to get most readers to agree to the Second Amendment's protection of the right to bear arms. It provides a shakier premise for argument, one that requires more backing. (See Chapter 8 for more on using evidence.)

George Sim Johnston offers another example of such a values argument in action when, in describing the beliefs of Pope John Paul II, he suggests what the consequences might be of failing to embrace specific principles:

> **Above all, the pope objects to the notion of the individual conscience as a little god, a supreme tribunal making categorical decisions about right and wrong. Along with a new generation of Catholic intellectuals, he is suggesting that the modern world either rediscover the principles of natural law . . . or prepare itself for an increasingly fragmented and unhappy existence.**
>
> **–George Sim Johnston, "Pope Culture"**

Not every reader will accept the either/or choice that Johnston presents (natural law versus fragmentation), but the argument clearly champions a specific value over its alternatives: if people accept the reality of a natural law, they will enjoy more coherent and satisfying lives.

Adrienne Rich, a poet and writer, provides a clear example of a third type of value comparison, one in which a current value—in this case, power—is redefined for a different group so that it can be embraced in a new way. Watch especially how she unpacks the meaning of *power*:

> The word *power* is highly charged for women. It has been long associated for us with the use of force, with rape, with the stockpiling of weapons, with the ruthless accrual of wealth and the hoarding of resources, with the power that acts only in its own interest, despising and exploiting the powerless—including women and children. . . . But for a long time now, feminists have been talking about redefining power, about that meaning of power which returns to the root—*posse, potere, pouvoir*: to be able, to have the potential, to possess and use one's energy of creation—*transforming power.*
>
> —Adrienne Rich, "What Does a Woman Need to Know?"

As you can see, arguments based on values are challenging and sophisticated. That's because they often take you right into the heart of issues.

RESPOND●

1. Listed here are groups whose members likely share some specific interests and values. Choose a group you recognize (or find another special interest group on your own), research it on the Web or in the library, and, in a paragraph, explain its core values for someone less familiar with the group.

   parrotheads

   Harley Davidson owners

   Trekkies

   slackers

   Beanie Babies collectors

   log cabin Republicans

   PETA members

   hip-hop fans

   survivalists

   cacophonists

2. The first two extracted examples in this chapter focus on the values associated with the United States, both historically and in the present. Crèvecoeur has his list (industry, individualism, equity), and

Crouch presents a quite different one (spectacle, conspicuous consumption). Can you list 30 values—core values—associated with the people of the United States? 100? 200? List as many as you can, and then ask yourself when the list stops being representative of core values. Why does this problem arise?

Now make a list of core values for a small group—the members of your college's English department, for instance, or a church philanthropy committee, or an athletic team. Any small group will do. How many core values can you list? How does the list compare to the list you generated for the people of the United States?

3. Using the list of core values you've developed for the smaller group, write a paragraph arguing that a public figure—such as Jesse Jackson, Madonna, or Wayne Gretzky—meets the standards of that group.

4. Recently a group of animal rights activists raided a mink "ranch" and released several thousand minks from their cages. Many of the animals died during and after their release. Soon thereafter, other animal rights groups criticized this action, arguing that it did not represent the values of *true* animal rights activists.

What might these values be? And how would those responsible for the release characterize their own values? Write a statement from one of the other groups, using arguments based on values to express your disapproval of the release. Then write a statement from the releasing group, explaining why its actions were consonant with the values of true animal lovers. In each of these letters, you'll have to decide whether you're writing to a public audience or directly to the opposing group; the values you refer to might change, depending on the audience.

chapter six

Arguments Based on Character

In the preface to a book about men, Dave Barry tries to draw a line between men and guys. Naturally, in making such a distinction, he leads readers to expect that he'll explain each term. Here is what he has to say about the second:

And what, exactly, do I mean by "guys"? I don't know. I haven't thought much about it. One of the major characteristics about guyhood is that guys don't spend a lot of time pondering our deep innermost feelings.

–Dave Barry, "Guys vs. Men"

Such prattle probably makes you laugh if you understand that Barry is a renowned humorist (there was even a TV sitcom based on his life) and that he's not writing a piece intended for deep scrutiny, a fact he stresses in the very first line of his preface:

> This is a book about guys. It's *not* a book about men. There are already way too many books about men and most of them are *way* too serious.

But imagine for an unlikely moment that you have never heard of Dave Barry and missed all earlier signals of comic intention. What might you think of a writer who confessed, "I don't know. I haven't thought much about it," it being the subject matter of his book? Chances are you'd close the volume and select another one written by someone competent.

That's because in argument, as in politics, character matters. Readers want to be sure that an argument they are considering is the work of someone they can trust—which means that in composing an argument you have to convey authority and honesty through an appeal based on character, or ethos (sometimes called an ethical appeal). You can do so in various ways, both direct and subtle.

UNDERSTANDING HOW ARGUMENTS BASED ON CHARACTER WORK

Given life's complications, people often need shortcuts to help make choices; they can't weigh every claim to its last milligram or trace every fragment of evidence to its original source. Yet they often have to make judgments about weighty matters: *Which college or university should I attend? For whom should I vote in the next election? How do I invest my retirement funds?*

To answer these and hundreds of other similar questions, people typically rely on authorities and experts to give wise, well-informed, and honest advice. People also look to trustworthy individuals with experience and training to guide them in thousands of less momentous matters. Depending on the subject, an *expert* might be anyone with knowledge and experience, from a professor of nuclear physics at a local college to a short-order cook at the local diner.

When experts or authorities make claims, readers usually transfer their personal respect for the authorities to their arguments. If readers don't automatically accept what the experts and authorities say, they at least pause to listen, signaling a willingness to engage in dialogue. Readers give experts a hearing they might not automatically grant to a stranger or to someone who hasn't earned their respect. That's the power of arguments based on character.

CLAIMING AUTHORITY

When you read an argument, especially one that makes an aggressive claim, you have every right to wonder about the writer's authority: *What does he know about the subject? What experiences does she have that make her especially knowledgeable? Why should I pay attention to this writer?*

When you offer an argument yourself, you have to anticipate queries exactly like these and be able to answer them, directly or indirectly. Sometimes the claim of authority will be bold and uncompromising, as it is in the opening sentences of Terry Tempest Williams's essay indicting those who poisoned the Utah deserts with nuclear radiation:

> **I belong to the Clan of One-Breasted Women. My mother, my grandmothers, and six aunts have all had mastectomies. Seven are dead. The two who survive have just completed rounds of chemotherapy and radiation.**
>
> **I've had my own problems: two biopsies for breast cancer and a small tumor between my ribs diagnosed as a "borderline malignancy."**
> **–Terry Tempest Williams, "The Clan of One-Breasted Women"**

What gives Williams the authority to speak on the hazards of living in areas affected by nuclear testing? Not scientific expertise, but gut-wrenching personal experience.

It's the same strategy Jill Frawley uses in reporting what she knows about appalling conditions in nursing homes. Hers is an attention-getting claim to authority, also delivered in the opening sentences of an essay:

> **I'm just one little nurse, in one little "care facility." Each shift I work, I carry in my soul a very big lie. I leave my job, and there aren't enough showers in the world to wash away my rage, my frustrations, my impotence.**
> **–Jill Frawley, "Inside the Home"**

Frawley knows what goes on inside nursing homes because she works there. But she tells us more. Her soul is troubled by what she sees, providing a rationale for her exposé. Readers are moved to trust her—especially if they identify with her sense of being just one person who is helpless to do much about the injustices she witnesses.

J. Michael Bishop, a scientist, also uses an argument based on character to defend the National Institutes of Health (NIH) against charges of mediocrity in its procedures:

> I have assisted the NIH with peer review for more than twenty years. Its standards have always been the same: it seeks work of the highest originality and demands rigor as well. I, for one, have never knowingly punished initiative or originality, and I have never seen the agencies of the NIH do so.
>
> —J. Michael Bishop, "Enemies of Promise"

Bishop might add, "Trust me," because as evidence of the NIH's integrity he offers his own character and experience as a respected scientist—not specific facts, objective evidence, or independent testimony. This argument in defense of an agency under attack depends on readers believing J. Michael Bishop personally.

When your readers are apt to be skeptical of both you and your claim—as is typically the problem when your subject is controversial—you may have to be even more specific about your credentials. That's exactly the strategy Richard Bernstein uses to establish his right to speak on the subject of multiculturalism. At one point in a lengthy argument, he challenges those who make simplistic pronouncements about non-Western cultures, specifically "Asian culture." But what gives a New York writer named Bernstein the authority to write about Asian peoples? Bernstein tells us in a sparkling example of an argument based on character:

> The Asian culture, as it happens, is something I know a bit about, having spent five years at Harvard striving for a Ph.D. in a joint program called History and East Asian Languages and, after that, living either as a student (for one year) or a journalist (six years) in China and Southeast Asia. At least I know enough to know there is no such thing as the "Asian culture."
>
> —Richard Bernstein, *Dictatorship of Virtue*

Clearly, Bernstein understates the case when he says he knows "a bit" about Asian culture and then mentions a Ph.D. program at Harvard and years of living in Asia. But the false modesty may be part of his argumentative strategy, too.

When you write for readers who trust you and your work, you may not have to make such an explicit claim to authority. But you should know that making this type of appeal is always an option. A second lesson is that it certainly helps to know your subject when you are making a claim.

Even if an author does not step directly into the fray, authority can be conveyed through lots of tiny signals that readers may pick up almost subconsciously. Sometimes it comes just from a style of writing that presents ideas with robust confidence. For example, when Allan Bloom wrote a controversial book about problems in American education, he used tough, self-assured prose to argue for what needed to be done:

> Of course, the only serious solution [to the problems of higher education] is the one that is almost universally rejected: the good old Great Books approach. . . . I am perfectly aware of, and actually agree with, the objections to the Great Books Cult. . . . But one thing is certain: wherever the Great Books make up a central part of the curriculum, the students are excited and satisfied.
>
> –Allan Bloom, *The Closing of the American Mind*

Bloom's "of course" seems arrogant; his concession—"I am perfectly aware"—is poised; his announcement of truth is unyielding—"one thing is certain." Writing like this can sweep readers along; the ideas feel carved in stone. Bloom was a professor at the University of Chicago, respected

CULTURAL CONTEXTS FOR ARGUMENT

In the United States, students are often asked to establish authority in their arguments by drawing on certain kinds of personal experience, by reporting on research they or others have conducted, and by taking a position for which they can offer strong evidence and support. But this expectation about student authority is by no means universal. Indeed, some cultures regard student writers as novices who can most effectively make arguments by reflecting back on what they have learned from their teachers and elders—those who hold the most important knowledge, wisdom, and, hence, authority. Whenever you are arguing a point with people from cultures other than your own, therefore, you need to think about what kind of authority you are expected to have:

- Whom are you addressing, and what is your relationship with him or her?

- What knowledge are you expected to have? Is it appropriate or expected for you to demonstrate that knowledge—and if so, how?

- What tone is appropriate? If in doubt, always show respect: politeness is rarely if ever inappropriate.

and knowledgeable and often able to get away with such a style even when his ideas provoked strong opposition. Indeed, there is much to be said for framing arguments directly and confidently, as if you really mean them. (And it helps if you do.)

ESTABLISHING CREDIBILITY

Writers with authority seem smart; those with credibility seem trustworthy. As a writer you usually want to convey both impressions, but sometimes, to seem credible, you have to admit limitations: *this is what I know; I won't pretend to fathom more.* Readers pay attention to writers who are willing to be honest and modest (sometimes even falsely) about their claims.

Imagine, for instance, that you are the commencement speaker at a prestigious women's college. You want the graduates to question all the material advantages they have enjoyed. But you yourself have enjoyed many of the same privileges. How do you protect your argument from charges of hypocrisy? The poet Adrienne Rich defuses this very conflict simply by admitting her status:

> And so I want to talk today about privilege and tokenism and about power. Everything I can say to you on this subject comes hard-won from the lips of a woman privileged by class and skin color, a father's favorite daughter, educated at Radcliffe.
> –Adrienne Rich, "What Does a Woman Need to Know?"

Candor is a strategy that can earn writers immediate credibility.

It's a tactic used by people as respected in their fields as was the late biologist Lewis Thomas, who in this example ponders whether scientists have overstepped their bounds in exploring the limits of DNA research:

> I suppose there is one central question to be dealt with, and I am not at all sure how to deal with it, although I am quite certain about my own answer to it. . . . Should we stop short of learning some things, for fear of what we, or someone, will do with the knowledge? My own answer is a flat no, but I must confess that this is an intuitive response and I am neither inclined nor trained to reason my way through it.
> –Lewis Thomas, "The Hazards of Science"

When advancing an argument, many people might be reluctant to write "I suppose" or "I must confess," but those are the very concessions that might increase a reader's confidence in Lewis Thomas.

Thus, a reasonable way to approach an argument—especially an academic or personal one—is to be honest with your readers about who you are and what you do and do not know. If it is appropriate to create a kind of dialogue with readers, as Thomas does, then you want to give them a chance to identify with you, to see the world from your perspective, and to appreciate why you are making specific claims.

In fact, a very powerful technique for building credibility is to acknowledge outright any exceptions, qualifications, or even weaknesses in your argument. Making such concessions to objections that readers might raise, called conditions of rebuttal, sends a strong signal to the audience that you've scrutinized your own position with a sharp critical eye and can therefore be trusted when you turn to arguing its merits. W. Charisse Goodman, arguing that the media promote prejudice against people who aren't thin, points out that some exceptions do exist:

> Television shows . . . occasionally make an effort. Ricki Lake, who has since lost weight, was featured in the defunct series *China Beach;* Delta Burke once co-starred in *Designing Women* and had her own series; and Roseanne's show has long resided among the Top 10 in the Nielsen ratings. Although these women are encouraging examples of talent overcoming prejudice, they are too few and far between. At best, TV shows typically treat large female characters as special cases whose weight is always a matter of comment, rather than integrating women of all sizes and shapes into their programs as a matter of course.
> —W. Charisse Goodman, "One Picture Is Worth a Thousand Diets"

Notice how pointing out these exceptions helps build Goodman's credibility as a critic. Conceding some effort on the part of television shows allows her to make her final judgment more compellingly.

You can also use language in other ways to create a relationship of trust with readers. Speaking to readers directly, using *I* or *you,* for instance, enables you to come closer to them when that strategy is appropriate. Using contractions will have the same effect because they make prose sound more colloquial. Consider how linguist Robert D. King uses such techniques (as well as an admission that he might be wrong) to add a personal note to the conclusion of a serious essay arguing against the notion that language diversity is endangering the United States:

> If *I'm wrong,* then the great American experiment will fail—not because of language but because it no longer means anything to be an American; because we have forfeited that "willingness of the heart"

that F. Scott Fitzgerald wrote was America; because we are no longer joined by Lincoln's "mystic chords of memory."

We are not even close to the danger point. I *suggest* that we relax and luxuriate in our linguistic richness and our traditional tolerance of language differences. Language does not threaten American unity. Benign neglect is a good policy for any country when it comes to language, and it's a good policy for America. (emphasis added)

–Robert D. King, "Should English Be the Law?"

On the other hand, you may find that a more formal tone gives your claims greater authority. Choices like these are yours to make as you search for the ethos that best represents you in a given argument.

Another fairly simple way of conveying both authority and credibility is to back up your claims with evidence and documentation—or, in an electronic environment, to link your claims to sites with reliable information. Citing trustworthy sources and acknowledging them properly shows that you have done your homework.

Indeed, any signals you give readers to show that you have taken care to present ideas clearly and fairly will redound to your credit. A helpful graph, table, chart, or illustration may carry weight, just as does the physical presentation of your work (or your Web site, for that matter). Even proper spelling counts.

RESPOND•

1. Consider the ethos of each of the following figures. Then describe one or two public arguments, campaigns, or products that might benefit from their endorsements as well as several that would not.

   Oprah Winfrey—TV talk-show host

   Jesse Ventura—governor of Minnesota and former professional wrestler

   Katie Holmes—actress featured on *Dawson's Creek*

   Ken Starr—special prosecutor during the Clinton era

   Jesse Jackson—civil rights leader

   Molly Ivins—political humorist and columnist

   Jeff Gordon—NASCAR champion

   Madeleine Albright—secretary of state in the Clinton administration

   Rush Limbaugh—radio talk-show host

   Marge Simpson—sensible wife and mother on *The Simpsons*

Jane Fonda—actress and political activist

Ricky Martin—pop singer from Puerto Rico

2. Voice is a choice. That is, writers modify the tone and style of their language depending on who they want to *seem to be*. Allan Bloom wants to appear poised and confident; his language aims to convince us of his expertise. Terry Tempest Williams wants to appear serious, knowledgeable, and personally invested in the problems of radiation poisoning; the descriptions of her family's illness try to convince us. In different situations, even when writing about the same topics, Bloom and Williams would adopt different voices. (Imagine Williams explaining "The Clan of One-Breasted Women" to a young girl in her family—she might use different words, a changed tone, and simpler examples.)

Rewrite the Williams passage on p. 66, taking on the voice—the character—of someone speaking to a congressional committee studying nuclear experiments in Utah. Then rewrite the selection in the voice of someone speaking to a fourth-grade class in New Hampshire. You'll need to change the way you claim authority, establish credibility, and demonstrate competence as you try to convince different audiences of your character.

3. A well-known television advertisement from the 1980s featured a soap-opera actor promoting a pain relief medication. "I'm not a doctor," he said, "but I play one on TV." Michael Jordan trades on his good name to star in Nike advertisements. Actress Susan Sarandon uses the entertainment media to argue for political causes. Each of these cases relies on explicit or implicit arguments based on character.

Develop a one-page print advertisement for a product or service you use often—anything from soap to auto repair to long-distance telephone service. There's one catch: your advertisement should rely on arguments based on character, and you should choose as a spokesperson someone who would seem the *least* likely to use or endorse your product or service (Elizabeth Taylor promoting a marriage-counseling program, for instance, or Al Gore promoting a gas-guzzling sport utility vehicle). The challenge is to turn an apparent disadvantage into an advantage by exploiting character.

chapter seven

Arguments Based on Facts and Reason

"Logic and practical information do not seem to apply here."

"You admit that?"

"To deny the facts would be illogical, Doctor."

–Spock and McCoy,
"A Piece of the Action"

When the choice is between logic and emotion, a great many of us are apt to side with *Star Trek*'s Dr. McCoy rather than the passionless Spock. Most people in Western society admire logical appeals—arguments based on facts, evidence, reason, and logic—but, like the good doctor, people are inclined to test the facts against their feelings. McCoy observes in another *Star Trek* episode, "You can't evaluate a man by logic alone."

The fortunate fact is that human beings aren't computers and most human issues don't present themselves like problems in geometry. When writers seek to persuade, they usually try their best to give readers or listeners good reasons to believe them or to enter into a dialogue with them. Sometimes their presentations get a sympathetic hearing; at other times, even their most reasonable efforts fail. Then they can try harder—by strengthening their good reasons with appeals to the heart and to authority. (For more on these types of appeals, see Chapters 4 and 6.)

Nevertheless, the resources of logical argument are formidable—far too numerous to catalog in a text this brief. Here we can only summarize some of the modes available to you. Aristotle provided one intriguing way of distinguishing among logical appeals when he divided them between inartistic and artistic. Inartistic appeals are those that people don't have to create themselves but find ready-made: facts, statistics, testimonies, witnesses. Artistic appeals are those shaped out of words, using informal logic and common understanding. We'll examine both types of appeals in this chapter.

INARTISTIC APPEALS

The term *inartistic appeal* sounds pejorative to modern ears, as if such an appeal comes up short in grace and subtlety. Nothing could be further from the truth. The arguments found in facts, statistics, and observations require just as much craft as artistic appeals invented by using informal logic. In fact, audiences today probably prefer evidence-based arguments to those grounded in reason. In a courtroom, for example, lawyers look for the "smoking gun"—the piece of *hard* evidence that ties a defendant unequivocally to a crime.

Often less compelling is the argument (perhaps about motive or opportunity) based on reason: *What is the likelihood that so wealthy a person would embezzle five thousand dollars? How could a defendant who had never shot a gun before kill the victim so readily with one clean shot through the heart?* After decades of exposure to science and the wonders of technology, people often have more faith in claims that can be counted, measured, photographed, or analyzed than in those that are merely defended with words.

Inartistic appeals come in many forms. Which ones you use will depend on the kind of argument you are writing.

Facts and Evidence

Facts can make compelling inartistic appeals, especially when readers believe they come from reputable sources. Assembling such evidence practically defines what contemporary writers mean by *scholarship*. Consider why a reviewer for the conservative journal *National Review* praises the work of William Julius Wilson, a liberal sociologist:

> In his eagerly awaited new book, Wilson argues that ghetto blacks are worse off than ever, victimized by a near-total loss of low-skill jobs in and around inner-city neighborhoods. In support of this thesis, he musters *mountains of data, plus excerpts from some of the thousands of surveys and face-to-face interviews* that he and his research team conducted among inner-city Chicagoans. It is a book that deserves a wide audience among thinking conservatives. (emphasis added)
>   –John J. Dilulio Jr., "When Decency Disappears"

Wilson's book is recommended precisely because of its formidable mustering of evidence; the facts are trusted even above ideology.

When facts are compelling, they may stand on their own in an argument, supported by little more than a reliable source of the information. Consider the power of phrases such as "reported by the *New York Times*," "according to CNN," or "in a book published by Oxford University Press." Such sources gain credibility if they have, in readers' experience, reported facts accurately in most cases.

But arguing with facts often involves disputing existing claims. That's a tactic used by Christina Hoff Sommers, who challenges a story widely reported in reputable newspapers:

> A story in the *Boston Globe* written by Lynda Gorov reported that women's shelters and hotlines are "flooded with more calls from victims [on Super Bowl Sunday] than on any other day of the year." Miss Gorov cited "one study of women's shelters out West" that "showed a 40 per cent climb in calls, a pattern advocates said is repeated nationwide, including in Massachusetts."
>
> In this roiling sea of credulity was a lone island of professional integrity. Ken Ringle, a *Washington Post* staff writer, took the time to call around. When he asked Janet Katz—professor of sociology and criminal justice at Old Dominion . . .—about the connection between violence and football games, she said: "That's not what we found at all." Instead, she told him, they had found that an increase in emergency room admissions "was not associated with the occurrence of football games in general."
>   –Christina Hoff Sommers, "Figuring Out Feminism"

In an ideal world, good evidence would always drive out bad. But as a writer, you'll soon learn that such is not always the case. That's why you have to present to readers not only the facts but also the contexts in which they make sense. You also must scrutinize any information you do collect before using it yourself, testing its reliability and reporting it with all appropriate qualifiers.

Providing evidence ought to become a habit whenever you write an argument. The evidence not only makes your case plausible; it also furnishes the details that make writing interesting. As noted earlier, Aristotle observed that arguments could be reduced to two basic parts:

Statement + Proof

These two basic parts of arguments are sometimes referred to as the claim and the supporting evidence. When you remember to furnish evidence for every disputable claim you make, you go a long way toward understanding argument. The process can be remarkably straightforward. For example, anthropologist Emily Martin believes that many scientific concepts—especially the operation of the human immune system—have been shaped by cultural metaphors that have racist, sexist, and classist implications. How does she prove such a thesis? She makes specific claims and then marshals supporting examples from professional literature, with each bit of evidence fully documented:

> *Although the metaphor of warfare against an external enemy dominates these accounts, another metaphor plays nearly as large a role: the body as police state.* **Every body cell is equipped with "'proof of identity' . . . The human body's police corps is programmed to distinguish between bona fide residents and illegal aliens—an ability fundamental to the body's power of self-defense" (Nilsson 1985:21). What identifies a resident is likened to speaking a national language: "An immune cell bumps into a bacterial cell and says, 'Hey, this guy isn't speaking our language, he's an intruder.' That's defense" (Levy, quoted in Jaret 1986:733). (emphasis added)**
>
> —Emily Martin, "The Body at War"

Remember, too, that you want readers to understand and identify with your notions. That's why the examples that provide support for claims also make the claims engaging. For example, in writing about evidence of job insecurity among young people, Caryn James draws on interesting evidence from popular culture:

> In music, alternative rock is the equivalent of the slacker film. In their song "Long View," the group Green Day proves there is no long view for its generation. The narrator watches television all day and sings: "My mother says to get a job/But she don't like the one she's got." A bleak future—a bad job or no job—is a legacy passed on from mom and dad.
>
> —Caryn James, "Pop Culture: Extremes but Little Reality"

The specific details here both support James's thesis and help older readers understand a subject they may find alien. The song lyric in particular gives the argument both support and texture.

Statistics

Let's deal with a cliché right up front: *figures lie and liars figure.* Like all clichés, it contains a grain of truth. It is possible to lie with numbers, even those that are accurate. Anyone either using or reading statistics has good reason to ask how the numbers were gathered and how they have been interpreted. Both factors bear on the credibility of statistical arguments.

But the fact remains that contemporary culture puts great stock in tables, graphs, reports, and comparisons of numbers. People use such numbers to understand the past, evaluate the present, and speculate about the future. These numbers almost always need writers to interpret them. And writers almost always have agendas that influence their interpretations.

For example, you might want to herald the good news that unemployment in the United States stands just a tick over 5 percent. That means 95 percent of Americans have jobs, a figure much higher than that of most other industrial nations. But let's spin the figure another way. In a country as populous as the United States, unemployment at 5 percent means that millions of Americans are without a daily wage. Indeed, one out of every twenty adults who wants work can't find it. One out of twenty! As you can see, the same statistics can be cited as a cause for celebration or shame.

We don't mean to suggest that numbers are meaningless or untrustworthy or that you have license to use them in any way that serves your purposes. Quite the contrary. But you do have to understand the role *you* play in giving numbers a voice and presence.

Look at how W. Michael Cox and Richard Alm first present an economic experiment and then interpret its results to support their thesis that inequality in a nation's economy is not necessarily the result of inequity:

In the early 1970s, three groups of unemployed Canadians, all in their 20s, all with at least twelve years of schooling, volunteered to take up residence in a stylized economy where the only employment was making woolen belts on small hand looms. They could work as much or as little as they liked, earning $2.50 for each belt. After 98 days, the results were anything but equal: 37.2 percent of the economy's income went to the 20 percent with the highest earnings. The bottom 20 percent received only 6.6 percent.

This economic microcosm tells us one thing: even among people with identical work options, differences in talent, motivation and preferences will lead some workers to earn more than others. Income inequality isn't some quirk or some aberration. Quite the opposite, it's perfectly consistent with the economic laws that govern a free enterprise system.

–W. Michael Cox and Richard Alm, "By Our Own Bootstraps"

Notice that the interpretation depends on readers agreeing to a key claim: "This economic microcosm tells us one thing." If you wanted to dispute Cox and Alm's argument, you'd probably begin by challenging their reading of the data and offering a second (or third) way of explaining the same experiment. But in either case, the statistical results of the experiment don't become an argument until a writer uses them.

Surveys, Polls, and Studies

Surveys and polls produce statistics. But they play so large a role in people's political and social lives that writers, whether using them or fashioning surveys themselves, need to give them special attention.

Surveys and polls provide persuasive appeals when they document the popularity of an idea or proposal since, in a democracy, majority opinion offers a compelling warrant: *a government should do what most people want.* Polls come as close to expressing the will of the people as anything short of an election—the most compelling and decisive poll of all. (For more on warrants, see Chapter 8, p. 95.)

However, surveys, polls, and studies can do much more than help politicians make decisions. They can also provide persuasive reasons for action or intervention. When studies show, for example, that most American sixth-graders don't know where France or Wyoming is on the map, that's an appeal for better instruction in geography. Here's Adrienne Rich arguing from a study for better education for women:

[I]t is well for us to remember that, in an age of increasing illiteracy, 60 percent of the world's illiterates are women. Between 1960 and 1970, the number of illiterate men in the world rose by 8 million, while the number of illiterate women rose by 40 million.[1] And the number of illiterate women is increasing.

–Adrienne Rich, "What Does a Woman Need to Know?"

By this point, however, you should appreciate the responsibility to question any cited study, even one offered to champion a cause as benign as improving education. What's Rich's source for these numbers? The superscript "1" provides the answer in a footnote: the United Nations' *Compendium of Social Statistics.* At this point, you might decide to trust the source or wonder whether the United Nations' numbers are influenced by a feminist social agenda. Perhaps you should also wonder why Rich doesn't use more recent figures. But you could check the date of her work: it turns out that the passage was written in 1979. And that fact might raise more questions about how relevant her numbers are today, decades later.

Are we picking on Rich? In fact, no. The scrutiny here is just the sort you should give to any claim in a study—and the sort you should anticipate from your readers whenever you use such material to frame an argument. Especially with polls and surveys, you should be confident that you or your source surveyed enough people to be accurate, that the people you chose for the study were representative of the selected population as a whole, and that you chose them randomly—not selecting those most likely to say what you hoped to hear.

Surveys and polls can be affected, too, by the way questions are asked. Professional pollsters generally understand that their reputations depend on asking questions in as neutral a way as possible. But some researchers aren't above skewing their results by asking leading questions. Consider how differently people might respond to the following queries on roughly the same subject:

Do you support cuts in Medicare to balance the budget?

Do you support adjustments in Medicare to keep the system solvent?

Do you support decisive action to prevent the bankruptcy of Medicare?

The simple lesson here is to use polls, surveys, and other studies responsibly.

Testimonies, Reports, and Interviews

We don't want to give the impression that numbers and statistics make the only good evidence. Writers support arguments with all kinds of human experiences, particularly those they or others have lived or reported. The testimony of reliable witnesses counts not only in courts but in almost any situation in which a writer seeks to make a case for action, change, or sympathetic understanding.

A writer's account of an event can support an argument when it helps readers identify with worlds otherwise unknown to them—as in the following passage, in which Maya Angelou explains what the black boxer Joe Louis meant to African Americans in the 1930s. The paragraph refers to a moment when Louis, facing a white opponent, seemed to be losing the fight that eventually earned him the heavyweight championship of the world:

> My race groaned. It was our people falling. It was another lynching, yet another Black man hanging on a tree. One more woman ambushed and raped. A Black boy whipped and maimed. It was hounds on the trail of a man running through slimy swamps. It was a white woman slapping her maid for being forgetful.
> —Maya Angelou, "Champion of the World"

Personal experience carefully reported can also support a claim convincingly, especially if a writer has earned the trust of readers. In the following excerpt, Christian Zawodniak describes his experiences as a student in a first-year college writing course. Not impressed by his instructor's performance, Zawodniak provides specific evidence of the instructor's failings:

> My most vivid memory of Jeff's rigidness was the day he responded to our criticisms of the class. Students were given a chance anonymously to write our biggest criticisms one Monday, and the following Wednesday Jeff responded, staunchly answering all criticisms of his teaching: "Some of you complained that I didn't come to class prepared. It took me five years to learn all this." Then he pointed to the blackboard on which he had written all the concepts we had discussed that quarter. His responses didn't seem genuine or aimed at improving his teaching or helping students to understand him. He thought he was always right. Jeff's position gave him responsibilities

> that he officially met. But he didn't take responsibility in all the ways
> he had led us to expect.
> –Christian Zawodniak, "Teacher Power, Student Pedagogy"

Zawodniak's portrait of a defensive instructor gives readers details by which to assess the argument. If readers believe Zawodniak, they learn something about teaching. (For more on establishing credibility with readers, see Chapter 6.)

Shifting from personal experience to more distanced observations of people and institutions, writers move into the arena of ethnographic observation, learning what they can from the close study of human behavior and culture. Ethnography is a discipline in itself with clearly defined methods of studying phenomena and reporting data, but the instinct to explore and argue from observation is widespread. Notice that instinct in play as English professor Shelby Steele assembles evidence to explain why race relationships on college campuses may be deteriorating:

> To look at this mystery, I left my own campus with its burden of familiarity and talked with black and white students at California schools where racial incidents had occurred: Stanford, UCLA, and Berkeley. I spoke with black and white students—not with Asians and Hispanics—because, as always, blacks and whites represent the deepest lines of division, and because I hesitate to wander into the complex territory of other minority groups. A phrase by William H. Gass—"the hidden internality of things"—describes, with maybe a little too much grandeur, what I hoped to find. But it is what I wanted to find, for this is the kind of problem that makes a black person nervous, which is not to say that it doesn't unnerve whites as well. Once every six months or so someone yells "nigger" at me from a passing car. I don't like to think that these solo artists might soon make up a chorus, or worse, that this chorus might one day soon sing to me from the paths of my own campus.
> –Shelby Steele, "The Recoloring of Campus Life"

Steele's method of observation also includes a rationale for his study, giving it both credibility and immediacy. Chances are, readers will pay attention to what he discovers. It may be worth noting that personal narratives and ethnographic reports can sometimes reach into the "hidden internality of things" where more scientific approaches cannot inquire so easily or reveal so much.

As you see, with appropriate caution and suitable qualifications you can offer personal experiences and careful observations as valid forms of argument.

ARTISTIC APPEALS

Artistic appeals are based on principles of reason rather than on specific pieces of evidence. In other words, writers base these cases on principles, assumptions, and habits of mind that they share with readers. Although these principles are formally known and studied as "logic," few people, except perhaps mathematicians and philosophers, present arguments using formal logic; the extent of what most people know about it is the most famous of all syllogisms (a vehicle of formal deductive logic):

> **All human beings are mortal.**
> **Socrates is a human being.**
> **Therefore, Socrates is mortal.**

Fortunately, even as gifted a logician as Aristotle recognized that most people could argue very well using informal logic (some might say common sense). Consciously or not, people are constantly stating propositions, drawing inferences, assessing premises and assumptions, and deriving conclusions whenever they read or write.

In the next chapter, we describe a system of informal logic you'll find useful in shaping credible arguments—Toulmin argument. Here we want to examine the way informal logic works in people's daily lives.

Once again, we begin with Aristotle, who used the term *enthymeme* to describe a very ordinary kind of sentence, one that includes both a claim and a reason.

> **Enthymeme = Claim + Reason**

Enthymemes are logical propositions that everyone makes almost effortlessly. The following sentences are all enthymemes:

> **We'd better cancel the picnic because it's going to rain.**

> **Flat taxes are fair because they treat everyone in the same way.**

> **I'll buy a Honda Civic because it's cheap and reliable.**

> **Alex Rodriguez ought to be a baseball all-star because he's hitting over 300.**

Enthymemes are persuasive statements when most readers agree with the assumptions hidden within them. Sometimes the statements seem so commonsensical that readers aren't even aware of the logical exercises they perform in accepting them. Consider the first example:

We'd better cancel the picnic because it's going to rain.

When a writer makes such a claim, it's usually derived from more specific information, so let's expand the enthymeme a bit to say what the writer really means:

We'd better cancel the picnic this afternoon because the weather bureau is predicting a 70 percent chance of rain for the remainder of the day.

Embedded in this little argument are all sorts of assumptions and bits of cultural information that help make it persuasive, among them:

Picnics are ordinarily held outdoors.

When the weather is bad, it's best to cancel picnics.

Rain is bad weather for picnics.

A 70 percent chance of rain means that rain is more likely than not.

When rain is more likely than not, it makes sense to cancel picnics.

The weather bureau's predictions are reliable enough to warrant action.

In most cases, it would be tedious and unnecessary to make all these points just to suggest that a picnic should be canceled because of rain. The enthymeme carries this baggage on its own; it is a *compressed* argument, acknowledging what audiences know and will accept.

Cultural Assumptions

Most logical arguments you are likely to make tote some of society's baggage in just this way — that is, the enthymemes likely rely on premises and assumptions that are acceptable to most readers. Where the premises or assumptions aren't acceptable, you'll have to make a conscious case for them. (After all, someone might object when you cancel the picnic that *you can't trust the weather bureau!*) Even when the premises are acceptable, you still have to prove that your particular claim is true — that the picnic will in fact be held outdoors and that the weather bureau has indeed predicted bad weather for the remainder of the day. So most informal arguments will involve presenting and proving enthymemes. And many enthymemes will be supported (consciously or not) by premises of argument widely endorsed by readers.

Some of those premises are grounded in culture and history. In the United States, for example, few arguments work better than those based on principles of fairness and equity. Most Americans believe that all people should be treated in the same way, no matter who they are or where they come from. That principle is announced even in the Declaration of Independence: *All men are created equal.*

Because fairness is culturally accepted, in American society enthymemes based on equity ordinarily need less support than those that challenge it. That's why, for example, both sides in debates over affirmative action programs seek the high ground of fairness: proponents claim that affirmative action is needed to correct enduring inequities from the past; opponents suggest that the preferential policies should be overturned because they cause inequity today. Here's Linda Chavez drawing deeply on this equity principle:

> Ultimately, entitlements based on their status as "victims" rob Hispanics of real power. The history of American ethnic groups is one of overcoming disadvantage, of competing with those who were already here and proving themselves as competent as any who came before. Their fight was always to be treated the same as other Americans, never to be treated as special, certainly not to turn the temporary disadvantages they suffered into permanent entitlement. Anyone who thinks this fight was easier in the earlier part of this century when it was waged by other ethnic groups does not know history.
> –Linda Chavez, "Towards a New Politics of Hispanic Assimilation"

Chavez expects Hispanics to accept her claims because she believes they do not wish to be treated differently than other ethnic groups in the society.

Other Artistic Appeals

Other lines of argument are less tightly bound to particular cultural assumptions. They seem to work on their own, making a plausible case that readers can readily comprehend—even when they don't necessarily agree with it. Arguments about *greater or lesser good* are of this type; they rarely need complex explanations. Consider the following argument from novelist Ayn Rand:

> If physical slavery is repulsive, how much more repulsive is the con-
> cept of servility of the spirit? The conquered slave has a vestige of
> honor. He has the merit of having resisted and of considering his con-
> dition evil. But the man who enslaves himself voluntarily in the name
> of love is the basest of creatures. He degrades the dignity of man and
> he degrades the conception of love. But this is the essence of altruism.
> —Ayn Rand, *The Fountainhead*

Although readers might disagree with this conclusion, the comparisons
posed help demonstrate why servility of spirit might be considered more
repulsive than physical slavery.

Gertrude Himmelfarb offers a less dramatic variation of this structure
when she presents a case for establishing orphanages to care for neglected
children:

> Orphanages are, to be sure, far more expensive than conventional
> relief. But the cost is not so excessive when compared with that of
> prisons, hospitals and asylums in which some of these children might
> otherwise spend a great deal of their adult lives, to say nothing of the
> cost of crime, delinquency, illiteracy and other social ills that these
> children might inflict on society.
> —Gertrude Himmelfarb, "The Victorians Get a Bad Rap"

Readers are much more likely to tolerate an expensive proposition if it
can be made to seem ultimately less costly than alternatives. This structure of support is one of the most common in deliberations about policy.

Analogies offer another appeal that people understand intuitively.
They usually involve illuminating something that is not well known by
comparing it to something much more familiar. We reject or accept such
analogies, depending on the quality of the comparison. For example, in
arguing that "full-body transplants" could present major ethical as well as
technical problems, Maia Szalavitz compares this operation to a horrify-
ing fountain of youth:

> Could full-body transplants become a macabre fountain of youth,
> offering people a chance at near immortality as they continually
> replace old bodies with new, younger ones? Will headless bodies be
> cloned as replacements, or would people need other sources of
> donors? Could this offer a bizarre new way to get a sex change? And
> what does it say about identity, humanity and the soul?
> —Maia Szalavitz, "Where's the Rest of Me?"

While the idea of a full-body transplant may offer attractions similar to
those connected with the fountain of youth, it may turn out not to be at

all like what we had traditionally imagined. Readers have to decide whether they are persuaded by the comparison.

As you can see, artistic appeals may require a bit of skill to construct and analyze. We give you a tool to do just that in the next chapter.

RESPOND•

1. Discuss whether the following statements are examples of inartistic or artistic appeals. Not all cases are clear-cut.

   "The bigger they are, the harder they fall."

   Drunk drivers are involved in more than 50 percent of traffic deaths.

   DNA tests of skin found under the victim's fingernails suggest that the defendant was responsible for the assault.

   Polls suggest that a large majority of Americans favor a constitutional amendment to ban flag burning.

   A psychologist testified that teenage violence could not be blamed on computer games.

   Honey attracts more flies than vinegar.

   Historical precedents demonstrate that cutting tax rates usually increases tax revenues because people work harder when they can keep more of what they earn.

   "We have nothing to fear but fear itself."

   Air bags ought to be removed from vehicles because they can kill young children and small adults.

2. We suggest in this chapter that statistical evidence—a kind of inartistic appeal—becomes useful only when responsible authors interpret the data fairly and reasonably. When Adrienne Rich argued in 1979 for better education for women, she used statistics to prove her point. Anyone making the same kind of argument today would need to do more statistical research before reaching a fair conclusion.

   Find several sources of information on men's and women's literacy rates worldwide (you might start with a recent edition of the United Nations' *Compendium of Social Statistics*). On the basis of your reading of the statistics, take a position on the need for more attention to women's literacy education, and write a paragraph for a general, educated audience arguing this position. Then write an opposing argument—many such arguments are available, not just simple pro versus con debates—using the same statistics.

We don't mean to suggest that you learn to use data disingenuously, but it is important that you see firsthand how the same statistics can serve a variety of arguments. After you've written the two opposing arguments, write a paragraph explaining which one you see as being fairer and more reasonable.

3. Testimony can be just as suspect as statistics. For example, movie reviews are often excerpted by advertising copywriters for inclusion in newspaper ads. A reviewer's stinging indictment of a shoot-'em-up film—"This summer blockbuster will be a great success at the box office; as a piece of filmmaking, though, it is a complete disaster"—could be reduced to "A great success."

   Bring to class a review of a recent film that you enjoyed. (If you haven't enjoyed any films lately, select a review of one you hated.) Using testimony from that review, write a brief argument to your classmates explaining why they should see that movie (or why they should avoid it at all costs). Be sure to use the evidence from the review fairly and reasonably, as support for a claim that you are making.

   Then exchange arguments with a classmate and decide whether the evidence in your peer's argument helps convince you about the movie. What is convincing about the evidence? If it does not convince you, why not?

4. For each excerpt in this chapter—from John J. Dilulio Jr.'s book review to Maia Szalavitz's passage on full-body transplants—determine the principal enthymeme (the claim and supporting reason) in the text. Remember that enthymemes are logical arguments that rely on assumptions the audience is likely to grant. For example, we could say that Linda Chavez's argument is built around the following enthymeme: Hispanics should not support policies that rely on their status as "victims" because such policies prevent them from proving themselves equal to other Americans. (This is just one version of the enthymeme; you might find other ways of stating the same general argument as a claim plus supporting reasons.)

   In the case of excerpts that are built on inartistic appeals, the enthymemes probably refer to the data. A few excerpts are logically very complex; you'll have to work hard to create simplified statements of claim and reasons without reducing the argument in an irresponsible way.

PART 3

WRITING arguments

chapter eight

Structuring Arguments

What do you do when you want to write an argument? The sheer variety of persuasive situations precludes simple guidelines: arguments serve too many audiences and purposes to wear one suit of clothes. All writing, moreover, is a process of discovery—thoroughly unpredictable and idiosyncratic. As a result, arguments can't be stamped out like sheet metal panels; they have to be treated like living things—cultivated, encouraged, and refined. Five-step plans for changing minds or scoring points don't work.

TOULMIN ARGUMENT

What we can offer, instead, is an informal method for constructing the kinds of arguments that can be expressed in thesis statements. This system—known as Toulmin argument after British philosopher Stephen Toulmin, who describes the method in *The Uses of Argument* (1958)—will help you think more clearly about basic elements of the writing process.

In the following pages, we'll introduce some key terms and processes of Toulmin argument as modified over the years by teachers of writing and rhetoric. Because it traces the ways many people really think rather than the paths of formal logic, Toulmin argument isn't airtight. But for exactly that reason, it has become a powerful and practical tool for shaping serious and persuasive prose. At the least, it opens up the dialogue at the heart of all inquiry.

Making Claims

In the Toulmin model, arguments begin with claims, which are statements of belief or truth. When you make an argument, you stake out a position others will likely find controversial and debatable. Notice that in this model the arguments depend on conditions set by others—your audience or readers. "It's raining" might be an innocent statement of fact in one situation; in another, it might provoke a debate: *No, it's not. That's sleet.* And in this way an inquiry begins, exploring a question of definition.

Claims worth arguing tend to be controversial; there's no point insisting on what most people freely acknowledge. For example, there are assertions in the statements *Twelve inches make a foot* or *Earth is the third planet from the sun.* But except in unusual circumstances, these claims aren't worth much debate. Life is too short to belabor the obvious.

Claims should also be debatable. That means that they can be demonstrated using logic or evidence, material offered to support an argument. Sometimes the line between what's debatable and what isn't can be thin. You push back your chair from the table in a restaurant and declare, "That was delicious!" A debatable point? Not really. If you thought the meal was appetizing, who can challenge your taste, particularly if your pronouncement touches no one but yourself?

But now imagine you're a restaurant critic working for the local newspaper, leaning back from the same table, making the same observation. Because of your job, your claim about the restaurant's cuisine has different status and wider implications. People's jobs may be at stake. "That was delicious!" suddenly becomes a matter for contention and demonstration, bite by bite.

CULTURAL CONTEXTS FOR ARGUMENT

In the United States, many people (especially those in the academic and business worlds) expect a writer to "get to the point" as directly as possible and to take on the major responsibility of articulating that point efficiently and unambiguously. Student writers are typically expected to make their claims explicit, leaving little unspoken. Such claims usually appear early on in an argument, often in the first paragraph. But not all cultures take such an approach. Some prefer that the claim or thesis be introduced subtly and indirectly, expecting that readers will be able to "read between the lines" to understand what is being said. Some even save the thesis until the very end of a written argument. Here are a couple of tips that might help you think about how explicitly you should (or should not) make your points:

- What general knowledge does your audience have about your topic? What information do they expect or need you to provide?
- Does your audience tend to be very direct, saying explicitly what they mean? Or are they more subtle, less likely to call a spade a spade? Look for cues to determine how much responsibility you have as the writer, and how you can most successfully argue your points.

Many writers stumble when it comes to making claims because facing issues squarely can take thought and guts. A claim answers the question: *What's your point?* If you haven't settled an issue in your own mind, it's hard to make a case to others. So writers and speakers sometimes avoid taking a stand, spewing out whole paragraphs to disguise the fact that they don't yet know enough about an issue to argue a case.

Is there a danger that a bold claim might oversimplify an issue? Of course. But making the claim is a logical first step toward complexity. Here are some fairly simple, undeveloped claims:

Grades in college should be abolished.

Flat taxes are fair.

NASA should launch a human expedition to Mars.

The federal government should support the arts.

Note that these claims are statements, not questions. There's nothing wrong with questions per se, but they're what you ask to reach a claim:

Questions   What should NASA's next goal be? Should the space agency establish a permanent moon base? Should NASA launch more robotic interstellar probes? Should NASA send people to Mars or Venus?

Statement   NASA should launch a human expedition to Mars.

Don't mistake one for the other.

Attaching Reasons

For every claim, there should be a reason—or two or three. A reason is a statement that offers evidence to support a claim. You can begin developing a claim, then, by drawing up a list of good reasons to support it. Doing so will provide a framework for your argument by generating a series of smaller claims that you can explore and, if necessary, shore up.

One student writer, for instance, wanted to gather good reasons in support of a claim that his college campus needed more space for motorcycle parking. He had been doing some research—gathering statistics about parking space allocation, numbers of people using particular parking lots, and numbers of motorcycles registered on campus. Before he went any further with this argument, however, he decided to list the good reasons he had identified for more motorcycle parking:

Personal experience: At least three times a week for two terms, he had been unable to find a parking space for his bike.

Anecdotes: Several of his best friends told similar stories; one had even sold her bike as a result.

Facts: He had found out that the ratio of car to bike parking spaces was 200 to 1, whereas the ratio of cars to bikes registered on campus was 25 to 1.

Authorities: The campus police chief had indicated in an interview with the college newspaper that she believed a problem existed for students trying to park motorcycles.

On the basis of his preliminary listing of possible reasons in support of the claim, this student decided that it would be worth his time to conduct extensive firsthand observation of campus parking conditions and to survey campus motorcycle owners. He was on the way to amassing a set of good reasons sufficient to support his claim.

In some arguments you read, claims might be widely separated from the reasons offered to support them. But in shaping your own arguments, try putting claims and reasons together early in the writing process to create what Aristotle called enthymemes, or arguments in brief. Think of these enthymemes as test cases:

Grades in college should be abolished *because I don't like them!*

Flat taxes are fairer than progressive taxes *because they treat all taxpayers in the same way.*

NASA should launch a human expedition to Mars *because Americans need a unifying national goal.*

Since the federal government supports the military, the federal government should support the arts.

As you can see, attaching a reason to a claim spells out the terms of an argument. In rare cases, the full enthymeme is all the argument you'll need:

Don't eat that mushroom—it's poisonous.

We'd better stop for gas because the gauge has been reading empty for more than thirty miles.

But more often, your work is just beginning when you've created an enthymeme. If your readers are capable—and you should always assume they are—they will then begin to question your enthymeme. At issue are the assumptions that connect your claim to the reason(s) you offer for supporting it. Also under scrutiny will be the evidence you introduce to make your case. You've got to address both issues: quality of assumptions, and quality of evidence. That connection between claim and reason(s) is a concern at the next level in Toulmin argument. (For more on enthymemes, see Chapter 7, p. 82.)

Determining Warrants

A crucial step in Toulmin argument is learning to state the warrants that support particular arguments. The warrant is the connection, often unstated and assumed, between your claim and your supporting reason(s), the glue that holds them together. Like the warrant in legal situations (a search warrant, for example), a sound warrant in an argument gives you authority to proceed with a case. If readers accept your warrant, you can then present specific evidence to prove your claim. If readers dispute your warrant, you'll have to defend it before you can move on to the claim itself.

Stating warrants can be tricky because they can be phrased in various ways. What you are looking for is the general principle that enables you to move from the reason to the specific claim.

The warrant is the assumption that makes the claim seem plausible. Let's demonstrate this logical movement with an easy example.

Don't eat that mushroom—it's poisonous.

The warrant supporting this enthymeme can be stated in several ways, always moving from the reason ("it's poisonous") to the claim ("Don't eat that mushroom"):

That which is poisonous shouldn't be eaten.

If something is poisonous, it's dangerous to eat.

Here is the relationship, diagrammed:

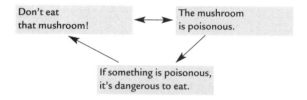

Perfectly obvious, you say? Exactly—and that's why the enthymeme is so convincing. If the mushroom in question is indeed a death angel or toadstool (and you might still need expert testimony to prove that's what it is), the warrant does the rest of the work, making the claim it supports seem logical and persuasive.

Let's look at a similar example, beginning with the argument in its enthymeme form:

We'd better stop for gas because the gauge has been reading empty for more than thirty miles.

There are at least two ways to express the warrant supporting this statement, beginning, as usual, with the reason ("because the gauge has been reading empty") and moving to the claim ("We'd better stop for gas"):

> If the fuel gauge of a car has been reading empty for more than thirty miles, the tank is nearly empty.

> When a fuel gauge has been reading empty for more than thirty miles, a car is about to run out of gas.

Since most readers would accept either of these warrants as reasonable, they would also likely accept the statement the warrants support.

Of course, cultural assumptions—beliefs considered obvious or commonsensical within a particular group—are operating in this statement. Such assumptions can function as warrants themselves: readers would understand without further explanation that running out of gas is no fun.

Naturally, factual information might undermine the whole argument—the fuel gauge might be broken, or the driver might know from previous experience that the car will go another ninety miles even though the fuel gauge reads empty. But in most cases, most readers would accept the warrant.

Let's look at a third easy case, one in which stating the warrant confirms the weakness of an enthymeme that doesn't seem convincing on its own merits:

> Grades in college should be abolished *because I don't like them!*

Moving from stated reason to claim, we see that the warrant is a silly and selfish principle:

> What I don't like should be abolished.

Most readers won't accept this assumption as a principle worth applying generally. It would produce a chaotic or arbitrary world, like that of the Queen of Hearts in *Alice in Wonderland. (Off with the heads of anyone I don't like!)*

So far so good. But how does understanding warrants make you better at writing arguments? Warrants suggest to you what arguments you have to make and at what level you have to make them. If your warrant isn't controversial, you can immediately begin to illustrate and defend your claim. If your warrant is controversial, you must explain the warrant—or modify it or shift your argument to different, more fertile grounds.

Let's consider how stating and exploring a warrant can help you determine the grounds on which you want to make a case. Here's a political enthymeme of a familiar sort:

> Flat taxes are fairer than progressive taxes *because they treat all taxpayers in the same way.*

Warrants that follow from this enthymeme have power because they appeal to a core American value—equal treatment under the law:

> That which treats all taxpayers in the same way is fair.

> Fair taxes are those that treat all taxpayers in the same way.

You certainly could make an argument on these grounds. But stating the warrant should also put you on alert about this line of approach. If the principle is so obvious and universal, why are federal income taxes progressive, requiring people at higher levels of income to pay at higher tax rates than people at lower income levels? Could it be that the warrant isn't as universally endorsed as it might seem at first glance? To explore the argument further, try stating the contrary enthymeme and warrant:

> Progressive taxes are fairer than flat taxes *because they tax people according to their ability to pay.*

> Fair taxes are those that tax people according to their ability to pay.

Now you see how different the assumptions behind opposing positions really are. In making the flat tax argument, you'll almost certainly want to address the issue raised by the contrary warrant. Or you may want to shift grounds in your presentation of the claim. After all, you aren't obligated to argue any particular proposition. So you might explore an alternative rationale for flat taxes:

> Flat taxes are preferable to progressive taxes *because they simplify the tax code and reduce fraud.*

Now you have two stated reasons, supported by two new warrants:

> Taxes that simplify the tax code are desirable.

> Taxes that reduce fraud are preferable.

You may find that warrants based on practicality provide surer grounds on which to erect your argument than warrants based on fairness. For example, middle-class taxpayers might question the equity of a flat tax system that expects them to pay at the same rate as wealthier people. But they might be willing to try out a simpler tax code if it actually relieved them of the burden of tax preparation and closed loopholes that made tax fraud possible. As always, you have to choose your warrant knowing your audience, the context of your argument, and your own feelings. But understanding how to state a warrant and how to assess its potential makes subsequent choices better informed.

Offering Evidence: Backing and Grounds

As you might guess, claims and warrants are only the skeleton of an argument; the bulk of a writer's work — the richest, most interesting part — still remains to be done after the argument has been assembled. Claims and warrants clearly stated do suggest the scope of the evidence you have yet to assemble.

An example will illustrate the point. Here's an enthymeme, suitably debatable and controversial, if somewhat abstract:

> NASA **should launch a human expedition to Mars** *because Americans need a unifying national goal.*

Here's the warrant that supports the enthymeme, at least one version of it:

> **What unifies the nation ought to be a national priority.**

To run with this claim and warrant, a writer needs, first, to place both in context because most points worth arguing have a rich history. Entering an argument can be like walking into a conversation already in progress. In the case of the politics of space exploration, the conversation has been a vigorous one, debated with varying intensity since the launch in 1957 of the Soviet Union's *Sputnik* satellite — the first human-engineered object to orbit the earth. A writer stumbling into this dialogue without a sense of history or context won't get far. Acquiring background knowledge (through reading, conversation, inquiry of all kinds) is the toll you have to pay to gain authority to speak on this subject. Without a minimum amount of information on this — or any comparable subject — all the subtleties of Toulmin argument won't do you much good. You've got to do the legwork before you're ready to make a case. (See Chapter 6 for more on gaining authority.)

Want examples of premature argument? Just listen to talk radio or C-SPAN phone-ins for a day or two. You'll soon learn that the better callers can hold a conversation with the host or guests, fleshing out their basic claims with facts, personal experience, and evidence. The weaker callers can usually offer a claim or even push as far as a full enthymeme. But then such callers begin to repeat themselves, as if saying over and over again that "Republicans are starving children" or "Democrats are scaring our senior citizens" will make the statement true.

If you are going to make a claim about the politics of space exploration, you need to defend both your warrant and your claim with authority, knowledge, and some passion (see Chapters 4–7), beginning with the warrant. Why? Because there is no point defending any claim until you've satisfied readers about the sturdiness of the foundation on which the claim is built. Evidence you offer in support of a warrant is called backing.

Warrant

What unifies the nation ought to be a national priority.

Backing

On a personal level, Americans want to be part of something bigger than themselves. (Emotional claim)

A country as regionally, racially, and culturally diverse as the United States of America needs common purposes and values to hold its democratic system together. (Ethical claim)

In the past, enterprises such as western expansion, World War II, and the Apollo moon program enabled many — though not all — Americans to work toward common goals. (Logical claim)

Once you are confident that most readers will grant your warrant, you can move on to demonstrate the truth of your enthymeme. Evidence you offer in support of your enthymeme is called the grounds.

Enthymeme

NASA should launch a human expedition to Mars *because Americans need a unifying national goal.*

Grounds

The American people are politically divided along racial, ethnic, religious, gender, and class lines. (Factual claim)

A common challenge or problem unites people to accomplish great things. (Emotional claim)

Successfully managing a Mars mission would require the cooperation of the entire nation — financially, logistically, and scientifically. (Logical claim)

A human expedition to Mars would be a worthwhile scientific project for the nation to pursue. (Logical claim)

Notice that backing and grounds may rely on information from outside sources—once again emphasizing the importance of context and background in any argument. Uninformed opinion doesn't have much status in argument.

Note, too, that backing and grounds can draw from a full range of argumentative claims. Appeals to values and emotions might be just as appropriate as appeals to logic and facts, and all such claims will be stronger if a writer presents a convincing ethos. Although one can study such appeals separately, they work together in arguments, reinforcing each other. (See Chapter 6 for more on ethos.)

Finally, evidence offered as either backing or grounds often involves additional enthymemes and, by implication, new warrants. For example, if you intend to back up the enthymeme

> NASA should launch a human expedition to Mars *because Americans need a unifying national goal.*

with the additional assertion that

> A human expedition to Mars would be a worthwhile scientific project for the nation to pursue. (Logical claim)

you've extended your argument. You may have to offer a supporting reason and possibly explore the resulting enthymeme:

Enthymeme

> A human expedition to Mars would be a worthwhile scientific goal *because human beings can explore the planet better than robots and other machines.*

Warrant

> We should use the best possible means when pursuing scientific goals.

If the warrant is convincing to most readers, the chain of argument can end here—if all factual claims are convincing. But, in fact, many planetary scientists would vigorously contest the claim that human beings can explore planets better than robots. So, as the writer, you would have to deal with this strong objection by either qualifying the supporting reason, defending it factually, or backing down from it entirely.

As you can see, arguments can readily shift downward from an original set of claims and warrants to deeper, more basic claims and reasons. In a philosophy course, you might dig many layers down to reach what seem to be first principles. In general, however, you need to pursue an argument only as far as critical readers require, always presenting them with adequate warrants and convincing evidence.

Using Qualifiers

If you begin to feel intimidated by the rigors of argument, remember that you control the terms of the argument. You can stipulate your responsibilities in an argument simply through the judicious use of qualifiers—terms and conditions that limit your claims and warrants. You can save yourself much time if you qualify a claim early in the writing process. But it often happens that the need to limit an argument becomes evident only as the argument develops.

One way to qualify an argument is by spelling out the terms of the claim as precisely as possible. Never assume that readers understand the limits you have in mind. Whenever you can, spell out what you mean precisely. You'll have less work to do as a result. In the following examples, the first claim in each pair would be much harder to argue convincingly and responsibly—and tougher to research—than the second claim.

> **Efforts to reduce drug use have failed. (Unqualified claim)**
>
> **Most efforts in Texas to reduce marijuana use among high school students have failed. (Qualified claim)**
>
> **Welfare programs should be cut. (Unqualified claim)**
>
> **Ineffective federal welfare programs should be identified, modified, and, if necessary, eliminated. (Qualified claim)**

Experienced writers cherish qualifying expressions because they make writing more precise and honest.

QUALIFIERS

few	it is possible
rarely	it seems
some	it may be
sometimes	more or less
in some cases	many
in the main	routinely

most	one might argue
often	perhaps
under these conditions	possibly
for the most part	if it were so

Understanding Conditions of Rebuttal

There's a fine old book on writing by Robert Graves and Alan Hodges enti-tled *The Reader over Your Shoulder* (1943). In it, Graves and Hodges advise writers always to imagine a crowd of "prospective readers" hovering over their shoulders, asking questions. At every stage in Toulmin argument—making a claim, offering a reason, or studying a warrant—you might con-verse with those nosy readers, imagining them as skeptical, demanding, even a bit testy. They may well get on your nerves. But they'll likely help you foresee the objections and reservations real readers will have regard-ing your arguments.

In the Toulmin system, potential objections to an argument are called conditions of rebuttal. Understanding and reacting to these conditions are essential not only to buttress your own claims where they are weak, but also to understand the reasonable objections of people who see the world differently.

For example, you may be a big fan of the Public Broadcasting Service (PBS) and the National Endowment for the Arts (NEA) and prefer that fed-eral tax dollars be spent on these programs. So you offer the following claim:

> *Claim* The federal government should support the arts.

Of course, you need reasons to support this thesis, so you decide to pres-ent the issue as a matter of values:

> *Claim + Reason* The federal government should support the arts because it also supports the military.

Now you've got an enthymeme and can test the warrant, or the premises of your claim:

> *Warrant* If the federal government can support the military, it can also support other programs.

But the warrant seems frail—something is missing to make a convincing case. Over your shoulder you hear your skeptical friends wondering what wouldn't be fundable according to your very broad principle. They restate your warrant in their own mocking fashion: *Because we pay for a military, we should pay for everything!* You could deal with their objection in the body of your paper, but revising your claim might be a more intelligent way to parry the objections. You give it a try.

> ***Revised Claim + Reason*** If the federal government can spend huge amounts of money on the military, it can afford to spend much less on arts programs.

Now you've got a new warrant, too:

> ***Revised Warrant*** A country that can fund expensive programs can also afford less expensive programs.

This is a premise you feel more able to defend, believing strongly that the arts are just as essential to the well-being of the country as is a strong military. (In fact, you believe the arts are *more* important, but remembering those readers over your shoulder, you decide not to complicate your case by overstating it.) To provide backing for this new and more defensible warrant, you plan to illustrate the huge size of the federal budget and the proportion of that budget that goes to various programs.

But though the warrant seems solid, you still have to offer strong grounds to support your specific and controversial claim. Once again you cite statistics from reputable sources, this time specifically comparing the federal budgets for the military and the arts, breaking them down in ways readers can visualize, demonstrating that much less than a penny of every tax dollar goes to support the arts.

But once more you hear those voices over your shoulder, pointing out that the "common defense" is a federal mandate; the government is constitutionally obligated to support a military. Support for public television or local dance troupes is hardly in the same league. And we still have a huge federal debt.

Hmmm. You'd better spend a paragraph explaining all the benefits the arts provide for the very few dollars spent, and maybe you should also suggest that such funding falls under the constitutional mandate to "promote the general welfare." Though not all readers will accept these grounds, they will at least see that you haven't ignored their point of view. You gain credibility and authority by anticipating a reasonable objection.

As you can see, dealing with conditions of rebuttal is a natural part of argument. But it is important to understand rebuttal as more than mere opposition. Anticipating objections broadens your horizons and likely makes you more open to change. One of the best exercises for you or for any writer is to learn to state the views of others in your own *favorable* words. If you can do that, you're more apt to grasp the warrants at issue and the commonalities you may share with others, despite differences.

Fortunately, today's wired world is making it harder to argue in sublime (or silly) isolation. Newsgroups and listservs on the Internet provide quick and potent responses to positions offered by participants in discussions. Email, too, an almost instantaneous form of communication, makes cross-country connections feel almost like face-to-face conversations. Even the links on Web sites encourage people to think of communication as a network, infinitely variable, open to many voices and different perspectives. Within the Toulmin system, conditions of rebuttal — the voices over the shoulder — remind us that we're part of this bigger world. (For more on arguments in electronic environments, see Chapter 16.)

BEYOND TOULMIN

Can most arguments be analyzed according to Toulmin's principles? The honest answer is no, if you expect most writers to express themselves in perfectly formulated enthymemes or warrants. The same neglect of Toulmin's conditions will likely be evident in arguments you compose yourself. Once you are into your subject, you'll be too eager to make a point to worry about whether you're buttressing the grounds or finessing a warrant.

But that's not a problem if you appreciate Toulmin argument for what it teaches:

- Claims should be stated clearly and qualified carefully.
- Claims should be supported with good reasons.
- Claims and reasons should be based on assumptions readers will likely accept.
- All parts of an argument need the support of solid evidence.
- Effective arguments anticipate objections readers might offer.

It takes considerable experience to write arguments that meet all these conditions. Using Toulmin's framework brings them into play automatically; if you learn it well enough, good arguments can become a habit.

CULTURAL CONTEXTS FOR ARGUMENT

As you think about how to organize your writing, remember that cultural factors are at work: the patterns that you find satisfying and persuasive are likely ones that are deeply embedded in your culture. The organizational patterns favored by U.S. engineers, for example, hold many similarities to the system recommended by Cicero some two thousand years ago. It is a highly explicit pattern, leaving little or nothing unexplained: introduction and thesis, background, overview of the parts that follow, evidence, other viewpoints, and conclusion. If a piece of writing follows this pattern, Anglo-American readers ordinarily find it "well organized."

But writers who are accustomed to different organizational patterns may not. Those accustomed to writing that is more elaborate or that sometimes digresses from the main point may find the U.S. engineers' writing overly simple, even childish. Those from cultures that value subtlety and indirection tend to favor patterns of organization that display these values.

When arguing across cultures, think about how you can organize material to get your message across effectively, but here are a couple of points to consider:

- Determine when to state your thesis—at the beginning? at the end? somewhere else? not at all?

- Consider whether digressions are a good idea, a requirement, or best avoided.

RESPOND•

1. Claims aren't always easy to find—sometimes they are buried deep within an argument, and sometimes they are not present at all. An important skill in reading *and* writing arguments is the ability to identify claims, even when they are not obvious.

   Collect a sample of eight to ten letters to the editor of a daily newspaper. Read each letter and reduce it to a single sentence, beginning with "I believe that . . ."—this should represent the simplest version of the writer's claim.

   When you have compiled your list of claims, look carefully at the words the writers use when stating their positions. Is there a common vocabulary? Can you find words or phrases that signal an impending claim? Which of these seem most effective? Which seem least effective? Why?

2. At their simplest, warrants can be stated as "X is good" or "X is bad." Consider the example from p. 96, "Don't eat that mushroom—it's poisonous." In this case, the warrant could be reduced to "poison is bad." Of course, this is an oversimplification, but it may help you to see how warrants are based in shared judgments of value. If the audience members agree that poison is bad (as they are likely to do), they will accept the connection the writer makes between the claim and the reason.

   As you might expect, warrants are often hard to find, relying as they do on unstated assumptions about value. Return to the letters to the editor that you analyzed in exercise 1, this time looking for the warrant behind each claim. As a way to start, ask yourself these questions: *If I find myself agreeing with the letter writer, what assumptions about the subject matter do I share with the letter writer? If I disagree, what assumptions are at the heart of that disagreement?* The list of warrants you generate will likely come from these assumptions.

3. Toulmin logic is a useful tool for understanding existing arguments, but it can also help you through the process of inventing your own arguments. As you decide what claim you would like to make, you'll need to consider the warrants, different levels of evidence, conditions of rebuttal, and qualifiers. The argument about federal support for the arts provides a good illustration of the Toulmin system's inventional power. By coming to terms with the conditions of rebuttal, you revised your claim and reconsidered the evidence you'd use.

   Using a paper you are writing for this class—it doesn't matter how far along you are in the process—do a Toulmin analysis of the argument. At first, you may struggle to identify the key elements, and you might not find all the categories easy to fill. When you're done, see which elements of the Toulmin scheme are least represented. Are you short of evidence to support the warrant? Have you considered the conditions of rebuttal?

   Next, write a brief revision plan: How will you buttress the argument in the places where your writing is weakest? What additional evidence will you offer for the warrant? How can you qualify your claim to meet the conditions of rebuttal? Having a clearer sense of the logical structure of your argument will help you revise more efficiently.

   It might be instructive to show your paper to a classmate and have him or her do a Toulmin analysis, too. A new reader will probably see your argument in a very different way than you do and suggest revisions that may not have occurred to you.

4. Formulate a specific claim about one or more of the following subjects:

> a current controversial film or TV show
>
> an influential or controversial political figure
>
> affirmative action in college admissions
>
> state laws permitting the carrying of concealed firearms
>
> a controversial issue in sports (the designated hitter in baseball; high school graduates playing in the NBA; Title IX closures of men's sports teams)
>
> violence or sex in video games or song lyrics
>
> transportation issues (public transportation; the safety of small cars; fuel economy regulation)
>
> religion in public life
>
> the role of computers or the Internet in education
>
> the role of the family

5. Turn any claim you wrote for exercise 4 into a full enthymeme by attaching major supporting reasons.

6. State the warrant that connects your claim to its supporting reasons. If necessary, qualify your initial claim.

Arguments of Definition

A traffic committee must define what a small car is in order to enforce parking restrictions in a campus lot where certain spaces are marked "Small Car Only!" Owners of compact luxury vehicles, light trucks, and motorcycles have complained that their vehicles are being unfairly ticketed.

A panel of judges must decide whether computer-enhanced images will be eligible in a contest for landscape photography. At what point is an electronically manipulated image no longer a photograph?

A scholarship committee must decide whether the daughter of two European American diplomats, born while her parents were assigned to the U.S. embassy in Nigeria, will be eligible to apply for grants designated specifically for "African American students." The student claims that excluding her from consideration would constitute discrimination.

A priest chastises some members of his congregation for being "cafeteria Catholics" who pick and choose which parts of Catholic doctrine they will accept and follow. A member of that congregation responds to the priest in a letter explaining her view of what a "true Catholic" is.

A young man hears a classmate describe hunting as a "blood sport." He disagrees and argues that hunting for sport has little in common with "genuine blood sports" such as cockfighting.

A committee of the student union is accused of bias by a conservative student group, which claims that the committee has brought a disproportionate share of left-wing speakers to campus. The committee defends its program by challenging the definition of "left wing" used to classify its speakers.

■ ■ ■

UNDERSTANDING ARGUMENTS OF DEFINITION

When Adam names the animals in the biblical book of Genesis, he acquires authority over them because to name things is, partly, to control them. That's why arguments of definition are so important and so often contentious. They can be about the power to say *what* someone or something is. As such, they can also be arguments about inclusion and exclusion: a creature is a mammal or it isn't; an act is harassment or it isn't; an athlete ought or ought not to be a Hall of Famer.

Another way of approaching definitional arguments, however, is to explore the fertile middle ground between "is" and "is not." Indeed, the most productive definitional arguments probably occur in this realm. Consider the controversy over how to define human intelligence. Some might argue that human intelligence is a capacity measurable by tests of verbal and mathematical reasoning. Others might define it as the ability to perform specific practical tasks. Still others might interpret intelligence in emotional terms, as a competence in relating to other people. Any of these positions could be defended reasonably, but perhaps the wisest approach would be to construct a definition of intelligence that is rich enough to incorporate all three perspectives—and maybe more.

In fact, it's important to realize that many definitions in civil, political, and social (and some scientific) arenas are constantly "under construction," reargued and reshaped whenever they prove inaccurate or inadequate for the times. For example, Gretel Ehrlich's "About Men," one of the definitional essays included at the end of this chapter, reworks the meaning of a very familiar term, *cowboys,* and broadens readers' understanding of the storied ranch hands in light of the labor they actually do:

> **Because these men work with animals, not machines or numbers, because they live outside in landscapes of torrential beauty, because they are confined to a place and a routine embellished with awesome variables, because calves die in the arms that pulled others into life, because they go to the mountains as if on a pilgrimage to find out what makes a herd of elk tick, their strength is also a softness, their toughness, a rare delicacy.**
>
> **–Gretel Ehrlich, "About Men"**

And in case you are wondering, important arguments of definition usually *can't* be solved by consulting dictionaries. Indeed, dictionaries themselves are compilations that reflect the way words are used at a particular time and place by particular classes of people. Like any form of writing, dictionaries reflect the prejudices of their makers — as shown, perhaps most famously, in the entries of lexicographer Samuel Johnson (1709–1784), who gave the English language its first great dictionary. For example, Johnson defined *oats* as "a grain which in England is generally given to horses, but in Scotland supports the people." (To be fair, he also defined *lexicographer* as "a writer of dictionaries, a harmless drudge.") So it is quite possible to disagree with dictionary definitions or to regard them merely as starting points for new explorations of meaning.

CHARACTERIZING DEFINITION

The scope of a definitional argument is often determined by the kind of definition being explored. In most cases, you will probably not even recognize the specific type of definitional question at issue. Fortunately, identifying the type is less important than recognizing the fact that an issue of definition may be involved. Let's explore some common definitional issues.

Formal Definitions

The formal definition is what is typically encountered in dictionaries. It involves placing a term in its proper genus and species—that is, establishing the larger class to which it belongs and then specifying the features that distinguish it from other members of that class. For example, a violin might first be identified by placing it among its peers—musical instruments or stringed instruments. Then the definition would identify the features necessary to distinguish violins from other musical or stringed instruments—four strings, an unfretted fingerboard, a bow.

Given the genus-and-species structure of a formal definition, arguments might evolve from (1) the larger class to which a thing or idea is assigned, or (2) the specific features that distinguish it from other members of the class:

QUESTIONS RELATED TO GENUS

- What is a violin?
- Is tobacco a drug or a crop?
- Is female prostitution a freely chosen profession or an exploitation of women?
- Is *Nightline* a news program? A tabloid? Both?

QUESTIONS RELATED TO SPECIES

- Is a fiddle a type of violin?
- Is tobacco a harmless drug? A dangerously addictive one? Something in between?
- Is female prostitution a profession that empowers or that demeans the women involved?
- Do tabloids report or sensationalize the news?

Operational Definitions

Operational definitions identify an object by what it does or by the conditions that create it: *A line is the shortest distance between two points; Sexual harassment is an unwanted and unsolicited imposition.* Arguments that evolve from operational definitions can be about the conditions that define the object or about whether those conditions have been met. (See also "Stasis Theory" in Chapter 1.)

QUESTIONS RELATED TO CONDITIONS

- Must sexual imposition be both unwanted and unsolicited to be considered harassment?
- Can institutional racism occur in the absence of individual acts of racism?
- Is a volunteer who is paid still a volunteer?
- Does someone who ties the record for home runs in one season deserve the title Hall of Famer?

QUESTIONS RELATED TO FULFILLMENT OF CONDITIONS

- Was the act sexual harassment if the accused believed the imposition was solicited?
- Has the institution kept in place traditions or policies that might lead to racial inequities?
- Was the compensation given to volunteers really "pay"?
- Has a person actually tied a home-run record if the player has hit the same number of homers in a long season that someone else has hit in a shorter season?

Definitions by Example

Resembling operational definitions are definitions by example, which define a class by listing its individual members. For example, one might define *planets* by listing all nine planets in orbit around the sun, or *true American sports cars* by naming the Corvette and the Viper.

Definitional arguments of this sort focus on what may or may not be included in a list of examples. Such arguments often involve comparisons and contrasts with the items most readers would agree from the start belong in this list. One might, for example, wonder why planet status is denied to asteroids, when both planets and asteroids are bodies in orbit around the sun. A comparison between planets and asteroids might suggest that size is one essential feature of the nine recognized planets that asteroids don't meet.

Similarly, one might define *great American presidents* simply by listing Washington, Lincoln, and Franklin Roosevelt. Does President Reagan belong in this company? You might argue that he does if he shares the qualities that place the other presidents in this select group.

QUESTIONS RELATED TO MEMBERSHIP IN A NAMED CLASS

- Is any rock artist today in a class with Chuck Berry, Elvis, Bob Dylan, the Beatles, or the Rolling Stones?
- Is the Mustang a Viper-class sports car?
- Who are the Freuds or Einsteins of the current generation?
- Does Washington, D.C., deserve the status of a state?

Other Issues of Definition

Many issues of definition cross the line between the types described here and some other forms of argument. For example, if you decided to explore whether banning pornography on the Internet violates First Amendment guarantees of free speech, you'd first have to establish a definition of *free speech*—either a legal one already settled on by, let's say, the Supreme Court, or another definition closer to your own beliefs. Then you'd have to argue that types of pornography on the Internet are (or are not) in the same class or share (or do not share) the same characteristics as free speech. In doing so, you'd certainly find yourself slipping into an evaluative mode since matters of definition are often also questions of value. (See Chapter 10.)

When exploring or developing an idea, you shouldn't worry about such slippage—it's a natural part of the process of writing. But do try to focus an argument on a central issue or question, and appreciate the fact that any definition you care to defend must be examined honestly and rigorously. Be prepared to explore every issue of definition with an open mind and with an acute sense of what will be persuasive to your readers.

DEVELOPING A DEFINITIONAL ARGUMENT

Definitional arguments don't just appear out of the blue; they evolve out of the occasions and conversations of daily life, both public and private, such as the following:

- Watching *Washington Journal* on C-SPAN while breakfasting with the kids, you're drawn into a dialogue between two politicians during the "Newspaper Roundtable" segment. They're exploring whether a volunteer who is paid for services is, in fact, a volunteer. You send a fax to C-SPAN expressing your opinion, and Brian Lamb reads it on the air!

- At work, you are asked your opinion about a job description your department is posting. Does it define the position adequately? Does the way the job is defined limit the pool of potential applicants too selectively or unfairly? You don't have many minority employees in your organization.

- Hot under the collar, Grandpa calls you long distance to complain that ten or twenty acres he intended to drain on his farm in Idaho are about to be declared "wetlands" by a busybody federal agent. He wants to know what the difference is between a no-good, mosquito-infested bog and a federally managed wetland.

- Your local newspaper claims, in an editorial, that a hefty new municipal fee on airport parking and hotel rooms shouldn't be considered a "tax." You vehemently disagree and decide to write a letter to the editor—after you cool down.

- Your favorite radio talk show host spends a whole segment explaining why Washington, D.C., ought not to be considered for statehood. "It's not a state," she says; "it's a city." You think about what makes a state a state.

- Just before you turn in one evening, you read an essay entitled "About Men" by Gretel Ehrlich. She says cowboys are the midwives of the plains. This shakes up your comfortable notions about cowboys.

Formulating Claims

In first addressing matters of definition, you'll likely formulate tentative claims—declarative statements that represent your first response to such situations. Note that these initial claims usually don't follow a single definitional formula.

CLAIMS OF DEFINITION

- A person paid to do public service is not a volunteer.
- Institutional racism can exist—maybe even thrive—in the absence of overt civil rights violations.
- A wetland is just a swamp with powerful friends.
- A municipal fee is the same darn thing as a tax.
- The District of Columbia has nothing in common with states.

- Gretel Ehrlich, who writes that "th[e] macho, cultural artifact the cowboy has become is simply a man who possesses resilience, patience, and an instinct for survival," may be on to something.

None of the claims listed here could stand on its own. The claims reflect first impressions and gut reactions because stating a claim is typically a starting point, a moment of bravura that doesn't last much beyond the first serious rebuttal or challenge. Statements of this sort aren't arguments until they're attached to reasons, warrants, and evidence. (See Chapter 8.)

Finding good reasons to support a claim of definition usually requires formulating a general definition by which to explore the subject. To be persuasive, the definition must be broad and *not* tailored to the specific controversy:

- A volunteer is . . .
- Institutional racism is . . .
- A wetland is . . .
- A tax is . . .
- A state is . . .
- A cowboy is . . .

Now consider how the following claims might be expanded in order to become full-fledged definitional arguments:

ARGUMENTS OF DEFINITION

- Someone paid to do public service is not a volunteer because volunteers are people who . . .
- Institutional racism can exist even in the absence of overt violations of civil rights because, by definition, institutional racism is . . .
- A swampy parcel of land becomes a federally protected wetland when . . .
- A municipal fee is the same darn thing as a tax. Both fees and taxes are . . .
- Washington, D.C., ought not to be considered eligible for statehood because states all . . . —and the District of Columbia doesn't!

Notice, too, that some of the issues here involve comparisons between things: swamp/wetland; fees/taxes.

Crafting Definitions

Imagine, now, that you decide to tackle the concept of "paid volunteer" in the following way:

> Participants in the federal AmeriCorps program are not really volunteers because they are paid for their public service. *Volunteers are people who work for a cause without compensation.*

In Toulmin terms, the argument looks like this:

Claim	Participants in AmeriCorps aren't volunteers . . .
Reason	. . . because they are paid for their service.
Warrant	Those who are paid for services are employees, not volunteers.

As you can see, the definition of *volunteers* will be crucial to the shape of the argument. In fact, you might think you've settled the matter with this tight little formulation. But now it's time to listen to the readers over your shoulder (see Chapter 8) pushing you further. Do the terms of your definition account for all pertinent cases of volunteerism, in particular any related to types of public service AmeriCorps volunteers might be involved in?

Consider, too, the word *cause* in your original statement of the definition:

Volunteers are people who work for a cause *without compensation.*

Cause has political connotations that you may or may not intend. You'd better clarify what you mean by *cause* when you discuss your definition in your paper. Might a phrase such as "the public good" be a more comprehensive or appropriate substitute for "a cause"?

And then there's the matter of compensation in the second half of your definition:

Volunteers are people who work for a cause without compensation.

Aren't people who volunteer to serve on boards, committees, and commissions sometimes paid, especially for their expenses? What about members of the so-called all-volunteer military? Certainly they are financially compensated for their years of service, and they enjoy substantial benefits after they complete their service.

As you can see, you can't just offer up a definition as part of your argument and assume that readers will understand or accept it. Every part of the definition has to be weighed, critiqued, and defended. That means you'll want to investigate your subject in the library, on the Internet, or in dialogue with others. You might then be able to present your definition in a single paragraph, or you may have to spend several pages coming to terms with the complexity of the core issue.

Were you to argue about the meaning of *wetlands,* for instance, you might have to examine a range of definitions from any number of sources before arriving at the definition you believe will be acceptable to your readers (or to Grandpa). Here are just three definitions of *wetlands* we found on the Internet, suggesting the complexity of the issue:

> **In general terms, wetlands are lands where saturation with water is the dominant factor determining the nature of soil development and the types of plant and animal communities living in the soil and on its surface.**
>
> –<http://www.nwi.fws.gov/contents.html#wetlands>
> U.S. Fish and Wildlife Service

> **WETLANDS are lands transitional between terrestrial and aquatic systems where the water table is usually at or near the surface or the land is covered by shallow water.**
>
> –<http://www.nwi.fws.gov/contents.html#wetlands>
> U.S. Fish and Wildlife Service

> **Part 303 of the Natural Resources and Environmental Protection Act, PA 451 of 1994, defines a wetland as "land characterized by the presence of water at a frequency and duration sufficient to support, and that under normal circumstances does support, wetland vegetation or aquatic life and is commonly referred to as a bog, swamp or marsh. . . ."**
>
> –<http://www.deq.state.mi.us/lwm/rrs/part303.html>

The definitions, taken together, do help distinguish the conditions that are essential and sufficient for determining wetlands. Essential conditions are those elements that must be part of a definition but that—in themselves—aren't enough to define the term. Clearly, the presence of water and land together in an environment is an essential component of a wetland, but not quite a sufficient condition since a riverbank or beach might meet that condition without being a wetland. In other words, land and water can be in proximity without being a wetland, but there can't be a wetland without there being land and water.

A sufficient condition is any element or conjunction of elements adequate to define a term. The sufficient condition for wetlands seems to be a combination of land and water sufficient to form a regular (if sometimes temporary) ecological system.

One might add accidental conditions to a definition as well—elements that are often associated with a term but are not present in every case or sufficient to identify it. An important accidental feature of wetlands, for example, might be specific forms of plant life or species of birds.

After conducting research of this kind you might be in a position to write an extended definition sufficient to explain to your readers what you believe makes a wetland a wetland; a volunteer a volunteer; a tax a tax; and so on.

Matching Claims to Definitions

Once you've formulated a definition readers will accept—a demanding task in itself—you should place your particular subject in relationship to that general definition, providing evidence to show that

- it is a clear example of the class defined
- it falls outside the defined class
- it falls between two closely related classes

    or

- it defies existing classes and categories and requires an entirely new definition

Thus, your presentation of an issue of definition will depend on the presentation of evidence that may or may not support your initial claim. It is remarkable how often seemingly clear issues of definition become blurry—and open to compromise and accommodation—when the available evidence is examined. So as you assemble evidence, you should be willing to modify your original claim or at least be prepared to deal with objections to it. (See Chapter 8.)

Grandpa, for example, might insist that for half the year his soon-to-be-reclassified property doesn't have a bird on it and is as dry as a bone, so it can't possibly be a wetland. But the federal agent might point out that it meets the sufficient conditions for a wetland from January through June, when it's as mushy as a Slurpee and, moreover, serves as a breeding ground for several endangered species of birds. Needless to say, this kind of argument of definition is often resolved in court.

KEY FEATURES OF DEFINITIONAL ARGUMENTS

Arguments of definition take many shapes. A piece like Gretel Ehrlich's "About Men" (which appears at the end of this chapter) follows a logic of its own in defining *cowboy*, yet it evolves steadily from evidence offered to support a thesis in its first paragraph: "In our hellbent earnestness to romanticize the cowboy we've ironically disesteemed his true character." In writing an argument of definition of your own, consider that it is likely to include the following parts:

- a claim involving a question of definition
- an attempt to establish a general definition acceptable to readers
- an examination of the claim in terms of the accepted definition and all its conditions
- evidence for every part of the argument
- a consideration of alternative views and counterarguments
- a conclusion, drawing out the implications of the argument

It is impossible, however, to predict in advance what emphasis each of those parts ought to receive or what the ultimate shape of an argument of definition will be, especially if it appears in an electronic environment. In a listserv, for example, an argument might evolve over days or weeks, the property of no one person, each separate email message sharpening, qualifying, or complicating the argument. And certainly an argument of definition presented on the Web will offer possibilities that are simply not available on paper. (See Chapter 16.)

Whatever form an argument takes, the draft should be shared with others who can examine its claims, evidence, and connections. It is remarkably easy for a writer in isolation to conceive of ideas narrowly—and not to imagine that others might define *volunteer* or *institutional racism* in a completely different way. It is important to keep a mind open to criticism and suggestions. Look very carefully at the terms of any definitions you offer. Do they really help readers distinguish one concept from another? Are the conditions offered sufficient or essential? Have you mistaken accidental features of a concept or object for more important features?

Don't hesitate to look to other sources for comparisons with your definitions. If you can't depend on dictionaries to offer the last word about any serious or contested term, you can at least begin there to gain control over a concept. Check the meaning of terms in encyclopedias and other reference works. And search the Web intelligently to find how your key terms are presented there. (Searching for the definition of *wetland*, for example, you could type the following into a search engine like Excite and get a limited number of useful hits: *wetland + definition of.*)

Finally, be prepared for surprises in writing arguments of definition. That's part of the delight in expanding the way you see the world. "You're not a terrier; you're a police dog," exclaims fictional detective Nick Charles after his fox terrier, Asta, helps him solve a case. Such is the power of definition.

Finding a Topic

You are likely entering an argument of definition when you

- formulate a controversial definition: *Discrimination is the act of judging someone on the basis of unchangeable characteristics.*

- challenge a definition: *Judging someone on the basis of unchangeable characteristics is not discrimination.*

- try to determine whether something fits an existing definition: *Affirmative action is/is not discrimination.*

Look for issues of definition in your everyday affairs—for instance, in the way jobs are classified at work; in the way key terms are described in your academic major; in the way politicians characterize the social issues that concern you; in the way you define yourself or others try to define you. Be especially alert to definitional arguments that may arise whenever you or others deploy adjectives such as *true, real, actual,* or *genuine: a true* Texan, *real* environmental degradation, *actual* budget projections, *genuine* rap music.

Researching Your Topic

You can research issues of definition using the following sources:

- college dictionaries and encyclopedias
- unabridged dictionaries
- specialized reference works and handbooks, such as legal and medical dictionaries
- your textbooks (check their glossaries)
- newsgroups and listservs that focus on particular topics

Be sure to browse in your library reference room. Also, use the search tools of electronic indexes and databases to determine whether or how often controversial phrases or expressions are occurring in influential materials: major online newspapers, journals, and Web sites.

Formulating a Claim

After exploring your subject, begin to formulate a full and specific claim, a thesis that lets readers know where you stand and what issues are at stake. In moving toward this thesis, begin with the following types of questions of definition:

- questions related to genus: *Is assisting in suicide a crime?*
- questions related to species: *Is tobacco a relatively harmless drug or a dangerously addictive one?*
- questions related to conditions: *Must the imposition of sexual attention be both unwanted and unsolicited to be considered sexual harassment?*
- questions related to fulfillment of conditions: *Has our college kept in place traditions or policies that might constitute racial discrimination?*
- questions related to membership in a named class: *Is any rock artist today in a class with Elvis, Dylan, the Beatles, or the Rolling Stones?*

Your thesis should be an actual statement. In one sentence, you need to *make a claim of definition and state the reasons that support your claim.* In your paper or project itself, you may later decide to separate the claim from the reasons supporting it. But your working thesis should be a fully expressed thought. That means spelling out the details and the qualifications: *Who? What? Where? When? How many? How regularly? How completely?* Don't expect readers to fill in the blanks for you.

Preparing a Proposal

If your instructor asks you to prepare a proposal for your project, here's a format you might use:

State your thesis completely. If you are having trouble doing so, try outlining it in Toulmin terms:

> Claim:
>
> Reason(s):
>
> Warrant(s):

Explain why this argument of definition deserves attention. What is at stake? Why is it important for your readers to consider?

Explain whom you hope to reach through your argument and why this group of readers would be interested in it.

Briefly discuss the key challenges you anticipate in preparing your argument. Defining a key term? Establishing the essential and sufficient elements of your definition? Demonstrating that your subject will meet those conditions?

Determine what strategies you will use in researching your definitional argument. What sources do you expect to consult? Dictionaries? Encyclopedias? Periodicals? The Internet?

Consider what format you expect to use for your project. A conventional research essay? A letter to the editor? A Web page?

Thinking about Organization

Your argument of definition may take various forms, but it is likely to include elements such as the following:

- a claim involving a matter of definition: *Pluto ought not to be considered a genuine planet.*

- an attempt to establish a definition of a key term: *A genuine planet must be a body in orbit around the sun, spherical (not a rock fragment), large enough to sustain an atmosphere, and. . . .*

- an explanation or defense of the terms of the definition: *A planet has to be large enough to support an atmosphere in order to be distinguished from lesser objects within the solar system. . . .*

- an examination of the claim in terms of the definition and all its criteria: *Although Pluto does orbit the sun, it may not in fact be spherical or have sufficient gravity to merit planetary status. . . .*

- evidence for every part of the argument: *Evidence from radio telescopes and other detailed observations of Pluto's surface suggest . . . , and so. . . .*

- a consideration of alternative views and counterarguments: *It is true, perhaps, that Pluto is large enough to have a gravitational effect on. . . .*

Getting and Giving Response

All arguments benefit from the scrutiny of others. Your instructor may assign you to a peer group for the purpose of reading and responding to each other's drafts; if not, make the effort yourself to get some careful response. You can use the following questions to evaluate a draft. If you are evaluating someone else's draft, be sure to illustrate your points with specific examples. Specific comments are always more helpful than general observations.

The Claim

- Is the claim clearly a question of definition?
- Is the claim significant enough to interest readers?

- Are clear and specific criteria established for the concept being defined? Do the criteria define the term adequately? Using this definition, could most readers identify what is being defined and distinguish it from other related concepts?

Evidence for the Claim

- Is enough evidence furnished to explain or support the definition? If not, what kind of additional evidence is needed?
- Is the evidence in support of the claim simply announced, or are its significance and appropriateness analyzed? Is a more detailed discussion needed?
- Are all the conditions of the definition met in the concept being examined?
- Are any objections readers might have to the claim, criteria, or evidence, or to the way the definition is formulated, adequately addressed?
- What kinds of sources are cited? How credible and persuasive will they be to readers? What other kinds of sources might be more credible and persuasive?
- Are all quotations introduced with appropriate signal phrases (such as "As Himmelfarb argues,") and blended smoothly into the writer's sentences?

Organization and Style

- How are the parts of the argument organized? Is this organization effective, or would some other structure work better?
- Will readers understand the relationships among the claim, supporting reasons, warrants, and evidence? If not, what could be done to make those connections clearer? Are more transitional words and phrases needed? Would headings or graphic devices help?
- Are the transitions or links from point to point, paragraph to paragraph, and sentence to sentence clear and effective? If not, how could they be improved?
- Is the style suited to the subject? Is it too formal? Too casual? Too technical? Too bland?
- Which sentences seem particularly effective? Which ones seem weakest, and how could they be improved? Should some short sentences be combined, or should any long ones be separated into two or more sentences?
- How effective are the paragraphs? Do any seem too skimpy or too long?

- Which words or phrases seem particularly effective, vivid, and memorable? Do any seem dull, vague, unclear, or inappropriate for the audience or the writer's purpose? Are definitions provided for technical or other terms that readers might not know?

Spelling, Punctuation, Mechanics, Documentation, Format

- Are there any errors in spelling, punctuation, capitalization, and the like?

- Is an appropriate and consistent style of documentation used for parenthetical citations and the list of works cited or references? (See Chapter 22.)

- Does the paper or project follow an appropriate format? Is it appropriately designed and attractively presented? If it is a Web site, do all the links work?

RESPOND●

1. Briefly discuss the criteria you might use to define the italicized terms in the following controversial claims of definition. Compare your definitions of the terms with those of classmates.

    Burning a nation's flag is a *hate crime*.

    The Kennedys are America's *royal family*.

    Matt Drudge and Larry Flynt are legitimate *journalists*.

    College sports programs have become *big businesses*.

    Plagiarism can be an act of *civil disobedience*.

    Satanism is a *religion* properly protected by the First Amendment.

    Wine (or beer) is a *health food*.

    Campaign contributions are acts of *free speech*.

    The District of Columbia should have all the privileges of an American *state*.

    Committed gay couples should have the legal privileges of *marriage*.

2. This chapter opens with sketches of six rhetorical situations that center on definitional issues. Select one of these situations, and write definitional criteria using the strategy of formal definition. For example, identify the features of a photograph that make it part of a larger class (art, communication method, journalistic technique). Next, identify the features of a photograph that make it distinct from other members of that larger class.

    Then use the strategy of operational definition to establish criteria for the same object: What does it *do*? Remember to ask questions related to conditions (*Is a computer-scanned photograph still a photograph?*) and questions related to fulfillment of conditions (*Does a good photocopy of a photograph achieve the same effect as the photograph itself?*).

3. In the essay at the end of this chapter, Gretel Ehrlich makes a variety of definitional claims—about men, about cowboys, about nature. Find the other terms that she defines, either explicitly or implicitly, and list all the criteria she uses to support her definitions.

    Keep in mind that since criteria are warrants, they are always audience-specific. What audiences are likely to accept Ehrlich's arguments about men? What audiences will likely not accept those arguments? Why not? Who is Ehrlich's *intended* audience? On what grounds do you make these judgments?

4. World chess champion Garry Kasparov lost a much-publicized match to a computer (IBM's "Deep Blue") in 1997. In the days following the

match, there was much speculation in the press and elsewhere over the computer's "intelligence" and its abilities relative to a human's.

Using Internet search engines, find several Web sites that discuss the results of the match between Kasparov and Deep Blue and that offer definitions of *intelligence*. What are the criteria that each site offers for the term? (You might have to analyze the sites carefully; not all arguments of definition provide obvious lists of criteria.)

Next, match the criteria to the sites' audiences. How have the authors of the various Web sites tailored their definitional arguments to the audiences they expect? What are the differences between chess-related sites that discuss the match and computer-related sites, or sites whose primary focus is artificial intelligence?

Before you begin, you might find it useful to make a short list of relevant terms to use during your searches. Start with the obvious terms *(intelligence, chess, Kasparov, Deep Blue)*, and then develop a more complete list as you search.

TWO SAMPLE ARGUMENTS OF DEFINITION

Creating a Criminal

....

MICHAEL KINGSTON

In reaction to the Vietnamese American practice of raising canines for food, Section 598b of the California Penal Code was recently amended to read as follows:

> (a) Every person is guilty of a misdemeanor who possesses, imports into this state, sells, buys, gives away, or accepts any carcass or part of any carcass of any animal traditionally or commonly kept as a pet or companion with the sole intent of using or having another person use any part of that carcass for food.

The California Penal Code defines what actions constitute a misdemeanor.

> (b) Every person is guilty of a misdemeanor who possesses, imports into this state, sells, buys, gives away, or accepts any animal traditionally or commonly kept as a pet or companion with the sole intent of killing or having another person kill that animal for the purpose of using or having another person use any part of the animal for food.

This is a fascinating new law, one that brings up a complex set of moral, political, and social questions. For example: What constitutes a "pet"? Do pets have special "rights" that other animals aren't entitled to? How should these "rights" be balanced with the real political rights of the human populace? How do we define the civil rights of an ethnic minority whose actions reflect cultural values that are at odds with those of the majority? Section 598b does not mention these issues. Rather, it seems to simply walk around them, leaving us to figure out for ourselves whose interests (if any) are being served by this strange new law.

All the questions Kingston raises here arise from an issue of definition: What is a pet?

Michael Kingston wrote "Creating a Criminal" while he was a student at the University of California, Riverside. Kingston argues that a law banning the consumption of animals regarded as pets targets specific immigrant groups. Key to the argument are definitions of *pet* and *racial discrimination*.

The first thing one might wonder is whether the purpose of Section 598b is to improve the lot of pets throughout California. What we do know is that it seeks to prevent
people from eating animals traditionally regarded as pets
(dogs and cats). But for the most part, the only people who
eat dogs or cats are Vietnamese Americans. Furthermore,
they don't consider these animals "pets" at all. So, pets
aren't really being protected. Maybe Section 598b means
to say (in a roundabout manner) that *all* dogs and cats are
special and therefore deserve protection. Yet, it doesn't
protect them from being "put to sleep" in government
facilities by owners who are no longer willing to have
them. Nor does it protect them from being subjected to
painful, lethal experiments designed to make cosmetics
safe for human use. Nor does it protect them from un-
scrupulous veterinarians who sometimes keep one or two
on hand to supply blood for anemic pets of paying cus-
tomers. No, the new law simply prevents Vietnamese
Americans from using them as food.

*Kingston compares
the ostensible
purpose of the new
statutes with what
he regards as their
real purpose.*

Is the consumption of dogs or cats so horrible that it
merits its own law? One possible answer is that these
practices pose a special threat to the trust that the pet-
trading network relies upon. Or in other words: that
strange man who buys one or more of *your* puppies might
just be one of those dog-eaters. But this scenario just
doesn't square with reality. A Vietnamese American,
canine-eating family is no more a threat to the pet-trading
industry than is a family of European heritage that
chooses to raise rabbits (another popular pet) for its food.
Predictably, there is a loophole in Section 598b that allows
for the continued eating of pet rabbits. Its circular logic
exempts from the new law any animal that is part of an
established agricultural industry.

*The case for
prejudice can be
built on a loophole
in the law's
definition of* pet —
*one that favors the
culinary habits
of the European
American majority.*

It seems as though Vietnamese Americans are the only
ones who can't eat what they want, and so it is hard not to
think of the issue in terms of racial discrimination. And
why shouldn't we? After all, the Vietnamese community
in California has long been subjected to bigotry. Isn't it
conceivable that latent xenophobia and racism have found
their way into the issue of dog-eating? One needs only to

look at the law itself for the answer. This law protects animals "traditionally . . . kept as a pet." *Whose* traditions? Certainly not the Vietnamese's.

The meaning of traditions *now becomes a key issue.*

Of course, the typical defense for racially discriminatory laws such as this one is that they actually protect minorities by forcing assimilation. The reasoning here is that everything will run much smoother if we can all just manage to fall in step with the dominant culture. This argument has big problems. First, it is morally bankrupt. How does robbing a culture of its uniqueness constitute a protection? Second, it doesn't defuse racial tensions at all. Racists will always find reasons for hating the Vietnamese. Finally, any policy that seeks to label minorities as the cause of the violence leveled against them is inherently racist itself.

A counterargument is considered and refuted.

Whatever the motives behind Section 598b, the consequences of the new law are all too clear. The government, not content with policing personal sexual behavior, has taken a large step toward dictating what a person can or cannot eat. This is no small infringement. I may never have the desire to eat a dog, but I'm rankled that the choice is no longer mine, and that the choice was made in a climate of racial intolerance. Whatever happened to the right to life, liberty, and the pursuit of happiness?

In this paragraph, Kingston draws on emotional and ethical appeals.

Unfortunately, we may suffer more than just a reduction in personal choice. Crimes such as dog-eating require a certain amount of vigilance to detect. More than likely, the police will rely upon such dubious measures as sifting through garbage left at curbside, or soliciting anonymous tips. Laws that regulate private behavior, after all, carry with them a reduction in privacy.

The threat the new law poses to privacy rights adds an emotional kick to the conclusion.

We sure are giving up a lot for this new law. It's sad that we receive only more criminals in return.

About Men

GRETEL EHRLICH

When I'm in New York but feeling lonely for Wyoming I look for the Marlboro ads in the subway. What I'm aching to see is horseflesh, the glint of a spur, a line of distant mountains, brimming creeks, and a reminder of the ranchers and cowboys I've ridden with for the last eight years. But the men I see in those posters with their stern, humorless looks remind me of no one I know here. In our hellbent earnestness to romanticize the cowboy we've ironically disesteemed his true character. If he's "strong and silent" it's because there's probably no one to talk to. If he "rides away into the sunset" it's because he's been on horseback since four in the morning moving cattle and he's trying, fifteen hours later, to get home to his family. If he's "a rugged individualist" he's also part of a team: ranch work is teamwork and even the glorified open-range cowboys of the 1880s rode up and down the Chisholm Trail in the company of twenty or thirty other riders. Instead of the macho, trigger-happy man our culture has perversely wanted him to be, the cowboy is more apt to be convivial, quirky, and softhearted. To be "tough" on a ranch has nothing to do with conquests and displays of power. More often than not, circumstances —like the colt he's riding or an unexpected blizzard—are overpowering him. It's not toughness but "toughing it out" that counts. In other words, this macho, cultural artifact the cowboy has become is simply a man who possesses resilience, patience, and an instinct for survival. "Cowboys are just like a pile of rocks—everything happens to them. They get climbed on, kicked, rained and snowed on, scuffed up by wind. Their job is 'just to take it,'" one old-timer told me.

A cowboy is someone who loves his work. Since the hours are long—ten to fifteen hours a day—and the pay is $30 he has to. What's required of him is an odd mixture of physical vigor and maternalism. His part of the beef-raising industry is to birth and nurture calves and take care of their mothers. For the most part his work is done on horseback and in a lifetime he sees and comes to know more animals than people. The iconic myth surrounding him is built on American notions of heroism: the index of a man's value as meas-

A filmmaker, poet, novelist, and essayist, Gretel Ehrlich lives on a ranch in Wyoming, ten miles from the nearest paved road. In this essay, from her collection *The Solace of Open Spaces* (1985), she sets out to define what she sees as the real qualities of a misunderstood American archetype—the cowboy.

ured in physical courage. Such ideas have perverted manliness into a self-absorbed race for cheap thrills. In a rancher's world, courage has less to do with facing danger than with acting spontaneously—usually on behalf of an animal or another rider. If a cow is stuck in a boghole he throws a loop around her neck, takes his dally (a half hitch around the saddle horn), and pulls her out with horsepower. If a calf is born sick, he may take her home, warm her in front of the kitchen fire, and massage her legs until dawn. One friend, whose favorite horse was trying to swim a lake with hobbles on, dove under water and cut her legs loose with a knife, then swam her to shore, his arm around her neck lifeguard-style, and saved her from drowning. Because these incidents are usually linked to someone or something outside himself, the westerner's courage is selfless, a form of compassion.

The physical punishment that goes with cowboying is greatly underplayed. Once fear is dispensed with, the threshold of pain rises to meet the demands of the job. When Jane Fonda asked Robert Redford (in the film *Electric Horseman*) if he was sick as he struggled to his feet one morning, he replied, "No, just bent." For once the movies had it right. The cowboys I was sitting with laughed in agreement. Cowboys are rarely complainers; they show their stoicism by laughing at themselves.

If a rancher or cowboy has been thought of as a "man's man"—laconic, hard-drinking, inscrutable—there's almost no place in which the balancing act between male and female, manliness and femininity, can be more natural. If he's gruff, handsome, and physically fit on the outside, he's androgynous at the core. Ranchers are midwives, hunters, nurturers, providers, and conservationists all at once. What we've interpreted as toughness—weathered skin, calloused hands, a squint in the eye and a growl in the voice—only masks the tenderness inside. "Now don't go telling me these lambs are cute," one rancher warned me the first day I walked into the football-field–sized lambing sheds. The next thing I knew he was holding a black lamb. "Ain't this little rat good-lookin'?"

So many of the men who came to the West were Southerners—men looking for work and a new life after the Civil War—that chivalrousness and strict codes of honor were soon thought of as western traits. There were very few women in Wyoming during territorial days, so when they did arrive (some as mail-order brides from places like Philadelphia) there was a standoffishness between the sexes and a formality that persists now. Ranchers still tip their hats and say, "Howdy, ma'am" instead of shaking hands with me.

Even young cowboys are often evasive with women. It's not that they're Jekyll and Hyde creatures—gentle with animals and rough on women—but rather, that they don't know how to bring their tenderness into the house and lack the vocabulary to express the complexity of what they feel. Dancing wildly all night becomes a metaphor for the explosive emotions pent up inside, and when these are, on occasion, released, they're so battery-charged and potent that one caress of the face or one "I love you" will peal for a long while.

The geographical vastness and the social isolation here make emotional evolution seem impossible. Those contradictions of the heart between respectability, logic, and convention on the one hand, and impulse, passion, and intuition on the other, played out wordlessly against the paradisical beauty of the West, give cowboys a wide-eyed but drawn look. Their lips pucker up, not with kisses but with immutability. They may want to break out, staying up all night with a lover just to talk, but they don't know how and can't imagine what the consequences will be. Those rare occasions when they do bare themselves result in confusion. "I feel as if I'd sprained my heart," one friend told me a month after such a meeting.

My friend Ted Hoagland wrote, "No one is as fragile as a woman but no one is as fragile as a man." For all the women here who use "fragileness" to avoid work or as a sexual ploy, there are men who try to hide theirs, all the while clinging to an adolescent dependency on women to cook their meals, wash their clothes, and keep the ranch house warm in winter. But there is true vulnerability in evidence here. Because these men work with animals, not machines or numbers, because they live outside in landscapes of torrential beauty, because they are confined to a place and a routine embellished with awesome variables, because calves die in the arms that pulled others into life, because they go to the mountains as if on a pilgrimage to find out what makes a herd of elk tick, their strength is also a softness, their toughness, a rare delicacy.

chapter ten

Evaluations

A library patron who has never worked on the Internet asks a librarian to recommend several books that introduce a computer novice to the World Wide Web, email, and newsgroups. The patron says she wants the most authoritative books written in the most accessible language.

After a twenty-two-year stint, the president of a small liberal arts college finally decides to retire. After the announcement a committee is formed to choose a new leader, with representatives from the faculty, administration, alumni, and student body. The first task the group faces is to describe the character of an effective college president in the twenty-first century.

A senior is frustrated by the "C" he received on an essay written for a history class, so he makes an appointment to talk with the teaching assistant who graded the paper. "Be sure to review the assignment sheet first," she warns. The student notices that the sheet, on its back side, includes a checklist of requirements for the paper; he hadn't turned it over before.

"We have a lousy home page," a sales representative observes at a district meeting. "What's wrong with it?" the marketing manager asks. "Everything," she replies, then quickly changes the subject when she notices the manager's furrowed brow. But the manager decides to investigate the issue. Web sites are so new: Who knows what a good one looks like—or does?

The waiter uncorks the wine and pours a little into the diner's glass. The diner swirls the Merlot, sniffs its bouquet, and then sips gently, allowing the flavor to bloom on her tongue. "Very good," she nods, and the waiter fills her glass.

You've just seen *Citizen Kane* for the first time and want to share the experience with your roommate. Orson Welles's masterpiece is playing at the Student Union for only one more night, but *Die Hard X: The Battery* is featured across the street in THX sound. Guess which movie Bubba wants to see? You intend to set him straight.

■ ■ ■

UNDERSTANDING EVALUATIONS

By the time you leave home in the morning, you've likely made a dozen informal evaluations. You've selected dressy clothes because you have a job interview in the afternoon with a law firm; you've chosen low-fat yogurt and shredded wheat over artery-clogging eggs and bacon; you've spun the remote past cheery Matt Lauer for what you consider more adult programming on C-SPAN. In each case, you've applied criteria—standards used to measure the quality or value of something—to a particular problem and then made a decision.

Because all people have opinions and most people can—when pressed—even defend them, evaluations may in fact be the most familiar type of argument. Some professional evaluations might require elaborate proto-cols, but they don't differ much structurally from simpler choices that people make routinely. And, of course, people do love to voice their opin-ions, and always have: a whole mode of classical rhetoric—called the cer-emonial, or epideictic—was devoted entirely to speeches of praise and blame. (See Chapter 1.)

Today, rituals of praise and blame are part of American life. Adults who'd choke at the very notion of debating causal or definitional claims will happily spend hours appraising the Dallas Cowboys or the Cleveland Indians. Other evaluative spectacles in our culture include award shows, beauty pageants, most-valuable-player presentations, lists of best-dressed or worst-dressed celebrities, "sexiest people" magazine covers, lit-erary prizes, political opinion polls, consumer product magazines, and—the ultimate formal public gesture of evaluation—elections.

However, many arguments of evaluation do not produce simple rank-ings, ratings, or winners. Instead, they lead people to make decisions, explore alternative courses of action, or even change their lives. In such cases, questions of evaluation can become arguments about core values that affect the way people think and live. Identifying criteria of evaluation can lead to individual insights into motives and preferences.

Why make such a big deal about criteria when many acts of evaluation seem almost effortless? Because in social, cultural, and political realms, evaluations need to be reexamined precisely when they become routine; embedded in many acts of evaluation are important "why" questions that typically go unasked:

- You may find yourself willing to dispute the grade you received in a course, but not the act of grading itself.

- You argue that Miss Alabama would have been a better Miss America than the contestant from New York, but perhaps you don't wonder loudly enough whether such competitions make sense at all.

- You argue passionately that a Republican Congress is better for America than a Democratic alternative, but you fail to ask why voters get only two choices.

- You may have good reasons for preferring a Ford pickup to a Chevy, but you never consider that a bike might be a better alternative than either truck.

- You prize books and reading over any other forms of cultural experi-ence, but you never ask precisely why that should be the case.

Push an argument of evaluation hard enough, and its relatively simple structure can raise deep questions about the values people hold in common and the consequences of those beliefs. Rosa Parks provides an effective example of the relationship between criteria and values when she points out, quite simply, what made Martin Luther King Jr. a hero to her:

> **Dr. King was a true leader. I never sensed fear in him. I just felt that he knew what had to be done and took the leading role without regard to consequences.**
>
> —Rosa Parks, "Role Models"

Her criterion for heroism could not be more evident or compelling: a fearless commitment to do what is right, regardless of the consequences. (For more on arguments based on values, see Chapter 5.)

CHARACTERIZING EVALUATION

For a society that regards itself as pluralistic, especially in matters of taste and values, U.S. citizens are remarkably feisty when it comes to making judgments. That's because even the strongest patrons of relativism—the belief that there are no absolute standards of value—find it hard to act on the principle. People prefer to think that their *own* beliefs are grounded in something more solid than mere rhetoric.

But "mere rhetoric," properly understood, is not to be sniffed at either. As an art of persuasion, rhetoric attunes writers to the power of audiences. Because audiences come to writers with values of their own, part of what writers must do is adjust their messages to the values of readers. But audiences can be moved as well by powerful words and good reasons, so writers also have the power to define values. This tension between existing values (tradition) and innovative perspectives (change) can spark healthy debates and move audiences toward new forms of consensus. That's what makes arguments of evaluation both powerful and exciting: they really do shape our worlds.

One way of classifying evaluative arguments is to consider the types of evidence they use. A distinction we explored in Chapter 7 between inartistic and artistic arguments is helpful here. You may recall that we defined inartistic arguments as those found ready-made as facts, statistics, testimony—what is sometimes now called "hard" evidence. Artistic arguments are those shaped chiefly in and through language, using informal logic. For evaluative arguments, the inartistic/artistic distinction can be expressed in terms of quantity versus quality. Quantitative arguments of evaluation rely on criteria that can be measured, counted, or demonstrated in a mechanical fashion. In contrast, qualitative arguments rely on nonnumerical criteria supported by reason, tradition, precedent, or logic. Needless to say, a claim of evaluation might be supported by arguments of both sorts. We separate them below merely to present them more clearly.

Quantitative Evaluations

At first glance, quantitative evaluations would seem to hold all the cards, especially in a society as enamored of science and technology as our own. Once you have defined a quantitative standard, making judgments should be as easy as measuring and counting—and in a few cases, that's the way things work out. *Who is the tallest or heaviest or loudest person in class?* If your colleagues allow themselves to be measured, you can find out easily enough, using the right equipment and internationally sanctioned standards of measurement: the meter, the kilo, or the decibel.

But what if you were to ask, *Who is the smartest person in class?* You could answer this more complex question quantitatively too, using IQ tests or college entrance examinations that report results numerically. In fact, almost every college-bound student in the United States submits to this kind of evaluation, taking either the SAT or ACT to demonstrate his or her verbal and mathematical prowess. Such measures are widely accepted by educators and institutions, but they are also vigorously challenged. Although scores generated by the SAT or ACT seem objective, they are based on responses to questions that measure particular kinds of skills, most of them related to academic success. Just how closely those numbers actually correlate with intelligence can be disputed, since many believe that academic achievement is far from the only measure of knowing, and that intelligence itself is not a single thing that can be measured quantitatively.

Like any standards of evaluation, quantitative criteria must be scrutinized carefully to make sure that what they measure relates to what is being evaluated. For example, in evaluating a car, you might use 0–60 mph times as a measure of acceleration, 60–0 mph distances as a measure of braking capability, skidpad numbers (0.85) as a measure of handling ability, and coefficient of drag (0.29) as a test of aerodynamic efficiency. But all these numbers are subject to error. A driver has to be on board to shift a manual transmission car through the gears, slam on the brakes, or steer a skidpad; the human variable tempers the absolute reliability of the measurements. Even when the numbers are gathered accurately and then compared, one vehicle with another, they may not tell the whole story, since some cars generate great test numbers and yet still feel less competent than vehicles with lower scores. The same disparity between numbers and feel occurs with other items—compact disc recordings, for example. CDs can produce awesome sonic accuracy numbers, but some listeners feel the music they produce may lack aural qualities important to listening pleasure. Educators, too, acknowledge that some students test better than others.

This is not to disparage quantitative measures of quality, only to offer a caveat: even the most objective measures have limits. They have been devised by fallible people looking at the world from their own inevitably limited perspectives. Just a few decades ago, teachers hoped that they might figure out how to measure quality of writing by applying quantitative measures relating to "syntactical maturity." The endeavor now seems almost comical because the more complex the human activity, the more it resists quantification. And writing is very complicated.

Yet experts in measurement assert with confidence that quantitative measures are almost always more reliable than qualitative criteria—no matter what is being evaluated. It is a sobering claim, and one not easily dismissed.

Qualitative Evaluations

Many issues of evaluation closest to people's hearts simply aren't subject to quantification. *What makes a movie great?* If someone suggested length, people would probably chuckle. Get serious! But what about box office receipts, especially if they could be adjusted to reflect changes in the value of the dollar over time? Would films that earned the most revenue—a definitely quantifiable measure—have a claim on the title "best picture"? In that select group would be movies such as *Star Wars, The Sound of Music, Gone with the Wind,* and *Titanic.* An interesting group of films, but the best? To argue for box office revenue as a criterion of film greatness, you'd have to defend the claim vigorously because many people in the audience would express doubts about it—substantial ones, based on prevailing prejudices that generally distinguish between artistic quality and popularity.

More likely, then, in defining the criteria for "great movie," you would look for standards to account for the merit of films such as *Citizen Kane,*

Casablanca, 8½, and *Jules et Jim*—works widely respected among serious critics. You might talk about directorial vision, societal impact, cinematic technique, dramatic rhythm—qualities that could be defined with some precision, but measured only with great difficulty. Lacking hard numbers, you would have to convince the audience to accept your standards and make your case rhetorically, providing evidence that connected artistic achievement to particular techniques or components. As you might guess, a writer using qualitative measures could spend as much time defending criteria of evaluation as providing evidence that these standards are present in the film under scrutiny.

But establishing subtle criteria is what can make arguments of evaluation so interesting if you take them seriously. They require you, time and again, to challenge conventional wisdom. Or they force you to give backbone to opinions you *think* you hold. In the following passage from one of the sample evaluative essays at the end of this chapter, the author provides a lively example of attacking a standard of evaluation she believes has survived too long:

> **Valorization of reading over television . . . is often based on the vague and groundless notion that reading is somehow "active" and television "passive." Why it is that the imaginative work done by a reader is more strenuous or worthwhile than that done by a viewer—or why watching television is more passive than, say, watching a play—is never explained.**
> **–Larissa MacFarquhar, "Who Cares If Johnny Can't Read?"**

Predictably, MacFarquhar's challenge to conventional wisdom provoked a strong response from readers when it appeared in the online magazine *Slate,* a response that generated perhaps more heat than light. Harvey Scodel writes in a letter to the editor: " 'Who Cares If Johnny Can't Read?' by Larissa MacFarquhar is a truly stupid article . . . a good example of supposedly skeptical and revisionist garbage." Ann W. Schmidt claims the article "is so off base that it is difficult to fathom that she [MacFarquhar] really believes what she is saying." Oh well, at least you know exactly where Scodel and Schmidt stand.

DEVELOPING AN EVALUATIVE ARGUMENT

Developing an argument of evaluation can seem like a simple process, especially if you already know what your claim is likely to be:

- *Citizen Kane* is the finest film ever made by an American director.
- Most serious drivers would prefer a 5-Series BMW to an E-Class Mercedes.
- A value-added tax would be a dreadful replacement for the federal income tax.
- John Paul II will likely be regarded as one of the three or four most important leaders of the twentieth century.

Having established a claim, you would then explore the implications of your belief, drawing out the reasons, warrants, and evidence that might support it.

Claim	**Citizen Kane is the finest film ever made by an American director . . .**
Reason	**. . . because it revolutionizes the way we see the world.**
Warrant	**Great films change viewers in fundamental ways.**
Evidence	**Shot after shot, Citizen Kane presents the life of its protagonist through cinematic images that viewers can never forget.**

The warrant here is, in effect, a statement of criteria—in this case, the quality that defines "great film" for the writer.

In developing an evaluative argument, you'll want to pay special attention to criteria, claims, and evidence.

Formulating Criteria

Most often neglected in evaluations is the discussion of criteria. Although even casual evaluations ("Da Bears bite!") could be traced to reasonable criteria, most people don't bother defending their positions unless they are pressed ("Oh yeah?"). This reluctance to state criteria can be especially unfortunate whenever unexamined judgments are either inaccurate or indefensible to the point of stereotype or prejudice, as in the following examples:

> **It's an ugly sport coat, probably from off the rack at Kmart.**
>
> **I doubt that the movie is any good. It stars Madonna.**
>
> **Henley may not be the lawyer you want—she was admitted to law school only because of affirmative action.**

Yet when writers address audiences whom they understand well or with whom they share core values, full statements of evaluative criteria are usually unnecessary. One wouldn't expect a film critic like Roger Ebert to restate all his principles every time he writes a movie review. Ebert assumes his readers will—over time—come to appreciate his standards.

Criteria are often embedded in statements rather than stated explicitly, because writers assume that readers will follow their meaning. For example, a newspaper columnist assessing President Clinton's policy toward North Korea might observe that "it lacks the imagination and risk of Nixon's China gambit." Packed in that clause is a wealth of implied meaning. First, there's implicit approval of a foreign policy widely agreed to have succeeded: in going to China in 1972, President Nixon reduced tensions between the United States and the huge Asian power. Since the China "gambit" worked, one can assume that the writer also approves of the "imagination" and "risk" that accompanied it. In other words, the writer is suggesting that foreign policy should be clever and daring: that's the implied criterion, a standard likely clear (even obvious) to readers familiar with the writer's historical allusion. But you can see the dangers of implied criteria. A reader who is ignorant of Nixon's policy won't appreciate the writer's point about President Clinton. So you see why you have to consider who your readers might be when you write arguments of evaluation. Readers must either share your criteria or be convinced to accept them.

Don't take criteria of evaluation for granted, especially when tackling a new subject. If you offer vague and unsupported principles, expect to be challenged. And you are most likely to be vague about your beliefs when you haven't thought enough about your subject. So push yourself at least as far as you imagine readers will. Imagine those readers over your shoulder, asking difficult questions.

Say, for example, that you intend to argue that serious drivers will obviously prefer a 5-Series BMW to an E-Class Mercedes. What standards would serious drivers apply to these sedans? Razor-sharp handling? But what does that mean? Perhaps it's the ability to hold the road in tight curves with minimal steering correction. That's a criterion you could defend. Serious drivers would likely expect precise braking, too. Might that mean that the brake pedal should be firm, responding linearly to driver input? Are such standards getting too technical? Or do you need to assert such sophisticated criteria to establish your authority to write about the subject? These are appropriate questions to ask.

Don't hesitate to be bold or idealistic in stating standards. Part of the appeal of Allan Bloom's now-classic discussion of American higher education, *The Closing of the American Mind,* was his ability to offer clear criteria to support the reforms he proposed:

A good program of liberal education feeds the student's love of truth and passion to live the good life. It is the easiest thing in the world to devise courses of study, adapted to the particular conditions of each university, which thrill those who take them. The difficulty is getting them accepted by the faculty. (emphasis added)
                                   –Allan Bloom, "The Student and the University"

Making Claims

Claims can be stated directly or, in rare instances, strongly implied. For most writers the direct evaluative claim probably works better, with the statement carefully qualified. Consider the differences between the following claims and how much less the burden of proof would be for the second and third ones:

> John Paul II is the most important leader of the twentieth century.

> John Paul II may be one of the three or four most influential leaders of the twentieth century.

> John Paul II may come to be regarded as one of the three or four most influential spiritual leaders of the twentieth century.

The point of qualifying a statement is not to make evaluative claims bland, but to make them responsible and manageable. Of course, claims themselves might be more responsible if they were always written after a sober study of facts and evidence. But most people don't operate that way, particularly if they are working in isolation or within a closed community. Most people start with an opinion and then seek reasons and evidence to support it. If people are honest, though, they'll at least modify their claims in the face of contrary evidence.

But bringing strongly held claims to the table can work well in situations where different opinions meet. That's what makes discussions on listservs so potentially exciting: people with different values make contradictory claims and then negotiate their differences, sometimes over days and weeks. Committees and study groups can work in this way, too. For example, imagine Congress contemplating alternatives to the current federal income tax system. A committee assigned to explore better systems of taxation would likely work best if it included people willing to champion the merits of different plans, everything from a flat tax to the current progressive income tax. Each of these positions, well argued, would broaden the scope of what the committee knew and might help the group move toward consensus. Or it might not.

Presenting Evidence

The more evidence the better in an evaluation, provided that the evidence is relevant. In evaluating the performance of two computers, the speed of their processors would certainly be important, but the quality of their keyboards or the availability of service might be less crucial, perhaps irrelevant.

Just as important as relevance in selecting evidence is presentation. Not all pieces of evidence are equally convincing, nor should they be treated as such. Select evidence most likely to impress your readers, and arrange the paper to build toward your best material. In most cases, that *best material* will be evidence that is specific, detailed, and derived from credible sources. To support her point that reading is not inherently "better" than watching television, Larissa MacFarquhar points to examples that most readers will recognize and remember:

> **The best books might be better than the best television, but further down the pile the difference gets murkier. Most of the time the choice between books and television is not between Virgil and *Geraldo* but between *The Celestine Prophecy* and *Roseanne*. Who wouldn't pick *Roseanne?***
> –Larissa MacFarquhar, "Who Cares If Johnny Can't Read?"

Don't be afraid, either, to concede a point when evidence goes contrary to the overall claim you wish to make. If you are really skillful, you can even turn a problem into an argumentative asset, as Bob Costas does in acknowledging the flaws of baseball great Mickey Mantle in the process of praising him:

> **None of us, Mickey included, would want to be held to account for every moment of our lives. But how many of us could say that our best moments were as magnificent as his?**
> –Bob Costas, "Eulogy for Mickey Mantle"

When you are developing evidence for an evaluative paper, the Internet can be a remarkably helpful source, particularly when your subject falls within the realms of popular culture. By checking out particular newsgroups (even some that might not be considered authoritative sources for a traditional academic paper), you'll likely gain insight into popular feelings and attitudes. If, for example, you find the popularity of a show like *The X-Files* or *Roswell* puzzling, checking its Web site or related newsgroups may lead you to appreciate what has captured the imagination of fans. Evidence drawn from such material represents legitimate research.

KEY FEATURES OF EVALUATIONS

In drafting an evaluation, you should consider three basic elements:

- an evaluative claim about a particular object, concept, or class related to the stated criteria

- a statement and (if necessary) an examination of criteria applicable to a given object, concept, or class: "This is what makes a *great film,* an *effective leader,* a *feasible solution:* . . ."

- evidence that the particular subject meets or falls short of the stated criteria

All these elements will be present in one way or another in arguments of evaluation, but they won't follow a specific order. In addition, you'll often need an opening paragraph to set the context for your evaluation, explaining to readers why they should care about the opinion you are about to present.

Nothing adds more depth to an opinion than offering it for discussion. When you can, use the resources of the Internet or more local online networks to get response to your opinions. It can be eye-opening to realize how strongly people react to ideas or points of view that you regard as perfectly conventional. When you are ready, share your draft with colleagues, asking them to identify places where you need additional support for your ideas, either in the discussion of criteria or in the presentation of evidence.

Finding a Topic

You are entering an argument of evaluation when you

- make a judgment about quality: *Citizen Kane is probably the finest film ever made by an American director.*
- challenge such a judgment: *Citizen Kane is vastly overrated by most film critics.*
- construct a ranking or comparison: *Citizen Kane is a more intellectually challenging movie than* Casablanca.

Issues of evaluation arise daily—in the judgments you make about public figures or policies; in the choices you make about instructors and courses; in the recommendations you make about books, films, or television programs; in the preferences you exercise in choosing products, activities, or charities. Be alert to evaluative arguments whenever you read or use terms that indicate value or rank: *good/bad, effective/ineffective, best/worst, competent/incompetent, successful/unsuccessful.* Finally, be aware of your own areas of expertise. Write about subjects or topics about which others regularly ask your opinion or advice.

Researching Your Topic

You can research issues of evaluation using the following sources:

- journals, reviews, and magazines (for current political and social issues)
- books (for assessing judgments about history, policy, etc.)
- biographies (for assessing people)
- research reports and scientific studies
- books, magazines, and Web sites for consumers
- periodicals and Web sites that cover entertainment and sports

Surveys and polls can be useful in uncovering public attitudes: *What books are people reading? Who are the most admired people in the country? What activities or businesses are thriving or waning?* You'll discover that Web sites, newsgroups, and listservs thrive on evaluation. Browse these public forums for ideas and, when possible, explore your own topic ideas there.

Formulating a Claim

After exploring your subject, begin to shape a full and specific claim, a thesis that lets readers know where you stand and on what criteria you will base your judgments. Look for a thesis that is challenging enough to attract readers' attention, not one that merely repeats views already widely held. In moving toward this thesis, you might begin with questions of this kind:

- What exactly is my opinion? Where do I stand?
- Can I make my judgment more specific?
- Do I need to qualify my claim?
- According to what standards am I making my judgment?
- Will readers accept my criteria, or will I have to defend them, too?
- What major reasons can I offer in support of my evaluation?

Your thesis should be a complete statement. In one sentence, you need to *make a claim of evaluation and state the reasons that support your claim.* Be sure your claim is specific enough. Anticipate the questions readers might have: *Who? What? Where? Under what conditions? With what exceptions? In all cases?* Don't expect readers to guess where you stand.

Preparing a Proposal

If your instructor asks you to prepare a proposal for your project, here's a format you might use.

State your thesis completely. If you are having trouble doing so, try outlining it in Toulmin terms:

  Claim:

  Reason(s):

  Warrant(s):

Explain why this issue deserves attention. What is at stake?

Specify whom you hope to reach through your argument and why this group of readers would be interested in it.

Briefly discuss the key challenges you anticipate. Defining criteria? Defending them? Finding quantitative evidence to support your claim? Developing qualitative arguments to bolster your judgment?

Determine what research strategies you will use. What sources do you expect to consult?

Consider what format you expect to use for your project. A conventional research essay? A letter to the editor? A Web page?

Thinking about Organization

Your evaluation may take various forms, but it is likely to include elements such as the following:

- a specific claim: *Most sport utility vehicles (SUVs) are unsuitable for the kind of driving most Americans do.*

- an explanation or defense of the criteria (if necessary): *The overcrowding and pollution of American cities and suburbs might be relieved if more Americans drove small, fuel-efficient cars. Cars do less damage in accidents than heavy SUVs and are also less likely to roll over.*

- an examination of the claim in terms of the stated criteria: *Most SUVs are unsuitable for the kind of driving Americans do because they are not designed for contemporary urban driving conditions.*

- evidence for every part of the argument: *SUVs get very poor gas mileage; they are statistically more likely than cars to roll over in accidents. . . .*

- consideration of alternative views and counterarguments: *It is true, perhaps, that SUVs make drivers feel safer on the roads and give them a better view of traffic conditions because of their height. . . .*

Getting and Giving Response

All arguments benefit from the scrutiny of others. Your instructor may assign you to a peer group for the purpose of reading and responding to each other's drafts; if not, make the effort yourself to get some careful response. You can use the following questions to evaluate a draft. If you are evaluating someone else's draft, be sure to illustrate your points with specific examples. Specific comments are always more helpful than general observations.

The Claim

- Is the claim clearly an argument of evaluation? Does it make a judgment about something?

- Does the claim establish clearly what is being evaluated?

- Is the claim too sweeping? Does it need to be qualified?

- Will the criteria used in the evaluation be clear to readers? Do the criteria need to be defined more explicitly or precisely?

- Are the criteria appropriate ones to use for this evaluation? Are they controversial? Does evidence of their validity need to be added?

Evidence for the Claim

- Is enough evidence provided to ensure that what is being evaluated meets the criteria established for the evaluation? If not, what kind of additional evidence is needed?

- Is the evidence in support of the claim simply announced, or are its significance and appropriateness analyzed? Is a more detailed discussion needed?

- Are any objections readers might have to the claim, criteria, or evidence adequately addressed?

- What kinds of sources are cited? How credible and persuasive will they be to readers? What other kinds of sources might be more credible and persuasive?

- Are all quotations introduced with appropriate signal phrases (for instance, "As Will argues,") and blended smoothly into the writer's sentences?

Organization and Style

- How are the parts of the argument organized? Is this organization effective, or would some other structure work better?

- Will readers understand the relationships among the claims, supporting reasons, warrants, and evidence? If not, what could be done to make those connections clearer? Are more transitional words and phrases needed? Would headings or graphic devices help?

- Are the transitions or links from point to point, paragraph to paragraph, and sentence to sentence clear and effective? If not, how could they be improved?

- Is the style suited to the subject? Is it too formal? Too casual? Too technical? Too bland?

- Which sentences seem particularly effective? Which ones seem weakest, and how could they be improved? Should some short sentences be combined, or should any long ones be separated into two or more sentences?

- How effective are the paragraphs? Do any seem too skimpy or too long?

- Which words or phrases seem particularly effective, vivid, and memorable? Do any seem dull, vague, unclear, or inappropriate for the audience or the writer's purpose? Are definitions provided for technical or other terms that readers might not know?

Spelling, Punctuation, Mechanics, Documentation, Format

- Are there any errors in spelling, punctuation, capitalization, and the like?

- Is an appropriate and consistent style of documentation used for parenthetical citations and the list of works cited or references? (See Chapter 22.)

- Does the paper or project follow an appropriate format? Is it appropriately designed and attractively presented? If it is a Web site, do all the links work?

RESPOND•

1. Choose one item from the following list that you understand well enough to evaluate. Develop several criteria of evaluation you could defend to distinguish excellence from mediocrity in the area. Then choose another item from the list, this time one you do not know much about at all, and explain the research you might do to discover reasonable criteria of evaluation for it.

   fashion designers

   sport utility vehicles

   action films

   hip-hop music

   American presidents

   NFL quarterbacks

   landscape design

   contemporary painting

   professional journalists

   TV sitcoms

   fast food

   rock musicians

2. Local news-and-entertainment magazines often publish "best of" issues or articles that list readers' and editors' favorites in such categories as "best place to go on a first date," "best softball field," and "best dentist." Sometimes the categories are very specific: "best places to say, 'I was retro before retro was cool,'" or "best movie theater seats." Imagine that you are the editor of your own local magazine and that you want to put out a "best of" issue tailored to your hometown. Develop ten categories for evaluation. For each category, list the evaluative criteria you use to make your judgment. (You might want to review Chapter 9 to decide which of the criteria are essential, sufficient, or accidental to your evaluation.)

   Next, consider that since your criteria are warrants, they are especially tied to audience. (The criteria for "best dentist," for example, might be tailored to people whose major concern is avoiding pain, to those whose children will be regular visitors, or to those who want the cheapest possible dental care.) For several of your evaluative categories, imagine that you have to justify your judgments to a completely different audience. Write a new set of criteria for that audience.

3. Read Larissa MacFarquhar's article "Who Cares If Johnny Can't Read?" and the two readers' letters of response, both of which appear at the end of this chapter. MacFarquhar makes several evaluative claims, some of them more explicit than others. What are the categories that she evaluates? What are the criteria that she uses to evaluate them? Pick one category and list her evaluative criteria. Then turn to the readers' letters, and determine the criteria *they* use to evaluate the same category. Which criteria do the readers accept? Which do they not accept? How can you account for the strength of the readers' reactions?

TWO SAMPLE EVALUATIONS

The Simpsons: *A Mirror of Society*

BEN McCORKLE

In recent years, a certain animated sitcom has caught the public's attention, evoking reactions that are both favorable and unfavorable, but hardly ever apathetic. As a brilliant, socially aware satire, Matt Groening's *The Simpsons* has effectively stirred different emotions from different factions of the culturally deadened American populace, and for this alone it should be recognized as "quality programming."

The first paragraph offers a criterion for quality entertainment.

Often, *The Simpsons* is truly brutal parody, hurling barbs of hostile commentary at our materialistic and gluttonous American lifestyle. Many in the audience might be offended by this bullying, except that it seems like harmless fun. For example, when father Homer Simpson decides he would rather sleep in on a Sunday than attend church, Groening is obviously pointing out a corruption of traditional values within the family structure. But recognizing that people don't like to be preached to, the show takes a comic approach, having God come to talk to Homer, telling him to start his own religious sect. The hedonism that Homer extols in the name of the Lord is both ludicrous and hilariously funny, and viewers who might be offended are disarmed, so that even the most conservative Republican grandmother is receptive to the comic message.

Effective parody exposes the flaws of society — another important standard for judging the show.

Because it is a cartoon, some might scoff at *The Simpsons* and call it a children's show. But this cartoon is clearly meant for a mass audience, including adults: it is shown during prime time rather than on Saturday morn-

McCorkle anticipates a potential objection to his argument.

Ben McCorkle wrote "The Simpsons: A Mirror of Society" while he was a student at Augusta College in Augusta, Georgia. McCorkle argues that the television cartoon series *The Simpsons* merits serious attention because it exposes the deepest flaws in our society while making us laugh.

ings, and, moreover, it appears on the Fox network, that paragon of broadcast debauchery. The cartoon format allows for visual freedom artistically and, because many people believe cartoons to be childish and incapable of making any real commentary on social values, may aid as well in the subtle presentation of the show's message.

The Simpson family has occasionally been described as a "nuclear" family, which obviously has a double meaning: first, the family consists of two parents and three children, and, second, Homer works at a nuclear power plant with very relaxed safety codes. The overused label *dysfunctional*, when applied to the Simpsons, suddenly takes on new meaning. Every episode seems to include a scene in which son Bart is being choked by his father, the baby is being neglected, or Homer is sitting in a drunken stupor transfixed by the television screen. The comedy in these scenes comes from the exaggeration of commonplace household events (although some talk shows and news programs would have us believe that these exaggerations are not confined to the madcap world of cartoons).

The next several paragraphs provide detailed evidence to support the claim of evaluation.

While Bart represents the mischievous demon-spawn and Homer the dim-witted plow ox, the female characters serve as foils to counterbalance these male characters' unredeeming characteristics. Marge, the mother, is rational, considerate, and forgiving, always aware of her husband's shortcomings; younger sister Lisa is intelligent, well behaved, and an outstanding student; and baby Maggie is an innocent child. (Could the fact that the "good" members of the family all happen to be female reflect some feminist statements on Groening's part?)

It is said that "to err is human," in which case the Simpsons may appear to be a little more human than the rest of us. They are constantly surrounded by their failures, yet seemingly unaware that their lives are often less than ideal. Their ability to accept the hand dealt them and endure without complaint is their most charming quality. Although not very bright as a whole, the Simpsons are survivors. Moreover, they exhibit a patriotic dedication to life, liberty, and the pursuit of happiness that should make every true American proud.

The Simpsons' targets are listed to suggest the breadth of the program's satire.

Ultimately, viewers find this family to be unwitting heroes, enduring the incompetence and corruption of contemporary education, industry, government, religion, and, ironically, even television. Yet in spite of all the disheartening social problems it portrays, *The Simpsons* nevertheless remains funny. Whenever a scene threatens to turn melodramatic or raise an inescapably deep issue, the moment is saved by some piece of nonsense, often an absurdly gratuitous act of violence.

The conclusion reinforces the overall claim and offers one final rationale for the show's success.

At a time when it seems that society is being destroyed by its own designs, it is good to be able to hold up a mirror that shows us the extent of our problems. Neither escapist nor preachy, *The Simpsons* provides such a satiric mirror, a metaphoric reflection of our dissolving social foundation. More than that, *The Simpsons* is therapeutic: to be able to laugh in the face of such problems is the ultimate catharsis.

Who Cares If Johnny Can't Read?

LARISSA MacFARQUHAR

Among the truisms that make up the eschatology of American cultural decline, one of the most banal is the assumption that Americans don't read. Once, the story goes—in the 1950s, say—we read much more than we do now, and read the good stuff, the classics. Now, we don't care about reading anymore, we're barely literate, and television and computers are rendering books obsolete.

None of this is true. We read much more now than we did in the '50s. In 1957, 17 percent of people surveyed in a Gallup poll said they were currently reading a book; in 1990, over twice as many did. In 1953, 40 percent of people

---

Larissa MacFarquhar is a contributing editor of *Lingua Franca*, a magazine about higher education, and an advisory editor at the *Paris Review*, a literary journal. In this article, which originally appeared in the online magazine *Slate* in 1997, she brashly challenges the traditional evaluation that the reading of books is the pinnacle of cultural achievement. As you might expect, the article provoked a torrent of outraged email to *Slate*'s editors; two examples follow her piece here.

polled by Gallup could name the author of *Huckleberry Finn;* in 1990, 51 percent could. In 1950, 8,600 new titles were published; in 1981, almost five times as many.

In fact, Americans are buying more books now than ever before—over 2 billion in 1992. Between the early '70s and the early '80s, the number of bookstores in this country nearly doubled—and that was before the Barnes & Noble superstores and Amazon.com. People aren't just buying books as status objects, either. A 1992 survey found that the average adult American reads 11.2 books per year, which means that the country as a whole reads about 2 billion—the number bought. There are more than 250,000 reading groups in the country at the moment, which means that something like 2 million people regularly read books and meet to discuss them.

In his book about Jewish immigrants in America at the turn of the century, *World of Our Fathers,* Irving Howe describes a time that sounds impossibly antiquated, when minimally educated laborers extended their workdays to attend lectures and language classes. Howe quotes an immigrant worker remembering his adolescence in Russia: "How can I describe to you . . . the excitement we shared when we would discuss Dostoyevsky? . . . Here in America young people can choose from movies and music and art and dancing and God alone knows what. But we—all we had was books, and not so many of them, either."

Hearing so much about the philistinism of Americans, we think such sentiments fossils of a bygone age. But they're not. People still write like that about books. Of course, most aren't reading Dostoyevsky. The authors who attract thousands and thousands of readers who read everything they write and send letters to them begging for more seem to be the authors of genre fiction—romances, science fiction, and mysteries.

Romance readers are especially devoted. The average romance reader spends $1,200 a year on books, and often comes to think of her favorite authors as close friends. Romance writer Debbie Macomber, for instance, gets thousands of letters a year, and when her daughter had a baby, readers sent her a baby blanket and a homemade Christmas stocking with the baby's name embroidered on it. It's writers like Macomber who account for the book boom. In 1994, a full 50 percent of books purchased fell into the category of "popular fiction." (Business and self-help books were the next biggest group at 12 percent, followed by "cooking/crafts" at 11 percent, "religion" at 7 percent, and "art/literature/poetry" at 5 percent.)

These reading habits are not new. Genre fiction and self-help books have made up the bulk of the American book market for at least 200 years. A survey conducted in 1930 found that the No. 1 topic people wanted to read about was personal hygiene. And you just have to glance through a list of best sellers through the ages to realize how little we've changed: *Daily Strength for Daily Needs* (1895); *Think and Grow Rich* (1937); *Games People Play: The Psychology of Human Relationships* (1964); *Harlow: An Intimate Biography* (1964).

Romance writers tend to be cleareyed about what it is they're doing. They don't think they're creating subversive feminine versions of Proust. They're producing mass-market entertainment that appeals to its consumers for much the same reason as McDonald's and Burger King appeal to theirs: It's easy, it makes you feel good, and it's the same every time. The point of a romance novel is not to dazzle its reader with originality, but to stimulate predictable emotions by means of familiar cultural symbols. As romance writer Kathleen Gilles Seidel puts it: "My reader comes to my book when she is tired. . . . Reading may be the only way she knows how to relax. If I am able to give her a few delicious, relaxing hours, that is a noble enough purpose for me."

But then, if romance novels are just another way to relax, what, if anything, makes them different from movies or beer? Why should the activity "reading romances" be grouped together with "reading philosophy" rather than with "going for a massage"? The Center for the Book in the Library of Congress spends lots of time and money coming up with slogans like "Books Make a Difference." But is the mere fact of reading something—*anything*—a cultural achievement worth celebrating?

We haven't always thought so. When the novel first became popular in America in the latter half of the 18th century, it was denounced as a sapper of brain cells and a threat to high culture in much the same way that television is denounced today. In the 1940s, Edmund Wilson declared that "detective stories [are] simply a kind of vice that, for silliness and minor harmfulness, ranks somewhere between smoking and crossword puzzles." You almost never hear this kind of talk anymore in discussions of American reading habits: *Not all reading is worth doing. Some books are just a waste of time.*

As fears of cultural apocalypse have been transferred away from novels onto a series of high-tech successors (radio, movies, television, and now computers), books have acquired a reputation for educational and even moral worthiness. Books are special: You can send them through the mail for lower rates, and there are no customs duties imposed on books imported into this country. There have, of course, been endless culture wars fought over what kind of books should be read in school, but in discussions of adult reading habits these distinctions tend to evaporate.

The sentimentalization of books gets especially ripe when reading is compared with its supposed rivals: television and cyberspace. Valorization of reading over television, for instance, is often based on the vague and groundless notion that reading is somehow "active" and television "passive." Why it is that the imaginative work done by a reader is more strenuous or worthwhile than that done by a viewer—or why watching television is more passive than, say, watching a play—is never explained. Sven Birkerts' maudlin 1994 paean to books, *The Gutenberg Elegies: The Fate of Reading in an Electronic Age,* is a classic example of this genre. *Time* art critic Robert Hughes made a similarly sentimental and mysterious argument recently in the *New York Review of Books*:

> Reading is a collaborative act, in which your imagination goes halfway to meet the author's; you visualize the book as you read it, you participate in making up the characters and rounding them out. . . . The effort of bringing something vivid out of the neutral array of black print is quite different, and in my experience far better for the imagination, than passive submission to the bright icons of television, which come complete and overwhelming, and tend to burn out the tender wiring of a child's imagination because they allow no re-working.

I cannot remember ever visualizing a book's characters, but everyone who writes about reading seems to do this, so perhaps I'm in a minority. Still, you could equally well say that you participate in making up TV characters because you have to imagine what they're thinking, where in a novel, you're often provided with this information.

Another reason why books are supposed to be better than television is that books are quirky and individualistic and real, whereas television is mass-produced corporate schlock. But of course popular books can be, and usually are, every bit as formulaic and "corporatized" as television. The best books might be better than the best television, but further down the pile the difference gets murkier. Most of the time the choice between books and television is not between Virgil and *Geraldo* but between *The Celestine Prophecy* and *Roseanne.* Who wouldn't pick *Roseanne?*

If the fertility of our culture is what we're concerned about, then McLuhanesque musing on the intrinsic nature of reading (as if it had any such thing) is beside the point. Reading per se is not the issue. The point is to figure out why certain kinds of reading and certain kinds of television might matter in the first place.

LINKS

BookWeb, the site of the American Booksellers Association, includes a "Reference Desk," which tracks some trends in book selling, book buying, books as gifts, etc. You can get a quick summary of the Center for the Book and its campaigns to promote readership. Book groups have made their way onto the Web, and publishers are, quite understandably, promoting them. The Bantam Doubleday Dell site serves up a minihistory of book groups and tells you how to join or form one of your own. Not surprisingly, aficionados of romance fiction have a plethora of sites to choose from: For starters, try the Romance Reader, with its many reviews, and the online version of the magazine *Romance Times*. Mystery-fiction sites are equally abundant—see Mystery/Net.com and the Mysterious Home Page. You can read excerpts from Sven Birkerts' *The Gutenberg Elegies,* as well as a response to the book in the *Atlantic Monthly*. Finally, for some academic resources on reading, turn to the Society for the History of Authorship, Reading & Publishing.

Two Responses to This Article

"Who Cares If Johnny Can't Read?" by Larissa MacFarquhar is a truly stupid article, whose only point is that there is a big difference between basic reading and highbrow reading. But this is not a crucial distinction for people concerned about literacy in this country. There has been a palpable decline in literacy in America over the last 30 years. Even the average university student both knows less and, by common-sense measures, is less intelligent than his or her predecessors. And even if IQ has not declined on a mass scale (and I suspect that it has), there is a point at which lack of curiosity and sheer ignorance are indistinguishable from a deficiency of intelligence. This article was a good example of supposedly skeptical and revisionist garbage.

–Harvey Scodel, "Illiteracy Test"

"Who Cares If Johnny Can't Read?" by Larissa MacFarquhar is so off base that it is difficult to fathom that she really believes what she is saying. I am the president of the Literacy Council of Garland County, Ark., and I know that the functional illiteracy rate in our state is 52 percent.

Her data is obviously faulty. It is nonsense to ask an illiterate person if he's reading a book. Of course he's going to say "yes." The last thing an illiterate person wants to advertise is the fact that he can't read. Our culture is filled with ways to help people hide their illiteracy. Restaurants like Shoney's and Denny's feature pictures of their entrees on the menu so those who can't read can still order their meal. And people know who wrote *Huckleberry Finn* and other books because they have learned from television and the movies.

–Ann W. Schmidt, "Lying Illiterates"

chapter eleven

Causal Arguments

A local school board member notes that students at one high school consistently outscore all others in the district on standardized math tests. She decides to try to identify the cause(s) of these students' success.

Researchers at a national research laboratory note that a number of their colleagues have contracted skin cancer during the last five years. They decide to work together to investigate possible causes.

A large clothing manufacturer wants to increase its market share among teenage buyers of blue jeans. Its executives know that another company has been the overwhelming market leader for years—and they set out to learn exactly why.

Convinced that there is a strong and compelling causal link between smoking and lung cancer, you argue that your cousin should stop smoking immediately and at any cost.

A state legislator notes that gasoline prices are consistently between twenty-five and fifty cents higher in one large city in the state than elsewhere. After some preliminary investigation, the legislator decides to bring a class action lawsuit on behalf of the people of this city, arguing that price fixing and insider deals are responsible for the price difference.

■ ■ ■

UNDERSTANDING CAUSAL ARGUMENTS

Arguments about causes and effects inform many everyday decisions and choices: you decide to swear off desserts since they inevitably lead to weight gain; because you failed last week's midterm, you decide to work through all the problems with a group of other students in your class, convinced that the new study technique will bring about an improvement in your test scores. To take another example, suppose you are explaining, in a petition for a change of grade, why you were unable to submit the final assignment on time. You would probably try to trace the causes of your failure to submit the assignment—the death of your grandmother followed by an attack of the flu followed by the theft of your car—in hopes that the committee reading the petition would see these causes as valid and change your grade. In identifying the causes of the situation, you are implicitly arguing that the effect—your failure to turn in the assignment on time—should be considered anew.

Causal arguments exist in many forms and frequently appear as parts of other arguments (such as evaluations or proposals). But it may help focus your work on causal arguments to separate them into three major categories:

- arguments that state a cause and then examine its effect(s)
- arguments that state an effect and then trace the effect back to its cause(s)
- arguments that move through a series of links: A causes B, which leads to C and perhaps to D

Arguments that begin with a stated cause and then move to an examination of one or more of its effects

This type of argument might begin, for example, with a cause like putting women into combat and then demonstrate the effects that such a cause would have. In this type of argument, success depends on being able to show compellingly that the cause would indeed lead to the described effects. Producer Anita Gordon and zoologist David Suzuki mount such a causal argument in an essay about how current attempts to "engineer" nature will lead to environmental disaster. Here is the opening of their essay:

> There's a strange phenomenon that biologists refer to as "the boiled frog syndrome." Put a frog in a pot of water and increase the temperature of the water gradually from 20°C to 30°C to 40°C . . . to 90°C and the frog just sits there. But suddenly, at 100°C (212°F), something happens: the water boils and the frog dies.
>
> Scientists studying environmental problems, particularly the greenhouse effect, see "the boiled frog syndrome" as a metaphor for the human situation: we have figuratively, and in some ways literally, been heating up the world around us without realizing the danger.
> –Anita Gordon and David Suzuki, "How Did We Come to This?"

Arguments that begin with an effect and then trace the effect back to one or more causes

This type of argument might begin with a certain effect — for example, the facts of urban ghetto poverty — and then trace the effect or set of effects to the most likely causes — in this case, widespread racism and persistent job discrimination, or, from another point of view, an implicit but powerful class and economic system that demands a "bottom." Again, the special challenge of such arguments is to make the causal connection compelling to the audience. In 1962, scientist Rachel Carson seized the attention of millions with a causal argument about the effects of the overuse of chemical poisons in agricultural control programs. Here is an excerpt from the beginning of her book-length study of this subject:

> . . . a strange blight crept over the area and everything began to change. Some evil spell had settled on the community: mysterious maladies swept the flocks of chickens; the cattle and sheep sickened and died. Everywhere was a shadow of death. The farmers spoke of much illness among their families. . . . There had been several sudden and unexplained deaths, not only among adults but even among children, who would be stricken suddenly while at play and die within a few hours. . . .

The roadsides, once so attractive, were now lined with browned and withered vegetation as though swept by fire. These, too, were silent, deserted by all living things. Even the streams were now lifeless. Anglers no longer visited them, for all the fish had died.

In the gutters under the eaves and between the shingles of the roofs, a white granular powder still showed a few patches; some weeks before it had fallen like snow upon the roofs and the lawns, the fields and streams.

No witchcraft, no enemy action had silenced the rebirth of new life in this stricken world. The people had done it themselves. . . .

What has already silenced the voices of spring in countless towns in America? This book is an attempt to explain.

–Rachel Carson, *Silent Spring*

Arguments that move through a series of links: Cause A leads to B, which leads to C and possibly to D

In an environmental science class, for example, you might decide to argue that a national law regulating smokestack emissions from utility plants is needed because (A) emissions from utility plants in the Midwest cause acid rain, (B) acid rain causes the death of trees and other vegetation in eastern forests, (C) powerful lobbyists have prevented midwestern states from passing strict laws to control emissions from these plants, and (D) as a result, acid rain will destroy most eastern forests by 2020. In this case, the first link is that emissions cause acid rain; the second, that acid rain causes destruction in eastern forests; and the third, that states have not acted to break the cause-effect relationship established by the first two points. These links set the scene for the fourth link, which ties the previous points together to argue from effect: unless X, then Y.

At their most schematic, then, causal arguments may be diagrammed in relatively straightforward ways, as shown in Figure 11.1.

FIGURE 11.1 CAUSAL ARGUMENTS

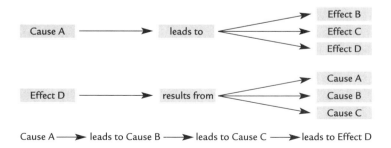

CHARACTERIZING CAUSAL ARGUMENTS

Causal arguments tend to share several characteristics.

They are often part of other arguments.

Causal arguments often work to further other arguments, especially proposals, so you should remember that they can be useful in establishing the good reasons for arguments in general. For example, a proposal to limit the amount of time children spend watching television would very likely draw on causal "good reasons" for support, ones that would attempt to establish that watching television causes negative results — such as increased violent behavior, decreased attention spans, and so on.

They are almost always complex.

The complexity of most causal arguments makes establishing causes and effects extremely difficult. For example, scientists and politicians continue to disagree over the extent to which acid rain is actually responsible for the so-called dieback of many eastern forests. If you can show that X *definitely* causes Y, though, you will have a powerful argument at your disposal. That is why, for example, so much effort has gone into establishing a definite link between smoking and cancer and between certain dietary habits and heart disease: providing the causal link amid the complex of factors that might be associated with cancer or heart disease would argue most forcefully for changing behavior in very significant ways.

They are often definition-based.

Part of the complexity of causal arguments arises from the need for very carefully worded definitions. Recent figures from the U.S. Department of Education, for example, indicate that the number of high school dropouts is rising and that this rise has caused an increase in youth unemployment. But exactly how does the study define *dropout*? A closer look may suggest that some students (perhaps a lot) who drop out actually "drop back in" later and go on to complete high school. Further, how does the study define *employment*? Until you can provide explicit definitions that answer such questions, you should proceed cautiously with a causal argument like this one.

They usually yield probable rather than absolute conclusions.

Because causal relationships are almost always extremely complex, they seldom yield more than a high degree of probability. Scientists in particular are wary of making causal claims—that eating certain foods causes cancer, for example, since it is highly unlikely that a disease as resistant and persistent as cancer could be linked to any one cause. Even after an event, causation can be difficult to prove. No one would disagree that the Japanese bombing of Pearl Harbor took place on December 7, 1941, or that the United States entered World War II shortly thereafter. But what is the causal connection? Did the bombing "cause" the U.S. entry into the war? Even if one is convinced that the bombing was the most immediate cause, what of other related causes: the unstable and often hostile relationship between the U.S. and Japanese governments in the years leading up to the bombing; U.S. policies toward Japanese immigration; common U.S. stereotypes of "Oriental" peoples; U.S. reactions to the Japanese invasion of China; and so on? As another example, during the campus riots of the late 1960s, a special commission was charged with determining the "causes" of riots on a particular campus. After two years of work—and almost a thousand pages of evidence and reports—the commission was unable to pinpoint anything but a broad network of contributing causes and related conditions. Thus, causal claims must be approached with care and supported with the strongest evidence available in order to demonstrate the highest probability possible that A caused B.

DEVELOPING CAUSAL ARGUMENTS

Formulating a Claim

Although you might decide to write a wildly exaggerated or parodic causal argument for humorous purposes (such as *Dave Barry's Complete Guide to Guys: A Fairly Short Book,* in which Barry traces the "causes" of "guy-dom"), most of the causal reasoning you do will be related to serious subjects of significance to you, to your family and friends, or to your society. To begin creating a strong causal claim, try listing some of the effects—events or phenomena—you would like to know the causes of. *Why do you tend to panic immediately before exams? What's responsible for the latest tuition hike? What has led to the postings of "contamination" along your favorite creek?* Or try moving in the opposite direction, listing some events or causes you are interested in and then hypothesizing what kinds of effects they may produce. *What will happen if your academic major begins requiring a six-year program for a B.S.? What may be the effects of a balanced federal budget?*

When you find several possible causal relationships that interest you, try them out on friends and colleagues. Can they suggest ways to refocus or clarify what you want to do? Can they offer leads to finding information about your subject? If you have hypothesized various causes or effects, can they offer counterexamples or refutations?

Finally, map out a rough statement about the causal relationship you want to explore:

A causes (or is caused by) B for the following reasons:

1. _____

2. _____

3. _____

Developing the Argument

Once you have drafted a claim, you can explore the cause-effect relationship(s), drawing out the reasons, warrants, and evidence that can support the claim most effectively.

Claim	Losing seasons caused the football coach to lose his job.
Reason	The team lost more than half its games for three seasons in a row.
Warrant	Winning is the key to success for Big Ten college coaches.
Evidence	For the last ten years, coaches with more than two losing seasons in a row have lost their jobs.

Claim	Certain career patterns cause women to be paid less than men.
Reason	Women's career patterns differ from men's, and in spite of changes in the relative pay of other groups, women's pay still lags behind that of men.
Warrant	Successful careers are made during the period between ages 25 and 35.
Evidence	Women often drop out of or reduce work during the decade between ages 25 and 35 in order to raise families.

In further developing a causal argument, you can draw on many of the strategies we have already touched on in this book. In the article from which the following passage is excerpted, for instance, Stephen King uses dozens of examples—from *The Texas Chainsaw Massacre, The Gory Ones,* and *Invasion of the Body Snatchers* to *Night of the Living Dead, Psycho, The Amityville Horror,* and *The Thing*—in explaining why people love horror movies:

> The mythic horror movie, like the sick joke, has a dirty job to do. It deliberately appeals to all that is worst in us. It is morbidity unchained, our most base instincts let free, our nastiest fantasies realized . . . and it all happens, fittingly enough, in the dark. For those reasons, good liberals often shy away from horror films. For myself, I like to see the most aggressive of them—*Dawn of the Dead,* for instance—as lifting a trap door in the civilized forebrain and throwing a basket of raw meat to the hungry alligators swimming around in that subterranean river beneath.
>
> Why bother? Because it keeps them from getting out, man. It keeps them down there and me up here. It was Lennon and McCartney who said that all you need is love, and I would agree with that.
>
> As long as you keep the gators fed.
>
> —Stephen King, "Why We Crave Horror Movies"

Another way to support a causal argument is through the use of analogies. In such an argument, the strength will lie in how closely you can relate the two phenomena being compared. In exploring why Americans are now involved in what he calls "The Worship of Art," journalist Tom Wolfe draws an analogy between religion and art, and he argues that the causes that have long linked humans with religious belief now link them with the arts:

> There was a time when well-to-do, educated people in America adorned their parlors with crosses, crucifixes, or Stars of David. These were marks not only of faith but of cultivation. Think of the great homes, built before 1940, with chapels. This was a fashionable as well as devout use of space. . . . Practically no one who cares about appearing cultivated today would display a cross or Star of David in the living room. It would be . . . *in bad taste.* Today the conventional symbol of devoutness is—but of course—the Holy Rectangle: the painting. The painting is the religious object we see today in the parlors of the educated classes.
>
> —Tom Wolfe, "The Worship of Art: Notes on the New God"

Establishing causes for physical effects—like diseases—often calls for another means of support: testing hypotheses, or theories about possible causes. This kind of reasoning helped to determine the causes of school poisonings in California recently, and some years ago it helped to solve a mystery disease that had struck some fifty people in Quebec City. Puzzled by cases all involving the same effects (nausea, shortness of breath, cough, stomach pain, weight loss, and a marked blue-gray coloration), doctors at first investigated the hypothesis that the cause was severe vitamin deficiency. But too many cases in too short a time made this hypothesis unlikely, because vitamin deficiency does not ordinarily appear as a sudden epidemic. In addition, postmortem examinations of the twenty people who died revealed severe damage to the heart muscle and the liver, features that were inconsistent with the vitamin-deficiency hypothesis. The doctors therefore sought a clue to the mysterious disease in something the fifty victims were found to have shared: all fifty had been lovers of beer and had, in fact, drunk a particular brand of beer.

It seemed possible that the illness was somehow connected to the beer, brewed in Quebec City and Montreal. But Montreal had no incidence of the disease. The hypothesis, then, was further refined: perhaps the significant difference existed in the process of brewing. Eventually, this hypothesis was borne out. The Quebec brewery had added a cobalt compound to its product in order to enhance the beer's foaminess; the Montreal brewery had not. Furthermore, the compound had been added only a month before the first victims became ill.

In spite of the strength of this causal hypothesis, doctors in this case were still cautious, since the cobalt had not been present in sufficient quantities to kill a normal person. Yet twenty had died. After persistent study, the doctors decided that this fact must be related to the victims' drinking habits, which in some way reduced their resistance to the chemical. For those twenty people, a normally nonlethal dose of cobalt had been fatal.

The difficulties of such causal analysis were in the news a lot after the 1996 explosion of TWA flight 800. Those who followed this case in the news and on the Internet saw investigators test—and reject—a number of hypotheses about the cause of the crash: a bomb, a missile, "friendly fire," pilot error. Only in the summer of 1997 did the head investigator put forward a hypothesis that the team felt was sufficiently supported by all the data at hand. In their analysis, air conditioning packs that had been running for over two hours prior to the plane's departure heated up a small amount of fuel in an almost-empty center tank. This heating in turn may have caused vapor to form and eventually explode, blowing out the bottom center of the plane. According to the team, the first explosion led to subsequent explosions that destroyed the entire aircraft.

Causal arguments can also be supported by experimental evidence that is based less on strictly scientific investigation than on ethnographic observation—the study of the daily routines of ordinary people in a particular community. In an argument that attempts to explain why, when people meet head-on, some step aside and some do not, investigators Frank Willis, Joseph Gier, and David Smith observed "1,038 displacements involving 3,141 persons" at a Kansas City shopping mall. In results that surprised the investigators, "gallantry" seemed to play a significant role in causing people to step aside for one another—more so than other causes the investigators had anticipated (such as deferring to someone who is physically stronger or higher in status).

Yet another method of supporting a causal argument is through the use of one or more correlations. In such an argument you try to show that if A occurs, B is also likely to occur. You may be most familiar with correlations from statistical procedures that allow you to predict, within a degree of certainty, how likely it is that two elements or events will occur together. Recent advances in the human genome project, for example, have identified "clusters" of genes that, when found in correlation with one another, strongly suggest the occurrence of certain cancers. But correlation works in more informal ways as well. Robert Coles, internationally known for his studies of childhood development, uses such a strategy in his study of affluent children in which he traces the effects that a correlation between wealth and power has on young people:

> **Wealth does not corrupt nor does it ennoble. But wealth does govern the minds of privileged children, gives them a peculiar kind of identity which they never lose, whether they grow up to be stockbrokers or communards, and whether they lead healthy or unstable lives. There is, I think, a message that virtually all quite well-off American families transmit to their children—an emotional expression of those familiar, classbound prerogatives, money and power. I use the word "entitlement" to describe that message.**
> **–Robert Coles, *Privileged Ones***

Finally, you may want to consider using personal experience in support of a causal argument. Indeed, people's experiences generally lead them to seek out or to avoid various causes and effects. If you are consistently praised for your writing ability, chances are that you will look for opportunities to produce that pleasant effect. If three times in a row you get sick after eating shrimp, you will almost certainly identify the shellfish as the cause of your difficulties and stop eating it. Personal experience can also help build your credibility as a writer, gain the empathy of your listeners, and thus support your cause. Although one person's experiences cannot ordinarily be universalized, they can still argue eloquently for causal relationships. Terry Tempest Williams explores one causal relationship, asking "If we poison Mother Earth, our home, will our own mothers (and we as well) not also be poisoned?" In pursuing this question, Williams draws on her own personal experience:

> **I belong to a Clan of One-Breasted Women. My mother, my grandmothers, and six aunts have all had mastectomies. Seven are dead. The two who survive have just completed rounds of chemotherapy and radiation. . . .**
>
> **I've had my own problems: two biopsies for breast cancer and a small tumor between my ribs diagnosed as "borderline malignancy."**
>
> **This is my family history.**
>
> **Most statistics tell us breast cancer is genetic, hereditary, with rising percentages attached to fatty diets, childlessness, or becoming pregnant after thirty. What they don't say is living in Utah may be the greatest hazard of all. . . .**
>
> **I cannot prove that my mother, Diane Dixon Tempest, or my grandmothers, Lettie Romney Dixon and Kathryn Blackett Tempest, along with my aunts developed cancer from nuclear fallout in Utah. But I can't prove they didn't.**
>
> **– Terry Tempest Williams, "The Clan of One-Breasted Women"**

All these strategies—the use of examples, analogies, testing hypotheses, experimental evidence, correlations, and personal experience—can help you build good reasons in support of a causal argument. However, the success of the argument may ultimately depend on your ability to convince your readers that the reasons you offer are indeed good ones. In terms of causal arguments, that will mean distinguishing among immediate, necessary, and sufficient reasons. In the case of the mysterious illness in Quebec City, the immediate reasons for illness were the symptoms themselves: nausea, shortness of breath, and so on. But they were not the base or root causes of the disease. Drinking the particular beer in question served as a necessary reason: without the tainted beer, the illness would not have occurred. However, the researchers had to search much harder for the sufficient reason—the reason that will cause the effect (the illness) if it is present. In the case of the Quebec City beer, that reason turned out to be the addition of cobalt.

This example deals with the scientific investigation of a disease, but everyday causal analysis can draw on this distinction among reasons as well. What caused you, for instance, to pursue a college education? Immediate reasons might be that you needed to prepare for a career of some kind or that you had planned to do so for years. But what are the necessary reasons, the ones without which your pursuit of higher education could not occur? Adequate funds? Good test scores and academic record? The expectations of your family? You might even explore possible sufficient reasons, those that—if present—will guarantee the effect of your pursuing higher education. In such a case, you may be the only person with enough information to determine what sufficient reasons might be.

KEY FEATURES OF CAUSAL ARGUMENTS

In drafting a causal argument, consider the following five elements:

- examination of each possible cause and effect
- description and explanation of the relationship among any links, especially in an argument based on a series of links in a causal chain
- evidence that your description and explanation are accurate and thorough
- evidence to show that the causes and effects you have identified are highly probable and that they are backed by good reasons, usually presented in order of their strength and importance
- consideration of alternative causes and effects, and evidence that you have considered them carefully before rejecting them

Fully developing a causal argument will probably call for addressing each of these elements, though you may order them in several ways. You may want to open your essay with a dramatic description of the effect, for example, and then "flash back" to multiple causes. Or you might decide to open with a well-known phenomenon, identify it as a cause, and then trace its effects. In the same way, you might decide to lead off the body of the argument with your strongest, most compelling piece of evidence, or to hold that evidence for the culmination of your argument. In any case, you should make a careful organizational plan and get a response to that plan from your instructor, friends, and colleagues before proceeding to a full draft. When the draft is complete, you should again seek a response, testing out the strength of your causal argument on at least several readers.

Finding a Topic

Chances are that a little time spent brainstorming—either with friends or other students, or on paper—will turn up some good possibilities for causal arguments of several kinds, including those that grow out of your personal experience. *Just exactly what did lead to your much higher GPA last term?* Beyond your own personal concerns, you may find a good number of public issues that lend themselves to causal analysis and argument: *What factors have led to the recent decline in reported cases of HIV infection? What will happen if the United States signs the Comprehensive Nuclear Test Ban Treaty? What effects have been caused by the move to pay professional basketball players astronomical sums of money?* Finally, as you are brainstorming possibilities for a causal argument of your own, don't ignore important current campus issues: *What have been the effects of recent increases in tuition (or what factors caused the increases)? What are the likely outcomes of shifting the academic calendar from a quarter to a semester system? If, as some argue, there has been a significant increase of racism and homophobia on campus, what has caused that increase? What are its consequences?*

Researching Your Topic

Causal arguments will lead you to a number of different resources:

- current news media—especially magazines and newspapers (online or in print)
- scholarly journals
- books written on your subject (here you can do a keyword search, either in your library or online)
- Web sites, listservs, or newsgroups devoted to your subject

In addition, you may decide to carry out some field research of your own—to conduct interviews with appropriate authorities on your subject, for instance, or to create a questionnaire aimed at getting a range of opinion on a particular aspect of your subject.

Formulating a Claim

You may begin to formulate your claim by identifying the particular kind of causal argument you want to make—one moving from cause(s) to effect(s); one moving from effect(s) to cause(s); or one involving a series of links, with cause A leading to B, which then leads to C. (See pp. 162–64 for a review of these kinds of arguments.)

Your next move may be to explore your own relationship to your subject. What do you know about the subject and its causes and effects? On what basis do you agree with the claim? What significant reasons can you offer in support of it?

In short, you should end this process of exploration by formulating a brief claim or thesis about a particular causal relationship. It should include *a statement that says, in effect, A causes (or is caused by) B, and a summary of the reasons supporting this causal relationship.* Remember to make sure that your thesis is as specific as possible and that it is sufficiently controversial or interesting to hold your readers' interest.

Preparing a Proposal

If your instructor asks you to prepare a proposal for your project, here's a simple format that may help.

State the thesis of your argument fully, perhaps using the Toulmin schema:

> Claim:
>
> Reason(s):
>
> Warrant(s):

Explain why this argument deserves attention. Why is it important for your readers to consider?

Specify those whom you hope to reach with this argument, and explain why this group of readers is an appropriate audience. What interest or investment do they have in the issue? Why will they (or should they) be concerned?

Briefly identify and explore the major challenges you expect to face in supporting your argument. Will demonstrating a clear causal link between A and B be particularly difficult? Will the data you need to support the claim be hard to obtain?

What strategies do you expect to use in researching your argument— Interviewing? Surveying opinion? Library or online searches? Other? What are the major sources you will need to consult—and are they readily available to you?

Briefly identify and explore the major counterarguments you might expect in response to your argument.

What format or genre do you expect to use for your argument? A press release? An editorial for the local newspaper? A Web site?

Thinking about Organization

Whatever genre or format you decide to use, your causal argument should address the following elements:

- a specific causal claim: *Devastating flash floods associated with El Niño were responsible for the dramatic loss of homes in central California in early 1998.*

- an explanation of the claim's significance or importance: *Claims for damage from flooding put some big insurance companies out of business; as a result, homeowners couldn't get coverage and many who lost their homes had to declare bankruptcy.*

- supporting evidence sufficient to support each cause or effect—or, in an argument based on a series of causal links, evidence to support the relationships among the links: *The amount of rain that fell in central California in early 1998 was 200 percent above normal, leading inexorably to rapidly rising rivers and creeks.*

- consideration of alternative causes and effects, and evidence that you understand these alternatives and have thought carefully about them before rejecting them: *Although some say that excessive and sloppy logging and poor building codes were responsible for the loss of homes, the evidence supporting these alternative causes is not convincing.*

Getting and Giving Response

All arguments can benefit from the scrutiny of others. Your instructor may assign you to a peer group for the purpose of reading and responding to each other's drafts; if not, make the effort yourself to get some careful response. You can use the following questions to evaluate a draft. If you are evaluating someone else's draft, be sure to supply specific examples to illustrate your points. Specific comments are always more helpful than general observations.

The Claim

- What is most effective about the claim? What are its strengths?
- Is the claim sufficiently qualified?
- Is the claim specific enough to be clear? Could it be narrowed and focused more clearly?
- How strong is the relationship between the claim and the reasons given to support it? Could that relationship be made more explicit?
- Is it immediately evident why the claim is important? Could it be rephrased in a way that more forcefully and clearly suggests its significance?

- Does the claim reveal a causal connection? Could it be revised to make the causal links clearer?

Evidence for the Claim

- What is the strongest evidence offered for the claim? Does any of the evidence need to be strengthened?

- Is enough evidence offered that these particular causes are responsible for the effect that has been identified, that these particular effects result from the identified cause, or that a series of causes and effects are linked? If not, what kind of additional evidence is needed? What kinds of sources might provide this evidence?

- How credible and persuasive will the sources likely be to potential readers? What other kinds of sources might be more credible and persuasive?

- Is the evidence in support of the claim simply announced, or is it analyzed in terms of its appropriateness and significance? Is a more detailed discussion necessary?

- Have all the major alternative causes and effects as well as objections to the claim been considered? What support is offered for rejecting these alternatives? Where is additional support needed?

Organization and Style

- How are the parts of the argument organized? Is this organization effective, or would some other structure work better?

- Will readers understand the relationships among the claims, supporting reasons, warrants, and evidence? If not, what could be done to make those connections clearer? Are more transitional words and phrases needed? Would headings or graphic devices help?

- Are the transitions or links from point to point, paragraph to paragraph, and sentence to sentence clear and effective? If not, how could they be improved?

- Is the style suited to the subject? Is it too formal? Too casual? Too technical? Too bland?

- Which sentences seem particularly effective? Which ones seem weakest, and how could they be improved? Should some short sentences be combined, or should any long ones be separated into two or more sentences?

- How effective are the paragraphs? Do any seem too skimpy or too long?

- Which words or phrases seem particularly effective, vivid, and memorable? Do any seem dull, vague, unclear, or inappropriate for the audience or the writer's purpose? Are definitions provided for technical or other terms that readers might not know?

Spelling, Punctuation, Mechanics, Documentation, Format

- Are there any errors in spelling, punctuation, capitalization, and the like?
- Is an appropriate and consistent style of documentation used for parenthetical citations and the list of works cited or references? (See Chapter 22.)
- Does the paper or project follow an appropriate format? Is it appropriately designed and attractively presented? If it is a Web site, do all the links work?

RESPOND.

1. The causes of the following events and phenomena are quite well known and frequently discussed. But do you understand them well enough yourself to spell out the causes to someone else? Working in a group, see how well (and in how much detail) you can explain each of the following events or phenomena. Which explanations are relatively clear-cut and which seem more open to debate?

   rain

   the collapse of communism in 1989

   earthquakes

   the common cold

   the popularity of the film *The Blair Witch Project*

   the itching caused by a mosquito bite

   the economic boom of the 1990s

   a skid in your car on a slippery road

   the explosion of the space shuttle *Challenger*

   the election of Minnesota Governor Jesse Ventura in 1998

2. One of the fallacies of argument discussed in Chapter 19 is the *post hoc, ergo propter hoc* fallacy: "after this, therefore because of this." Causal arguments are particularly prone to this kind of fallacious reasoning, in which a writer asserts a causal relationship between two entirely unconnected events. After Elvis Presley's death, for instance, oil prices in the United States rose precipitously—but it would be a real stretch to argue that the King's passing *caused* gas prices to skyrocket.

   Because causal arguments can easily fall prey to this fallacy, you might find it useful to take absurd causal positions and see where they go—if only to learn how to avoid such mistakes. As a class, create an argument that goes from cause to effect—or from effect to cause—in a series of completely ridiculous steps (A leads to B leads to C leads to D). Start with one person stating a cause (such as someone sleeping late or missing a test) and move on one by one through the class, building effects on effects. (For example: "Because I slept in, I missed my flight home for Thanksgiving break." Next person: "Because I missed my flight home, I had to call my parents and explain." Next person: "Because I was talking to my parents on the phone, . . .")

3. In the article at the end of this chapter, Lester C. Thurow tests a variety of hypotheses about the causes of gender-based wage inequality.

He rejects all but one of the hypotheses, claiming that they don't hold up as causal explanations. Using Toulmin logic, analyze the competing causal claims Thurow offers, the role that evidence plays in them, and the reasons he decides against them. (Incidentally, the latest government statistics reveal that women now earn 76 percent as much as men. What causes might have accounted for this change? Do you think they are related to the changes Thurow predicts would have to take place for the wage differential to diminish?)

TWO SAMPLE CAUSAL ARGUMENTS

What Makes a Serial Killer?

LA DONNA BEATY

Jeffrey Dahmer, John Wayne Gacy, Mark Allen Smith, Richard Chase, Ted Bundy — the list goes on and on. These five men alone have been responsible for at least ninety deaths, and many suspect that their victims may total twice that number. They are serial killers, the most feared and hated of criminals. What deep, hidden secret makes them lust for blood? What can possibly motivate a person to kill over and over again with no guilt, no remorse, no hint of human compassion? What makes a serial killer?

The cause-effect relationship is raised in a question: What (the causes) makes a serial killer (the effect)?

Serial killings are not a new phenomenon. In 1798, for example, Micajah and Wiley Harpe traveled the backwoods of Kentucky and Tennessee in a violent, year-long killing spree that left at least twenty — and possibly as many as thirty-eight — men, women, and children dead. Their crimes were especially chilling as they seemed particularly to enjoy grabbing small children by the ankles and smashing their heads against trees (Holmes and DeBurger 28). In modern society, however, serial killings have grown to near epidemic proportions. Ann Rule, a respected author and expert on serial murders, stated in a seminar at the University of Louisville on serial murder that between 3,500 and 5,000 people become victims of serial murder each year in the United States alone (qtd. in Holmes and DeBurger 21). Many others estimate that there are close to 350 serial killers currently at large in our society (Holmes and DeBurger 22).

An important term (serial killer) is defined through examples.

Authority is cited to emphasize the importance of the causal question.

La Donna Beaty wrote this essay while she was a student at Sinclair Community College in Dayton, Ohio. In the essay, she explores the complex web of possible causes — cultural, psychological, genetic, and others — that may help to produce a serial killer. The essay follows MLA style.

180

Fascination with murder and murderers is not new, but researchers in recent years have made great strides in determining the characteristics of criminals. Looking back, we can see how naive early experts were in their evaluations: in 1911, for example, Italian criminologist Cesare Lombrosco concluded that "murderers as a group [are] biologically degenerate [with] bloodshot eyes, aquiline noses, curly black hair, strong jaws, big ears, thin lips, and menacing grins" (qtd. in Lunde 84). Today, however, we don't expect killers to have fangs that drip human blood, and many realize that the boy-next-door may be doing more than woodworking in his basement. While there are no specific physical characteristics shared by all serial killers, they are almost always male and 92 percent are white. Most are between the ages of twenty-five and thirty-five and often physically attractive. While they may hold a job, many switch employment frequently as they become easily frustrated when advancement does not come as quickly as expected. They tend to believe that they are entitled to whatever they desire but feel that they should have to exert no effort to attain their goals (Samenow 88, 96). What could possibly turn attractive, ambitious human beings into cold-blooded monsters?

Evidence about general characteristics of serial killers is presented.

One popular theory suggests that many murderers are the product of our violent society. Our culture tends to approve of violence and find it acceptable, even preferable, in many circumstances (Holmes and DeBurger 27). According to research done in 1970, one out of every four men and one out of every six women believed that it was appropriate for a husband to hit his wife under certain conditions (Holmes and DeBurger 33). This emphasis on violence is especially prevalent in television programs. Violence occurs in 80 percent of all prime-time shows, while cartoons, presumably made for children, average eighteen violent acts per hour. It is estimated that by the age of eighteen, the average child will have viewed more than 16,000 television murders (Holmes and DeBurger 34). Some experts feel that children demonstrate increasingly aggressive behavior with each violent act they view (Lunde 15) and become so accustomed to violence that these acts

One possible cause is explored: violence in society.

Evidence, including statistics and authority, is offered to support the first cause.

seem normal (35). In fact, most serial killers do begin to show patterns of aggressive behavior at a young age. It is, therefore, possible that after viewing increasing amounts of violence, such children determine that this is acceptable behavior; when they are then punished for similar actions, they may become confused and angry and eventually lash out by committing horrible, violent acts.

A second possible cause is introduced: family context.

Another theory concentrates on the family atmosphere into which the serial killer is born. Most killers state that they experienced psychological abuse as children and never established good relationships with the male figures in their lives (Ressler, Burgess, and Douglas 19). As children, they were often rejected by their parents and received little nurturing (Lunde 94; Holmes and DeBurger 64–70). It has also been established that the families of serial killers often move repeatedly, never allowing the child to feel a sense of stability; in many cases, they are also forced to live outside the family home before reaching the age of eighteen (Ressler, Burgess, and Douglas 19–20). Our culture's tolerance for violence may overlap with such family dynamics: with 79 percent of the population believing that slapping a twelve-year-old is either necessary, normal, or good, it is no wonder that serial killers relate tales of physical abuse (Holmes and DeBurger 30; Ressler, Burgess, and Douglas 19–20) and view themselves as the "black sheep" of the family. They may even, perhaps unconsciously, assume this same role in society.

Evidence is offered in support of the second cause.

While the foregoing analysis portrays the serial killer as a lost, lonely, abused, little child, another theory, based on the same information, gives an entirely different view. In this analysis, the killer is indeed rejected by his family but only after being repeatedly defiant, sneaky, and threatening. As verbal lies and destructiveness increase, the parents give the child the distance he seems to want in order to maintain a small amount of domestic peace (Samenow 13). This interpretation suggests that the killer shapes his parents much more than his parents shape him. It also denies that the media can influence a child's mind and turn him into something that he doesn't already long to be. Since most children view similar amounts of violence,

An alternative analysis of the evidence in support of the second cause is explored.

the argument goes, a responsible child filters what he sees and will not resort to criminal activity no matter how acceptable it seems to be (Samenow 15–18). In 1930, the noted psychologist Alfred Adler seemed to find this true of any criminal. As he put it, "With criminals it is different: they have a private logic, a private intelligence. They are suffering from a wrong outlook upon the world, a wrong estimate of their own importance and the importance of other people" (qtd. in Samenow 20).

Most people agree that Jeffrey Dahmer or Ted Bundy had to be "crazy" to commit horrendous multiple murders, and scientists have long maintained that serial killers are indeed mentally disturbed (Lunde 48). While the percentage of murders committed by mental hospital patients is much lower than that among the general population (35), it cannot be ignored that the rise in serial killings happened at almost the same time as the deinstitutionalization movement in the mental health care system during the 1960s (Markman and Bosco 266). While reform was greatly needed in the mental health care system, it has now become nearly impossible to hospitalize those with severe problems. In the United States, people have a constitutional right to remain mentally ill. Involuntary commitment can only be accomplished if the person is deemed dangerous to self, dangerous to others, or gravely disabled. However, in the words of Ronald Markman, "According to the way that the law is interpreted, if you can go to the mailbox to pick up your Social Security check, you're not gravely disabled even if you think you're living on Mars"; even if a patient is thought to be dangerous, he or she cannot be held longer than ninety days unless it can be proved that the patient actually committed dangerous acts while in the hospital (Markman and Bosco 267). Many of the most heinous criminals have had long histories of mental illness but could not be hospitalized due to these stringent requirements. Richard Chase, the notorious Vampire of Sacramento, believed that he needed blood in order to survive, and while in the care of a psychiatric hospital, he often killed birds and other small animals in order to quench this desire. When he was

A third possible cause is introduced: mental instability.

Evidence in support of the third cause, including a series of examples, is offered.

released, he went on to kill eight people, one of them an eighteen-month-old baby (Biondi and Hecox 206). Edmund Kemper was equally insane. At the age of fifteen, he killed both of his grandparents and spent five years in a psychiatric facility. Doctors determined that he was "cured" and released him into an unsuspecting society. He killed eight women, including his own mother (Lunde 53–56). The world was soon to be disturbed by a cataclysmic earthquake, and Herbert Mullin knew that he had been appointed by God to prevent the catastrophe. The fervor of his religious delusion resulted in a death toll of thirteen (Lunde 63–81). All of these men had been treated for their mental disorders, and all were released by doctors who did not have enough proof to hold them against their will.

A fourth possible cause is introduced: genetic makeup.

Recently, studies have given increasing consideration to the genetic makeup of serial killers. The connection between biology and behavior is strengthened by research in which scientists have been able to develop a violently aggressive strain of mice simply through selective inbreeding (Taylor 23). These studies have caused scientists to become increasingly interested in the limbic system of the brain, which houses the amygdala, an almond-shaped structure located in the front of the temporal lobe. It has long been known that surgically altering that portion of the brain, in an operation known as a lobotomy, is one way of controlling behavior. This surgery was used frequently in the 1960s but has since been discontinued as it also erases most of a person's personality. More recent developments, however, have shown that temporal lobe epilepsy causes electrical impulses to be discharged directly into the amygdala. When this electronic stimulation is recreated in the laboratory, it causes violent behavior in lab animals. Additionally, other forms of epilepsy do not cause abnormalities in behavior, except during seizure activity. Temporal lobe epilepsy is linked with a wide range of antisocial behavior, including anger, paranoia, and aggression. It is also interesting to note that this form of epilepsy produces extremely unusual brain waves. These waves have been found in only 10 to 15 percent of the general population, but over 79 percent of known serial killers test positive for these waves (Taylor 28–33).

Statistical evidence in support of the fourth cause is offered.

The look at biological factors that control human behavior is by no means limited to brain waves or other brain abnormalities. Much work is also being done with neurotransmitters, levels of testosterone, and patterns of trace minerals. While none of these studies are conclusive, they all show a high correlation between antisocial behavior and chemical interactions within the body (Taylor 63–69).

One of the most common traits that all researchers have noted among serial killers is heavy use of alcohol. Whether this correlation is brought about by external factors or whether alcohol is an actual stimulus that causes certain behavior is still unclear, but the idea deserves consideration. Lunde found that the majority of those who commit murder had been drinking beforehand and commonly had a urine alcohol level of between .20 and .29, nearly twice the legal level of intoxication (31–32). Additionally, 70 percent of the families that reared serial killers had verifiable records of alcohol abuse (Ressler, Burgess, and Douglas 17). Jeffrey Dahmer had been arrested in 1981 on charges of drunkenness and, before his release from prison on sexual assault charges, his father had written a heartbreaking letter which pleaded that Jeffrey be forced to undergo treatment for alcoholism, a plea that, if heeded, might have changed the course of future events (Davis 70, 103). Whether alcoholism is a learned behavior or an inherited predisposition is still hotly debated, but a 1979 report issued by Harvard Medical School stated that "[a]lcoholism in the biological parent appears to be a more reliable predictor of alcoholism in the children than any other environmental factor examined" (qtd. in Taylor 117). While alcohol was once thought to alleviate anxiety and depression, we now know that it can aggravate and intensify such moods (Taylor 110), which may lead to irrational feelings of powerlessness that are brought under control only when the killer proves he has the ultimate power to control life and death.

A fifth possible cause—heavy use of alcohol—is introduced and immediately qualified.

"Man's inhumanity to man" began when Cain killed Abel, but this legacy has grown to frightening proportions, as evidenced by the vast number of books that line the shelves of modern bookstores—row after row of titles

The complexity of causal relationships is emphasized: one cannot say for certain what produces a particular serial killer.

The conclusion looks toward the future: the web of causes examined here suggests that much more work needs to be done to understand, predict, and ultimately control the behavior of potential serial killers.

dealing with death, anger, and blood. We may never know what causes a serial killer to exact his revenge on an unsuspecting society. But we need to continue to probe the interior of the human brain to discover the delicate balance of chemicals that controls behavior. We need to be able to fix what goes wrong. We must also work harder to protect our children. Their cries must not go unheard. Their pain must not become so intense that it demands bloody revenge. As today becomes tomorrow, we must remember the words of Ted Bundy, one of the most ruthless serial killers of our time: "Most serial killers are people who kill for the pure pleasure of killing and cannot be rehabilitated. Some of the killers themselves would even say so" (qtd. in Holmes and DeBurger 150).

WORKS CITED

Biondi, Ray, and Walt Hecox. *The Dracula Killer.* New York: Simon, 1992.

Davis, Ron. *The Milwaukee Murders.* New York: St. Martin's, 1991.

Holmes, Ronald M., and James DeBurger. *Serial Murder.* Newbury Park, CA: Sage, 1988.

Lunde, Donald T. *Murder and Madness.* San Francisco: San Francisco Book, 1976.

Markman, Ronald, and Dominick Bosco. *Alone with the Devil.* New York: Doubleday, 1989.

Ressler, Robert K., Ann W. Burgess, and John E. Douglas. *Sexual Homicide—Patterns and Motives.* Lexington, MA: Heath, 1988.

Samenow, Stanton E. *Inside the Criminal Mind.* New York: Times, 1984.

Taylor, Lawrence. *Born to Crime.* Westport, CT: Greenwood, 1984.

Why Women Are Paid Less Than Men

LESTER C. THUROW

In the 40 years from 1939 to 1979 white women who work full time have with monotonous regularity made slightly less than 60 percent as much as white men. Why?

Over the same time period, minorities have made substantial progress in catching up with whites, with minority women making even more progress than minority men. Black men now earn 72 percent as much as white men (up 16 percentage points since the mid-1950s) but black women earn 92 percent as much as white women. Hispanic men make 71 percent of what their white counterparts do, but Hispanic women make 82 percent as much as white women. As a result of their faster progress, fully employed black women make 75 percent as much as fully employed black men while Hispanic women earn 68 percent as much as Hispanic men.

This faster progress may, however, end when minority women finally catch up with white women. In the bible of the New Right, George Gilder's *Wealth and Poverty*, the 60 percent is just one of Mother Nature's constants like the speed of light or the force of gravity. Men are programmed to provide for their families economically while women are programmed to take care of their families emotionally and physically. As a result men put more effort into their jobs than women. The net result is a difference in work intensity that leads to that 40 percent gap in earnings. But there is no discrimination against women—only the biological facts of life.

The problem with this assertion is just that. It is an assertion with no evidence for it other than the fact that white women have made 60 percent as much as men for a long period of time.

"Discrimination against women" is an easy answer but it also has its problems as an adequate explanation. Why is discrimination against women not

Professor of economics at the Massachusetts Institute of Technology and former dean of the Sloan School of Management, Lester C. Thurow is noted for his many writings on U.S. and global economic issues. He is author or coauthor of more than sixteen books, including *The Future of Capitalism: How Today's Economic Forces Shape Tomorrow's World* (1997) and *Economics Explained: Everything You Need to Know about How the Economy Works and Where It's Going* (1998). In this brief essay, originally published in the *New York Times* in March 1981, Thurow examines possible reasons that women earn less money than men and predicts the conditions that must exist if the gap between earnings is to be reduced.

declining under the same social forces that are leading to a lessening of discrimination against minorities? In recent years women have made more use of the enforcement provisions of the Equal Employment Opportunities Commission and the courts than minorities. Why do the laws that prohibit discrimination against women and minorities work for minorities but not for women?

When men discriminate against women, they run into a problem. To discriminate against women is to discriminate against your own wife and to lower your own family income. To prevent women from working is to force men to work more.

When whites discriminate against blacks, they can at least think that they are raising their own incomes. When men discriminate against women they have to know that they are lowering their own family income and increasing their own work effort.

While discrimination undoubtedly explains part of the male-female earnings differential, one has to believe that men are monumentally stupid or irrational to explain all of the earnings gap in terms of discrimination. There must be something else going on.

Back in 1939 it was possible to attribute the earnings gap to large differences in educational attainments. But the educational gap between men and women has been eliminated since World War II. It is no longer possible to use education as an explanation for the lower earnings of women. Some observers have argued that women earn less money since they are less reliable workers who are more apt to leave the labor force. But it is difficult to maintain this position since women are less apt to quit one job to take another and as a result they tend to work as long, or longer, for any one employer. From any employer's perspective they are more reliable, not less reliable, than men.

Part of the answer is visible if you look at the lifetime earnings profile of men. Suppose that you were asked to predict which men in a group of 25-year-olds would become economically successful. At age 25 it is difficult to tell who will be economically successful and your predictions are apt to be highly inaccurate. But suppose that you were asked to predict which men in a group of 35-year-olds would become economically successful. If you are successful at age 35, you are very likely to remain successful for the rest of your life. If you have not become economically successful by age 35, you are very unlikely to do so later.

The decade between 25 and 35 is when men either succeed or fail. It is the decade when lawyers become partners in the good firms, when business managers make it onto the "fast track," when academics get tenure at good universities, and when blue collar workers find the job opportunities that will lead to training opportunities and the skills that will generate high earnings. If there is any one decade when it pays to work hard and to be consistently in the labor force, it is the decade between 25 and 35. For those who succeed, earnings will rise rapidly. For those who fail, earnings will remain flat for the rest of their lives.

But the decade between 25 and 35 is precisely the decade when women are most apt to leave the labor force or become part-time workers to have children. When they do, the current system of promotion and skill acquisition will extract an enormous lifetime price.

This leaves essentially two avenues for equalizing male and female earnings. Families where women who wish to have successful careers, compete with men, and achieve the same earnings should alter their family plans and have their children either before 25 or after 35. Or society can attempt to alter the existing promotion and skill acquisition system so that there is a longer time period in which both men and women can attempt to successfully enter the labor force. Without some combination of these two factors, a substantial fraction of the male-female earnings differentials are apt to persist for the next 40 years, even if discrimination against women is eliminated.

chapter twelve

Proposals

A couple looking forward to a much-needed vacation writes to four friends proposing that they all charter a sailboat for two weeks of exploring the Greek islands.

A blue-ribbon commission works for two years to develop a plan for instituting a national health care policy.

The members of a club for business majors begin to talk about their common need to create informative and appealing résumés. After lengthy discussion, three members suggest that the club develop a Web site that will guide members in building résumés and provide links to other resources.

A project team at a large consulting engineering firm works for three months developing a proposal in response to an RFP (request for proposal) to convert a military facility to a community camp.

Members of a church take up a question brought to them by their youth organization: Why are women disallowed from taking on certain roles in the church? After a series of discussions, the youth group decides to propose a change in church policy.

The undergraduate student organization at a large state university asks the administration for information about how long it takes to complete a degree in each academic major. Following an analysis of this information, the group recommends a reduction in the number of hours needed to graduate.

■ ■ ■

UNDERSTANDING AND CATEGORIZING PROPOSALS

Much everyday activity is related to proposals you make or consider, many of them very informal: your roommate suggests skipping breakfast in order to get in an extra hour of exercise; you and a colleague decide to go out to dinner rather than work late once again; you call your best friend to propose checking out a new movie; you decide to approach your boss about implementing an idea you've just had. In each case, the proposal implies that some action *should* take place and implicitly suggests that there are good reasons *why* it should.

In their simplest form, then, proposal arguments look something like this:

A should do B because of C.

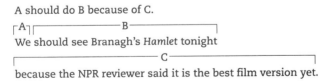

Because proposals are so pervasive in people's lives, it's no surprise that they cover a dizzyingly wide range of possibilities, from very local and concrete practices (*A company should switch from one supplier of paper to another*) to very broad matters of policy (*The United States should adopt a more inclusive immigration policy*). Thus, it may be helpful to think of proposal arguments as divided roughly into two kinds — those that focus on practices and those that focus on policies. Here are several examples:

PROPOSALS ABOUT PRACTICES

- The city should use brighter lightbulbs in employee parking garages.
- The college should adopt a new procedure allowing students to pay tuition on a month-by-month basis.
- The community center staff should authorize funds for a new interior paint job.

PROPOSALS ABOUT POLICIES

- Congress should institute a national youth service plan.
- The college should adopt a "forgiveness" policy allowing students to have one course each semester not count in their grade point average.
- The state should end affirmative action policies in every state agency.

CHARACTERIZING PROPOSALS

Proposals have three main characteristics:

- They are action-oriented.
- They are focused on the future.
- They are audience-centered.

Proposals always call for some kind of action; they aim at *getting something done*. Thus, although proposals may rely on analysis and on careful reflection about ideas and information, these strategies are in the service of urging a decision about what to do. This feature of proposals almost always presents a challenge to the writer or speaker. Most simply, this challenge is the one expressed in the old saying, "You can lead a horse to water, but you can't make it drink." You can present a proposal as cogently and compellingly as possible — but most of the time you can't *make* the audience take the action you propose. Thus, proposal arguments must stress the ethos of the writer: if your word and experience and judgment are all credible, the audience is more likely to carry out the action you propose.

In addition, proposal arguments focus on the future, which the actions proposed will affect. Aristotle referred to such arguments as "deliberative" and associated them with the work of government, which is most often concerned with what a society should do over the upcoming few years or decades. This future orientation also presents special challenges, since writers have no crystal balls that enable them to predict the future with absolute confidence. Proposal arguments must therefore concentrate on marshaling all available evidence to demonstrate that the proposed action is very likely to produce the effects it sets out to achieve.

Finally, proposal arguments are highly focused on audience and audience response, since the success of the argument often (if not always) depends on the degree to which the audience agrees to carry out the proposed action.

Let's say that as president of your church youth organization, you decide to propose that the group take on a community tutoring project. Your proposal aims at action: you want members to do volunteer tutoring in an after-school program at the local community center. Your proposal is also future-oriented: you believe that such a project would help teach your group's members about conditions in the inner city as well as help inner-city children in ways that could make them more successful in future schooling. And certainly your proposal is heavily audience-dependent, because only if you can convince members that such service is needed, that it is feasible and likely to achieve the desired effects, and that it will be beneficial to members and to the organization, is your proposal likely to be acted on positively.

In a proposal argument called "Let's Put Pornography Back in the Closet," Susan Brownmiller likewise focuses on action, on what she wants to happen—which is for legislatures and courts to draw a "distinction between permission to publish and permission to display publicly." Brownmiller argues that government restrictions on the public display of pornography would not endanger the free-speech guarantees of the First Amendment and would contribute to social harmony by removing from public view what she sees as a major vehicle for expression of hatred in our society. Her argument is thus action- and future-oriented. But it is also strongly audience-centered, for in it she mentions objections that readers might have and tries to answer them in a fair and evenhanded way.

DEVELOPING PROPOSALS

Developing effective proposals requires you to make a strong and clear claim, to show that the proposal meets a specific need or solves a significant problem, to present good reasons why adopting the proposal will effectively address the need or problem, and finally to show that the proposal is feasible and should therefore be adopted.

Making a Strong and Clear Claim

Formulating a strong claim means crafting a statement that features a claim (what X or Y should do) followed by the reason(s) why X or Y should act and the effects of adopting the proposal:

Claim	Communities should encourage the development of charter schools
Reason	because they are not burdened by the bureaucracy associated with most public schooling, and
Effects	because instituting such schools will bring more effective educational progress to the community and offer a positive incentive to the public schools to improve their programs as well.

Having established a claim, you can explore its implications by drawing out the reasons, warrants, and evidence that can support it most effectively:

Claim	Parents should shed old taboos and deal with new realities by providing extensive sex education at home and encouraging additional education in community centers and schools.
Reason	More than a million teenagers become pregnant each year, almost all of them unintentionally.
Warrant	Sex education helps prevent unwanted pregnancies.
Evidence	Evidence from Sweden, the Netherlands, France, and Canada demonstrates that extensive sex education results in reduced numbers of teenage pregnancies.

In this proposal argument the reason sets up the need for the proposal, whereas the warrant and evidence demonstrate that the proposal could indeed meet its objective.

Relating the Claim to a Need or Problem

To be effective, claims must be clearly related to a significant need or problem. Thus, establishing that the need or problem exists is one of the most important tasks the writer of a proposal argument faces. For this reason, you should explore this part of any proposal you wish to make very early on; if you can't establish a clear need for the proposal or show that it solves an important problem, you should probably work toward a revision or a new claim.

In practice, establishing the need or problem may occur at the beginning of your introduction as a way of leading up to your claim. Alternatively, it might appear right after your introduction as the major reason for adopting the proposal. In the preceding examples about charter schools and sex education, the writer might choose either strategy. Regardless of the practical choices about organization, the task of establishing a need or problem calls on you to

- evoke the need or problem in concrete and memorable ways
- show how the need or problem affects the larger society or group in general and the audience in particular
- indicate why the need or problem is significant

In an argument proposing that a state board of higher education institute courses that involve students in community service in all state colleges, a writer might begin by painting a fairly negative picture of a "me first and only" society that is self-absorbed and concentrated only on self-gratification. After evoking such a scene, the writer might explore how this particular problem affects society in general and the state's colleges in particular: it results in hypercompetition that creates a highly stressful "pressure-cooker" atmosphere on campuses; it leaves many of society's most vulnerable members without resources or helping hands; it puts the responsibility of helping these people solely in the hands of government, thereby adding to the size and cost of government and raising taxes for all; it deprives many of the satisfaction that helping others can bring, a satisfaction that should be a part of every student's education. Finally, the writer might demonstrate this problem's importance by relating it to the needs of the many people who would be benefited by various kinds of volunteer service: child care, elder care, health care, community learning, arts and cultural projects—the list of those affected could go on and on.

Note the way Craig R. Dean, a lawyer and executive director of the Equal Marriage Rights Fund, relates his claim—that the United States should legalize same-sex marriage—to a significant problem (and how he evokes, or renders, the problem):

> In November 1990, my lover, Patrick Gill, and I were denied a marriage license because we are gay. In a memorandum explaining the District's decision, the clerk of the court wrote that "the sections of the

District of Columbia code governing marriage do not authorize marriage between persons of the same sex." By refusing to give us the same legal recognition that is given to heterosexual couples, the District has degraded our relationship as well as that of every other gay and lesbian couple.

At one time, interracial couples were not allowed to marry. Gays and lesbians are still denied this basic civil right in the U.S.—and around the world. Can you imagine the outcry if any other minority group was denied the right to legally marry today?

Marriage is more than a piece of paper. It gives societal recognition and legal protection to a relationship. It confers numerous benefits to spouses; in the District alone, there are more than 100 automatic marriage-based rights. In every state in the nation, married couples have the right to be on each other's health, disability, life insurance and pension plans. Married couples receive special tax exemptions, deductions and refunds. Spouses may automatically inherit property and have rights of survivorship that avoid inheritance tax. Though unmarried couples—both gay and heterosexual—are entitled to some of these rights, they are by no means guaranteed.

For married couples, the spouse is legally the next of kin in case of death, medical emergency or mental incapacity. In stark contrast, the family is generally the next of kin for same-sex couples. In the shadow of AIDS, the denial of marriage rights can be even more ominous. . . .

Some argue that gay marriage is too radical for society. We disagree. According to a 1989 study by the American Bar Association, eight to 10 million children are currently being reared in three million gay households. Therefore, approximately 6 percent of the U.S. population is made up of gay and lesbian families with children. Why should these families be denied the protection granted to other families?

Allowing gay marriage would strengthen society by increasing tolerance. It is paradoxical that mainstream America perceives gays and lesbians as unable to maintain long-term relationships while at the same time denying them the very institutions that stabilize such relationships.

–Craig R. Dean, "Legalize Gay Marriage"

Showing That the Proposal Addresses the Need or Problem

A very important but potentially tricky part of making a successful proposal lies in relating the claim to the need or problem it seeks to address. Everyone you know may agree that rising tuition costs at your college constitute a major problem. But will your spur-of-the-moment letter to the college newspaper proposing to reduce the size of the faculty and eliminate all campus bus services really address the problem effectively? Chances are, you would have a very hard time making this connection. On the other hand, proposing that the college establish a joint commission of students, administrators and faculty, and legislative leaders charged with studying the problem and proposing a series of alternatives for solving it would be much more likely to establish a clear connection between the problem and the claim.

In the earlier example about charter schools, the writer would need to show that establishing such schools could significantly address at least one of the problems identified with currently available public education. And in the passage from "Legalize Gay Marriage," the writer must show explicitly how carrying out the recommended action would directly affect the problems he has identified.

Showing That the Proposal Is Feasible

To be effective, proposals must be feasible—the action proposed must be able to be carried out in a reasonable way. Demonstrating feasibility calls on you to present more evidence—from analogous cases, from personal experience, from observational data, from interview or survey data, from Internet research, or from any other sources that help show that what you propose can indeed be done. In addition, it will help your case if you can show that the proposal can be carried out with the resources available. If instead the proposal calls for personnel or funds far beyond reach or reason, the audience is unlikely to accept it. As you think about revising your proposal argument, you can test its feasibility against these criteria. In addition, you can try to think of proposals that others might say are better, more effective, or more feasible than yours—and you can ask colleagues and friends to help you think of such counterproposals. If your own proposal argument can stand the test of counterproposals, it is a strong one indeed.

Using Personal Experience

If you have personally had an experience that demonstrates the need or problem your proposal aims to address, or that can serve as backing for your claim, consider using it to develop your proposal (as Craig R. Dean does in the opening of his proposal to legalize gay marriage). Consider the following questions in deciding when to include your own experiences in making a proposal:

- Is your experience directly related to the need or problem you seek to address, or to your proposal?
- Will your experience be appropriate and speak powerfully to the audience? Will the audience immediately understand its significance, or will it require explanation?
- Does your personal experience fit logically with the other reasons you are using to support your claim?

KEY FEATURES OF PROPOSALS

In drafting a proposal, remember to include each of the following elements:

- a claim that proposes a practice or policy to address a problem or need and that is oriented toward action, directed at the future, and appropriate to your audience
- statements that clearly relate the claim to the problem or need
- evidence that the proposal will effectively address the need or solve the problem, and that it is feasible

Fully developing your proposal will call for addressing all these elements, though you may choose to order them in several different ways. As you organize your proposal, you may want to open with an introductory paragraph that evokes as dramatically as possible the problem you are addressing, and you may decide to conclude by recalling this opening dramatic scene in your final paragraphs. Or you may choose to start right off with your claim and offer strong support for it before showing the ways in which your proposal addresses a need or solves a problem. In any case you should organize your proposal carefully, seeking response to your organizational plan from your instructor and colleagues.

Considering Design

Since proposals often address very specific audiences, they can take any number of forms: a letter or memo, a feasibility report, a brochure, a prospectus. Each form has different design requirements; indeed, the design may add powerfully to—or detract significantly from—the effectiveness of the proposal. Even in a college essay that is produced on a computer, the use of white space and margins, headings and subheadings, and variations in type (such as boldface or italics) can guide readers through the proposal and enhance its persuasiveness. So before you produce a final copy of any proposal, make a careful plan for its design. Then get response to the proposal in terms of its content *and* its design, asking friends, colleagues, or instructors to read the proposal and give you their responses. Finally, revise to address all the concerns they raise.

Finding a Topic

Your everyday experience probably calls on you to make proposals all the time; for example, to spend the weekend doing a special activity, to change your academic major for some very important reasons, or to add to the family income by starting a small, home-based business. In addition, your community group work or your job may require you to make proposals—to a boss, a board of directors, the local school board, and so on. And in this age of electronic communication, you may have an opportunity or a need to make proposals to online groups or to Web sites you visit. In all these cases some sort of action is called for, which is the hallmark of proposal arguments. Why not make an informal list of proposals you'd like to explore in a number of different areas? Or do some freewriting on a subject of great interest to you and see if it leads to a proposal? Either method of exploration is likely to turn up several possibilities for a good proposal argument.

Researching Your Topic

Proposals often call for some research. Even a simple one like "Let's all paint the house this weekend" would raise questions that require some investigation: *Who has the time for the job? What sort of paint will be the best? How much will the job cost?* A proposal that your school board adopt block scheduling would call for careful research into evidence supporting the use of such a system. *Where has it been effective, and why?* And for proposals about social issues (for example, that information on the Internet be freely accessible to everyone, even youngsters), extensive research would be necessary to provide sufficient support. For many proposals, you can begin your research by consulting the following types of sources:

- newspapers, magazines, reviews, and journals (online and print)
- online databases
- government documents and reports
- Web sites and listservs or newsgroups
- books
- experts in the field, some of whom may be right on your campus

In addition, you may decide to carry out some field research: a survey of student opinion on Internet accessibility, for example, or online interviews with people who are well informed about your subject.

Formulating a Claim

As you are thinking about and exploring your topic, you can also begin formulating a claim about it. To do so, try to draft a clear and complete thesis that *makes a proposal and states the reasons why this proposal should be followed*. To get started on formulating a claim, explore and respond to the following questions:

- What do I know about the proposal I am making?
- What reasons can I offer to support my proposal?
- What evidence do I have that implementing my proposal will lead to the results I want?

Preparing a Proposal

If your instructor asks you to prepare a proposal for your project, here's a format that may help:

State the thesis of your proposal completely. If you are having trouble doing so, try outlining it in terms of the Toulmin system:

    Claim:

    Reason(s):

    Warrant(s):

Explain why your proposal is important. What is at stake in taking, or not taking, the action you propose?

Identify and describe those whom you most hope to reach with your proposal. Why is this group of readers most appropriate for your proposal? What are their interests in the subject?

Briefly discuss the major difficulties you foresee in preparing your argument. Demonstrating that the action you propose is necessary? Demonstrating that it is feasible? Moving the audience beyond agreement to action? Something else?

List the research you intend to do. What kinds of sources do you expect to consult? What formats or genre do you expect to use? An academic essay? A formal report? A Web site?

Thinking about Organization

Proposals can take many different forms, generally including the following elements:

- a clear and strong proposal, including the reasons for taking the action proposed and the effects that taking this action will have: *Our neighborhood should establish a "Block Watch" program that will help reduce break-ins and vandalism, and involve our children in building neighborhood pride.*

- a clear connection between the proposal and a significant need or problem: *Break-ins and vandalism have been on the rise in our neighborhood for the last three years.*

- a demonstration of ways in which the proposal addresses the need: *A Block Watch program establishes a rotating monitor system for the streets in a neighborhood and a voluntary plan to watch out for others' homes.*

- evidence that the proposal will achieve the desired outcome: *Block Watch programs in three other areas have significantly reduced break-ins and vandalism.*

- consideration of alternative ways to achieve the desired outcome, and a discussion of why these are not preferable: *We could ask for additional police presence, but funding would be hard to get.*

- a demonstration that the proposal is feasible and practical: *Because Block Watch is voluntary, our own determination and commitment are all we need to make it work.*

Getting and Giving Response

All arguments can benefit from the scrutiny of others. Your instructor may assign you to a peer group for the purpose of reading and responding to each other's drafts; if not, make the effort yourself to get some careful response. You can use the following questions to evaluate a draft. If you are evaluating someone else's draft, be sure to illustrate your points with specific examples. Specific comments are always more helpful than general observations.

The Claim

- Does the claim clearly call for action? Is the proposal as clear and specific as possible?

- Is the proposal too sweeping? Does it need to be qualified? If so, how?

- Does the proposal clearly address the problem it intends to solve? If not, how could the connection be strengthened?

- Is the claim likely to get the audience to act rather than just to agree? If not, how could it be revised to do so?

Evidence for the Claim

- Is enough evidence provided to get the audience to support the proposal? If not, what kind of additional evidence is needed? Does any of the evidence provided seem inappropriate or otherwise ineffective? Why?

- Is the evidence in support of the claim simply announced, or are its significance and appropriateness analyzed? Is a more detailed discussion needed?

- Are any objections readers might have to the claim or evidence adequately addressed?

- What kinds of sources are cited? How credible and persuasive will they be to readers? What other kinds of sources might be more credible and persuasive?

- Are all quotations introduced with appropriate signal phrases ("As Ehrenreich argues") and blended smoothly into the writer's sentences?

Organization and Style

- How are the parts of the argument organized? Is this organization effective, or would some other structure work better?

- Will readers understand the relationships among the claims, supporting reasons, warrants, and evidence? If not, what could be done to make those connections clearer? Are more transitional words and phrases needed? Would headings or graphic devices help?

- Are the transitions or links from point to point, paragraph to paragraph, and sentence to sentence clear and effective? If not, how could they be improved?

- Is the style suited to the subject? Is it too formal? Too casual? Too technical? Too bland?

- Which sentences seem particularly effective? Which ones seem weakest, and how could they be improved? Should some short sentences be combined, or should any long ones be separated into two or more sentences?

- How effective are the paragraphs? Do any seem too skimpy or too long?

- Which words or phrases seem particularly effective, vivid, and memorable? Do any seem dull, vague, unclear, or inappropriate for the audience or the writer's purpose? Are definitions provided for technical or other terms that readers might not know?

Spelling, Punctuation, Mechanics, Documentation, Format

- Are there any errors in spelling, punctuation, capitalization, and the like?

- Is an appropriate and consistent style of documentation used for parenthetical citations and the list of works cited or references? (See Chapter 22.)

- Does the paper or project follow an appropriate format? Is it appropriately designed and attractively presented? If it is a Web site, do all the links work?

RESPOND•

1. For each problem and solution, explain readers' likely objections to the outrageous solution offered. Then propose a more defensible solution of your own and explain why you think it is more feasible.

   Problem   Future bankruptcy of the Social Security system in the United States.

   Solution   Raise the age of retirement to eighty.

   Problem   Traffic gridlock in major cities.

   Solution   Allow only men to drive on Mondays, Wednesdays, and Fridays and only women on Tuesdays, Thursdays, and Saturdays. Everyone can drive on Sunday.

   Problem   Increasing rates of obesity in the general population.

   Solution   Ban the sale of all high-fat items in fast-food restaurants, including hamburgers, fries, and shakes.

   Problem   Threats of violence in schools.

   Solution   Authorize teachers and students to carry handguns.

   Problem   Unmanageable credit card debt among college students.

   Solution   Limit credit card use to people over age twenty-five.

2. People write proposal arguments to solve problems; when writers face some kind of practical or policy issue, they develop arguments that will (they hope) change the way things are. But problems are not always obvious; what troubles some people might be no problem at all to others.

   To get an idea of the range of problems people face on your campus—some of which you may not even have thought of as problems—divide into groups and brainstorm about things that annoy you on and around campus, including everything from short crosswalk-light timers to long lines at the registrar's office. Each group should aim for a list of twenty gripes. Then choose one problem and, as a group, discuss how you would go about writing a proposal to deal with it. Remember that you will need to (a) make a strong and clear claim, (b) show that the proposal meets a clear need or solves a significant problem, (c) present good reasons why adopting the proposal will effectively address the need or problem, and (d) show that the proposal is feasible and should be adopted.

3. In the essay "Don't Make English Official—Ban It Instead" at the end of this chapter, Dennis Baron makes a tongue-in-cheek proposal to

outlaw the English language. Using the Toulmin model discussed in Chapter 8, analyze the proposal's structure. What claim does Baron make, and what reasons does he give to support the claim? What are the warrants that connect the reasons to the claim? What evidence does he provide?

TWO SAMPLE PROPOSALS

Auto Liberation

BRENT KNUTSON

The driver of a late-model Japanese sports car grins as he downshifts into third gear, blips the throttle with his heel, and releases the clutch. The car's rear end abruptly steps out in the wide, sweeping corner. He cranks the wheel, gathering the tail while eagerly stabbing the accelerator. The engine emits a metallic wail and barks angrily as the driver pulls the gearshift into fourth. Controlled pandemonium ensues as the secondary turbocharger engages and slams the driver's cranium against the headrest. With adrenaline thumping in his temples, he watches the needle on the speedometer sweep urgently toward the end of the scale. The driver then flicks the turn signal and blasts onto the interstate like a guided missile launching from a fighter jet. Today, he will not be late for work.

An opening vignette captures readers' attention and piques interest in the title.

This scenario may seem a bit far-fetched, enough so that one might conclude that the driver is unnecessarily risking his life and the lives of other people on the road. But, on Germany's autobahns, people normally drive in excess of 80 miles per hour. Yet, these German superhighways are the safest in the world, filled with German drivers who are skilled, competent, and courteous. Using the autobahn system as a model, it is possible to examine whether national speed limits in the United States are necessary.

Background information on driving in Germany is presented.

In fact, there is solid reasoning to support the claim that the speed limits on U.S. interstate highways should be repealed. Not only are American speed limits unnecessarily restrictive, they also infringe upon the personal

The claim — that U.S. interstate speed limits should be repealed — is introduced and followed by a summary of reasons in support of the claim.

Brent Knutson wrote this essay while he was a student at Boise State University in Boise, Idaho. He calls for an end to speed limits on U.S. interstate highways—a proposal that requires him to spend much of the essay in refuting opposing views.

207

freedoms of American citizens. Although there are locations where speed limits are appropriate, in most cases these limits are arbitrarily imposed and sporadically enforced. Modern automobiles are capable of traveling safely at high speeds, and, despite what the auto-insurance consortium would have us believe, speed does not kill. With proper training, American drivers could be capable of driving "at speed" responsibly. Perhaps the most compelling reason to lift the national speed limit is the simplest: driving fast is enjoyable.

Those opposed to lifting the national speed limit argue that removing such restrictions would result in mayhem on the freeway; they're convinced that the countryside would be littered with the carcasses of people who achieved terminal velocity only to career off the road and explode into flames. Speed limit advocates also argue that American drivers do not possess the skill or capacity to drive at autobahn speeds. They contend that our driver-education programs do not sufficiently prepare drivers to operate vehicles, and obtaining a driver's license in most states is comically easy; therefore, lifting the speed limit would be irresponsible.

The major objection to the proposal — that repeal will lead to an increase in deaths — is considered, and a statistical counter-argument is offered.

The belief that a "no speed limit" highway system would result in widespread carnage appears to be based more on fear than fact. In 1987, Idaho senator Steve Symms introduced legislation allowing states to raise speed limits on rural interstates to 65 miles per hour (Csere, "Free" 9). Auto-insurance industry advocates responded that the accident rates would skyrocket and the number of fatalities caused by auto accidents would increase accordingly. Ironically, the Insurance Institute for Highway Safety (IIHS) reported in July 1994 that "[o]nly 39,235 deaths resulting from auto-related accidents were reported during 1992, the lowest number since 1961. The institute found that 1992 was the fourth year in which automotive deaths consistently declined" (qtd. in "Highways" 51). Coincidentally, that decline in fatalities began two years after many states raised interstate speed limits. Unfortunately, the insurance industry has made it a habit to manipulate statistics to suit its purposes. Later in the essay, I'll discuss evidence of this propensity to deceive.

The contention that American drivers are not capable of driving safely at higher speeds has some merit. During a drive around any city in this country, one is bound to witness numerous displays of behind-the-wheel carelessness. Because of poor driver-education programs, as well as general apathy, Americans have earned their standing among the worst drivers in the world. Regarding our poor driving habits, automotive journalist Csaba Csere wrote in the April 1994 issue of *Car and Driver*: "American drivers choose their lanes randomly, much in the way cows inexplicably pick a patch of grass on which to graze" ("Drivers" 9). Fortunately, Americans' poor driving habits can be remedied. Through intensive driver-education programs, stringent licensing criteria, and public-service announcement campaigns, we can learn to drive more proficiently.

Knutson concedes that Americans are poor drivers, but he offers a remedy.

I recently returned from a four-year stay in Kaiserslautern, Germany. While there, I learned the pleasure of high-speed motoring. I was particularly impressed by the skill and discipline demonstrated by virtually all drivers traveling on the network of superhighways that make up the autobahn system. Germany's automobile regulatory laws are efficient, practical, and serve as an example for all countries to follow. It is striking that automobiles and driving fast are such integral components of German culture. Germans possess a passion for cars that is so contagious I didn't want to leave the country. German chancellor Helmut Kohl summed up the German attitude regarding speed limits quite concisely: "For millions of people, a car is part of their personal freedom" (qtd. in Cote 12).

A comparison is offered as logical evidence: Germany has both high-speed motoring and efficient and responsible drivers.

It is apparent in the United States that there are not many old, junky cars left on the road. The majority of vehicles operating in the United States are newer cars that have benefited from automotive engineering technology designed to increase the performance of the average vehicle. With the advent of independent suspension, electronic engine-management systems, passive restraints, and

Factual evidence (improvements in automotive technology and stringent safety requirements) supports the proposal to repeal speed limits.

other technological improvements, modern automobiles are more capable than ever of traveling at high speeds, safely. Indeed, the stringent safety requirements imposed by the Department of Transportation for vehicles sold in the United States ensure that our cars and trucks are the safest in the world.

A mini-argument of definition is offered in support of the proposal argument: driving fast does not itself constitute a "hazard."

One of the biggest fallacies perpetrated by the auto-insurance industry and car-fearing legislators is that "speed kills." Driving fast in itself, however, is not a hazard; speed combined with incompetence, alcohol, or hazardous conditions is dangerous. A skilled motor-vehicle operator traveling at 90 miles per hour, in light traffic, on a divided highway does not present a significant risk. Psychologist and compensation theorist G. J. Wilde

An authority is cited in support of the proposal: drivers try to keep their level of risk constant, regardless of speed limits.

"developed the RHT (Risk Homeostasis Theory) to account for the apparent propensity of drivers to maintain a constant level of experienced accident risk" (qtd. in Jackson and Blackman 950). During a driving simulation experiment in which he changed "non-motivational factors," Wilde determined that "[n]either speed limit nor speeding fine had a significant impact on accident loss" (qtd. in Jackson and Blackman 956). Wilde's theory is convincing because he emphasizes the human tendency towards self-preservation. The impact of RHT could be far-reaching. As Wilde says, "The notion that drivers compensate fully for non-motivational safety countermeasures is significant because it is tantamount to the claim that most legislated safety measures will not permanently reduce the total population traffic accident loss" (qtd. in Jackson and Blackman 951). What this means is that drivers would not increase their personal risk by driving faster than their capabilities dictate, regardless of the speed limit.

Opposing statistical evidence is refuted.

Unfortunately, the IIHS doesn't see things this way. It has been busy manipulating statistics in an attempt to convince people that raising the interstate speed limits to 65 miles per hour has resulted in a veritable bloodbath. A headline in a recent edition of the IIHS status report states, "For Sixth Year in a Row, Deaths on U.S. Rural Interstates Are Much Higher Than before Speed Limits Were Raised to 65 mph" (qtd. in Bedard 20). That statistic is more than a little misleading because it does not compensate for the increased number of drivers on the road. Patrick Bedard explains: "What's the real conclusion? Rural interstate fatalities over the whole United States increased 19 percent between 1982 and 1992. But driving increased 44 percent. So the fatality rate is on a definite downward trend from 1.5 to 1.2 [percent]" (21).

One might ask what the insurance industry stands to gain by misrepresenting auto fatality statistics. The real issue is what it stands to lose if speed limits are deregulated. The lifting of speed limits translates into fewer traffic citations issued by police. Fewer tickets means fewer points assessed on Americans' driving records, which would remove the insurance industry's primary tool for raising premiums. Needless to say, the industry isn't thrilled about the prospect of less money in its coffers.

The credibility of opponents is challenged: insurance companies make a lot of money from enforcement of speed limits.

There is one lucid and persuasive argument to abolish interstate speed limits: Driving fast is pure, unadulterated, rip-snortin' fun. I experienced the thrill of a lifetime behind the wheel of a 1992 Ford Mustang while chasing a BMW 525i on the Frankfurt-Mainz Autobahn. I remember my heart racing as I glanced at my speedometer, which read 120 mph. When I looked up, I saw the high-beam flash of headlights in my rearview mirror. Moments after I pulled into the right lane, a bloodred Ferrari F-40 passed in a surreal symphony of sound, color, and power, dominated by the enraged howl of a finely tuned Italian motor at full tilt. At that moment, I was acutely aware of every nerve ending in my body, as I experienced the automotive equivalent of Zen consciousness. It was a sort of convergence of psyche and body that left me light-headed and giddy for ten minutes afterwards. I was glad to discover that my reaction to driving fast was not unique:

An appeal to emotion — that driving fast is fun — is supported by evidence from personal experience.

> Few people can describe in words the mixture of sensations they experience, but for some the effect is so psychologically intense that no other experience can match it [. . .]. For some people the psychological effects are experienced as pure fear. For others, however, this basic emotional state is modified to give a sharply tingling experience which is perceived as intensely

pleasurable. The fear, and the state of alertness are still there—but they have been mastered. (Marsh and Collett 179)

Conclusion reiterates proposal and emotional appeal to personal freedom.

Repealing interstate speed limits is an objective that every driver should carefully consider. At a time when our elected officials are striving to control virtually every aspect of our lives, it is imperative that we fight to regain our freedom behind the wheel. Like Germans, Americans have a rich automotive culture and heritage. The automobile represents our ingenuity, determination, and independence. It is time to return control of the automobile to the driver, and "free us from our speed slavery once and for all" (Csere, "Free" 9).

Bedard, Patrick. "Auto Insurance Figures Don't Lie, but Liars Figure." Editorial. *Car and Driver* Mar. 1994: 20–21.

Cote, Kevin. "Heartbrake on Autobahn." *Advertising Age* 26 Sept. 1994: 1+.

Csere, Csaba. "Drivers We Love to Hate." Editorial. *Car and Driver* Apr. 1994: 9.

———. "Free the Speed Slaves." Editorial. *Car and Driver* Nov. 1993: 9.

"Highways Become Safer." *Futurist* Jan.–Feb. 1994: 51–52.

Jackson, Jeremy S. H., and Roger Blackman. "A Driving Simulator Test of Wilde's Risk Homeostasis Theory." *Journal of Applied Psychology* 79.6 (1994): 950–58.

Marsh, Peter, and Peter Collett. *Driving Passion.* Winchester: Faber, 1987.

Don't Make English Official—Ban It Instead

DENNIS BARON

Congress is considering, and may soon pass, legislation making English the official language of the United States. Supporters of the measure say that English forms the glue that keeps America together. They deplore the dollars wasted translating English into other languages. And they fear a horde of illegal aliens adamantly refusing to acquire the most powerful language on earth.

On the other hand, opponents of official English remind us that without legislation we have managed to get over ninety-seven percent of the residents of this country to speak the national language. No country with an official language law even comes close. Opponents also point out that today's non-English-speaking immigrants are picking up English faster than earlier generations of immigrants did, so instead of official English, they favor "English Plus," encouraging everyone to speak both English and another language.

I would like to offer a modest proposal to resolve the language impasse in Congress. Don't make English official, ban it instead.

That may sound too radical, but proposals to ban English first surfaced in the heady days after the American Revolution. Anti-British sentiment was so strong in the new United States that a few superpatriots wanted to get rid of English altogether. They suggested replacing English with Hebrew, thought by many in the eighteenth century to be the world's first language, the one spoken in the garden of Eden. French was also considered, because it was thought at the time, and especially by the French, to be the language of pure reason. And of course there was Greek, the language of Athens, the world's first democracy. It's not clear how serious any of these proposals were, though Roger Sherman of Connecticut supposedly remarked that it would be better to keep English for ourselves and make the British speak Greek.

Denis Baron is professor of English and linguistics at the University of Illinois at Urbana-Champaign and head of the department of English. His books include *Grammar and Good Taste: Reforming the American Language* (1982) and the *Guide to Home Language Repair* (1994). He writes often on questions of language and efforts to reform it or legislate its use. This essay, originally published in the *Washington Post,* parodies the genre of proposals—and is a great model of an academic proposal.

Even if the British are now our allies, there may be some benefit to banning English today. A common language can often be the cause of strife and misunderstanding. Look at Ireland and Northern Ireland, the two Koreas, or the Union and the Confederacy. Banning English would prevent that kind of divisiveness in America today.

Also, if we banned English, we wouldn't have to worry about whose English to make official: the English of England or America? of Chicago or New York? of Ross Perot or William F. Buckley?

We might as well ban English, too, because no one seems to read it much lately, few can spell it, and fewer still can parse it. Even English teachers have come to rely on computer spell checkers.

Another reason to ban English: it's hardly even English anymore. English started its decline in 1066, with the unfortunate incident at Hastings. Since then it has become a polyglot conglomeration of French, Latin, Italian, Scandinavian, Arabic, Sanskrit, Celtic, Yiddish and Chinese, with an occasional smiley face thrown in.

More important, we should ban English because it has become a world language. Remember what happened to all the other world languages: Latin, Greek, Indo-European? One day they're on everybody's tongue; the next day they're dead. Banning English now would save us that inevitable disappointment.

Although we shouldn't ban English without designating a replacement for it, there is no obvious candidate. The French blew their chance when they sold Louisiana. It doesn't look like the Russians are going to take over this country any time soon—they're having enough trouble taking over Russia. German, the largest minority language in the U. S. until recently, lost much of its prestige after two world wars. Chinese is too hard to write, especially if you're not Chinese. There's always Esperanto, a language made up a hundred years ago that is supposed to bring about world unity. We're still waiting for that. And if you took Spanish in high school you can see that it's not easy to get large numbers of people to speak another language fluently.

In the end, though, it doesn't matter what replacement language we pick, just so long as we ban English instead of making it official. Prohibiting English will do for the language what Prohibition did for liquor. Those who already use it will continue to do so, and those who don't will want to try out what has been forbidden. This negative psychology works with children. It works with speed limits. It even worked in the Garden of Eden.

chapter thirteen

Humorous Arguments

When the local city council passes an ordinance requiring bicyclists to wear helmets to protect against head injuries, a cyclist responds by writing a letter to the editor of the local newspaper suggesting other requirements the council might impose to protect citizens—including wearing earplugs in dance clubs, water wings in city pools, and blinders in City Hall.

After staging a successful academic conference, participants in a listserv begin exchanging messages of congratulations, praising the cooperation and fine work done by members of the group. After the seventh or eighth syrupy communication, a member of the group posts a tongue-in-cheek message suggesting that his conference paper was the only one he found bearable and that he spent the other sessions sleeping—along with most other members of the audience.

An undergraduate who thinks his school's new sexual harassment policy amounts to puritanism parodies it for the school literary magazine by describing in a short fictional drama what would happen if Romeo and Juliet strayed onto campus.

Under fire for inviting political contributors to stay at the White House overnight, the president of the United States jokes that while he's sad his only child is going away to college, it does free up another bedroom!

Tired of looking at the advertisements that cover every square inch of the campus sports arena walls, a student sends the college newspaper a satirical "news" article entitled "Sports Arena for Sale—to Advertisers!"

■ ■ ■

UNDERSTANDING HUMOR AS ARGUMENT

Though tough to define and even harder to teach, humor can be a powerful form of argument. You can use humor as a strategy to make readers well disposed toward your own projects or to ridicule people and concepts you don't like. In recent years, late-night talk show hosts have become the barometers of political opinion, the day's events fodder for their comic monologues. A somber two minutes from Dan Rather probably does a politico less harm than a couple of zingers from Jay Leno.

By its very nature, humor is risky. Playing fast and loose with good taste and sound reason, writers turn what is comfortable and familiar inside out and then hope readers get the joke. Play it too safe with humor, and audiences groan; step over an unseen line, and they hiss or hurl tomatoes. Because of such pitfalls, humor may be the most rhetorically intense form of argument, requiring a shrewd assessment of audience, language, and purpose. At its best, humor amazes readers with its evanescent clarity. But one cannot revise bad humor or save it with better evidence or more careful documentation.

Neither can humor afford to be less than razor sharp. (John Dryden described great satire as severing the head from a body so cleanly as to leave it standing in place.) Comic timing is, in fact, a rhetorical skill, the ability to find suitable words for unanticipated situations. Because humor is so attached to the moment of its delivery and to the cultural context, retelling a funny story often ends with the comment, "You just had to be there." It's also why topical humor wears so poorly—and why even Shakespeare's comedies require so many footnotes. To manage humor, you must appreciate the rhetorical situation as well as the foibles of human nature. You've got to be fresh and witty, not crude and obscene (which reflects the most juvenile form of humor).

Obviously, then, humor cannot be learned quickly or easily. But it is too powerful a tool to leave to comedians. For writers and speakers, humor can quicken the major rhetorical strategies—appeals of the heart, character, and reason.

Humor is not itself an emotion, but it can be used to rouse powerful feelings in readers. In some circumstances, humor can simply make people feel good and, thus, move them to do what others ask. That's the rationale behind many "soft sell" commercials, from classic VW pitches of a generation ago ("Think small") to more recent, thoroughly silly spots for Mentos mint candies. Advertisers hope to associate the pleasure of a smile with particular products.

But humor has a darker side, too; it can make people feel superior to targets of ridicule. Naturally, one doesn't want to associate with people or ideas one finds ridiculous. So if a health care reform proposal can be lampooned as a ludicrously tangled web of government agencies, perhaps it won't be taken seriously by citizens who might fear a medical delivery system with the efficiency of the post office and the charm of the IRS.

Humor plays a large role, too, in arguments of character. One of the easiest ways to win the goodwill of readers is to make them laugh. It is no accident that all but the most serious speeches ritually begin with a few jokes or anecdotes. The humor puts listeners at ease and helps them identify with the speaker—*She's just a regular guy, who can crack a smile*. A little self-deprecating wit can endear writers or speakers to the toughest audience. You'll likely listen to people confident enough to make fun of themselves because their wit suggests both intelligence and an appealing awareness of their own limitations. After all, no one likes a stuffed shirt.

Humor also is related to reason and good sense. A funny remark usually has, at its core, an element of truth:

Political correctness is . . . another form of American insanity that forbids people from speaking their minds for fear they'll say exactly what everyone else is thinking.
                    –John Ruszkiewicz, "Politics, Political Correctness, and Sex"

Or humor may work off a particular logical structure. Dave Barry, for example, opens the sample argument at the end of this chapter with a carefully constructed, rather artful analogy between—odd as it may seem—Amtrak and sports:

> I mean, suppose you have a friend who, for no apparent reason, suddenly becomes obsessed with Amtrak. He babbles about Amtrak constantly, citing obscure railroad statistics from 1978; he puts Amtrak bumper stickers on his car; and when something bad happens to Amtrak, such as a train crashes and investigators find that the engineer was drinking and wearing a bunny suit, your friend becomes depressed for weeks. You'd think he was crazy, right? "Bob," you'd say to him as a loving and caring friend, "you're a moron. Amtrak has NOTHING TO DO WITH YOU."
>
> But if Bob is behaving exactly the same deranged way about, say, the Pittsburgh Penguins, it's considered normal guy behavior. He could name his child "Pittsburgh Penguin Johnson" and be considered only mildly eccentric.
>
> –Dave Barry, "A Look at Sports Nuts—And We Do Mean Nuts"

Many forms of humor, especially satire and parody, get their power from twists of logic. When Jonathan Swift in the eighteenth century suggested that Ireland's English rulers consider a diet of Irish children, he depended on readers perceiving the parallel between his outrageous proposal and actual policies of an oppressive English government. The satire works precisely because it is perfectly logical, given the political realities of Swift's time—though some of his contemporaries missed the joke.

> I profess, in the sincerity of my heart, that I have not the least personal interest in endeavoring to promote this necessary work, having no other motive but the public good of my country, by advancing our trade, providing for infants, relieving the poor, and giving some pleasure to the rich.
>
> –Jonathan Swift, "A Modest Proposal"

In our own era, columnist Molly Ivins, taking on opponents of gun control on a television talk show, seems to submit to their position—but then extends it with a twist that makes her own point and ridicules her opponents at the same time:

> I think that's what we need: more people carrying weapons. I support the legislation but I'd like to propose one small amendment. Everyone

should be able to carry a concealed weapon. But everyone who carries a weapon should be required to wear one of those little beanies on their heads with a little propeller on it so the rest of us can see them coming.

–Molly Ivins

CHARACTERIZING KINDS OF HUMOR

It's possible to write entire books about comic form, exploring variations such as satire, parody, burlesque, travesty, pastiche, lampoon, caricature, farce, and more. Almost every type of humor entails a kind of argument, laughter usually aiming at some purpose grander than a chuckle. Not all such purposes are laudable; schoolyard taunts and vicious editorial cartoons may share an intent to hurt or humiliate. But humor can also break down pretensions or barriers of prejudice and help people see the world in new ways. When it is robust and honest, humor is a powerful rhetorical form.

Humor

Though serious academic writing generally avoids sustained moments of comedy, humor can contribute to almost any argument. Appreciating when it is appropriate isn't always easy, however. One has to sense what humor can do before deploying it.

For instance, humor inserted in an otherwise serious piece readily catches a reader's attention and changes the tone. Here, for example, is the African American writer Zora Neale Hurston addressing the very real issue of discrimination, with a nod and a wink:

> Sometimes I feel discriminated against, but it does not make me angry. It merely astonishes me. How *can* any deny themselves the pleasure of my company? It's beyond me.
> –Zora Neale Hurston, "How It Feels to Be Colored Me"

Or a fairly serious point can be illustrated with comic examples that keep a reader engaged in the message, aware that what the author is describing comports with reality. Consider the following lengthy passage in which Prudence Makintosh, mother of three sons, illustrates, in part, why she believes that nurture and socialization alone don't account for certain differences between girls and boys:

How can I explain why a little girl baby sits on a quilt in the park thoughtfully examining a blade of grass, while my baby William uproots grass by handfuls and eats it? Why does a mother of very bright and active daughters confide that until she went camping with another family of boys, she feared that my sons had a hyperactivity problem? I am sure there are plenty of noisy, rowdy little girls, but I'm not just talking about rowdiness and noise. I'm talking about some sort of primal physicalness that causes the walls of my house to pulsate on rainy days. I'm talking about something inexplicable that makes my sons fall into a mad, scrambling, pull-your-ears-off-kick-your-teeth-in heap just before bedtime, when they're not even mad at each other. I mean something that causes them to climb the doorjamb with honey and peanut butter on their hands while giving me a synopsis of *Star Wars* that contains only five unintelligible words. . . . When Jack and Drew are not kicking a soccer ball or each other, they are kicking the chair legs, the cat, the baby's silver rattle, and inadvertently, Baby William himself, whom they have affectionately dubbed "Tough Eddy."

–Prudence Makintosh, "Masculine/Feminine"

The rich detail of the description is part of the argumentative strategy, capturing perfectly the exasperation of a mother who apparently thought she could raise her boys to be different. Readers chuckle at little William eating grass, the house pulsating, doorjambs sticky with peanut butter—and see Makintosh's point, whether they agree with it or not. Her intention, however, is not so much to be funny but to give her opinion presence.

That seems to be George Felton's strategy, too, in the following passage from his meditation on the American obsession with healthy living and natural foods. In this case, the humor may be gaining the upper hand, yet readers understand the writer's point (at least those readers of a certain age):

The cereal aisle at the grocery store now presents us with one trail mix after another designed for the long march through our large intestines, each another grainy way to combat cancer, cholesterol, our own weak desire for pleasure. I now walk down the aisle trying, not to satisfy my hunger, but to represent my colon. What would it like? What does it need? I wonder. "Bran!" the shelves shout back.

–George Felton, "The Selling of Pain"

Exaggeration of the kind evident in Felton's piece is an essential technique of humor. Sometimes readers see the world more clearly when a writer blows up the picture. Here's Dave Barry, again, arguing that computer enthusiasts might be just a tad odd:

> I am not the only person who uses his computer mainly for the purpose of diddling with his computer. There are millions of others. I know because I encounter them on the Internet, which is a giant international network of intelligent informed computer enthusiasts, by which I mean, "people without lives."
>
> —Dave Barry, "You Have to Be a Real Stud Hombre Cybermuffin to Handle 'Windows'"

Satire

Satire is a more focused form of humor, a genre in its own right. In satire, a writer uses humor and wit to expose — and possibly correct — human problems or failings. The most famous piece of satire in English literature is probably Jonathan Swift's *Gulliver's Travels,* which pokes fun at all human pretensions, targeting especially politics, religion, science, and sexuality. This satire is a sustained argument for change in human character and institutions.

Not all satires reach as far as Swift's masterpiece, but the impulse to expose human foibles to ridicule is quite strong. Political and social satire thrive on television programs such as *Saturday Night Live* and *Politically Incorrect.* Most editorial cartoons, like the one shown in Figure 13.1, also fall into the realm of satire when they highlight a defect in society that the cartoonist feels needs to be remedied.

Satire often involves a shift in perspective that compels readers to examine a situation in a new way. In *Gulliver's Travels,* for example, we see human society reduced in scale (in Lilliput), exaggerated in size (in Brobdingnang), even through the eyes of a superior race of horses (the Houyhnhnms). In the land of the giants, Gulliver comments on the defects of the ladies when he sees them up close in their boudoirs:

> Their skins appeared so coarse and uneven, so variously coloured, when I saw them near, with a mole here and there as broad as a trencher, and hairs hanging from it thicker than pack-threads, to say nothing further concerning the rest of their persons.
>
> —Jonathan Swift, *Gulliver's Travels*

So much for human beauty. You'll note that there's nothing especially funny in Gulliver's remarks. That's because satire is more likely to employ

FIGURE 13.1

"Do you solemnly swear to be truth-oriented?"

wit than humor, the point of a piece being to open readers' eyes rather than to make them laugh out loud. People are amused that the author of a satire is not altogether serious, but they also understand that there is a larger point to be made—if the satire works.

You can see this balancing act between satiric form and message in the following proposal to eliminate grades in college. Roberta Borkat, a college English instructor fed up with her students' whining about grades, is sure there's a better way to handle evaluation and offers a scheme:

> The plan is simplicity itself: at the end of the second week of the semester, all students enrolled in each course will receive a final grade of A. Then their minds will be relieved of anxiety, and they will be free to do whatever they want for the rest of the term.
>
> The benefits are immediately obvious. Students will be assured of high grade point averages and an absence of obstacles in their march toward graduation. Professors will be relieved of useless burdens and will have time to pursue their real interests. Universities will have achieved the long-desired goal of molding individual professors into interchangeable parts of a smoothly operating machine. Even the environment will be improved because education will no longer consume vast quantities of paper for books, compositions and examinations.
>
> –Roberta Borkat, "A Liberating Curriculum"

Readers know Borkat doesn't mean what she says, but they don't exactly laugh at her proposal either. For many teachers and some students, no doubt, the satire strikes too close to home. Borkat has made her case.

Parody

Like satire, parody typically offers an argument. What distinguishes the two forms is that parody makes its case by transforming the familiar—be it songs, passages of prose, TV shows, poems, films, even people—into something new. The argument sparkles in the tension between the original work and its imitation. That's where the humor lies, too.

Needless to say, parodies work best when audiences make that connection. Imagine how pointless a parody of the sitcom *Friends* might seem fifty years from now. Even today, allusions to President Gerald Ford's clumsiness seem about as funny (and topical) as digs at William Howard Taft's prodigious weight. Indeed, context is everything.

But if the half-life of parody is brief, the form is potent in its prime. Just a few years ago, when a men's movement danced briefly in the national consciousness, Joe Bob Briggs brought the nascent trend to its knees with a ruthless parody of Wild Man weekends, when boorish males finally got in touch with their inner selves:

> **I'll never forget it. I sweated a lot. I cried. I sweated *while* I was crying. Of course, I was crying because they made me sweat so much. We had this one part of the weekend where we went into a giant sauna and turned it up to about, oh, 280, until everybody's skin turned the color of strawberry Jell-O and the veins of our heads started exploding, and it turned into this communal out-of-body *male* thing, where everybody was screaming, "I want *out* of my body!"**
> —Joe Bob Briggs, "Get in Touch with Your Ancient Spear"

When a subject or work becomes the object of a successful parody, it's never seen in quite the same way again.

Signifying

One distinctive kind of humor found extensively in African American English is signifying, in which a speaker cleverly and often humorously needles the listener. In the following passage, two African American men (Grave Digger and Coffin Ed) signify on their white supervisor (Anderson), who ordered them to discover the originators of a riot:

"I take it you've discovered who started the riot," Anderson said.

"We knew who he was all along," Grave Digger said.

"It's just nothing we can do to him," Coffin Ed echoed.

"Why not, for God's sake?"

"He's dead," Coffin Ed said.

"Who?"

"Lincoln," Grave Digger said.

"He hadn't ought to have freed us if he didn't want to make provisions to feed us," Coffin Ed said. "Anyone could have told him that."

–Chester Himes, *Hot Day, Hot Night*

Coffin Ed and Grave Digger demonstrate the major characteristics of effective signifying: indirection, ironic humor, fluid rhythm—and a surprising twist at the end. Rather than insulting Anderson directly by pointing out that he's asked a dumb question, they criticize the question indirectly by ultimately blaming a white man (and not just *any* white man, but one they're all supposed to revere). This twist leaves the supervisor speechless, teaching him something *and* giving Grave Digger and Coffin Ed the last word.

You will find examples of signifying in the work of many African American writers. You may also hear signifying in NBA basketball, for it is an important element of trash talking; what Grave Digger and Coffin Ed do to Anderson, Reggie Miller regularly does to his opponents on the court.

DEVELOPING HUMOROUS ARGUMENTS

It's doubtful anyone can offer a formula for being funny; some would suggest that humor is a gift. But at least the comic perspective is a trait widely distributed among the population. Most people can be funny, given the right circumstances.

But the stars may not always be aligned when you need them in composing an argument. And just working hard may not help: laughter arises from spirited, not labored, insights. Yet once you strike the spark, a blaze usually follows.

Look for humor in obvious situations. Bill Cosby began a stellar career as a humorist with a comedy album that posed the rather simple question: *Why Is There Air?* The late columnist and author Erma Bombeck, too, endeared herself to millions of people by pointing out the humor in daily routines.

Look for humor in incongruity or in *what if* situations, and then imagine the consequences. *What if men had monthlies? What if reading caused flatulence? What if students hired special prosecutors to handle their grade complaints? What if broccoli tasted like chocolate? What if politicians always told the truth? What if the Pope wasn't Catholic?*

Don't look for humor in complicated ideas. You're more apt to find it in simple premises, like Barry's potent question: "How come guys care so much about sports?" There are, of course, serious answers to the question. But the humor practically bubbles up on its own once you ponder men and their games. You can write a piece of your own just by listing details: *Monday Night Football, sports bars, beer commercials, sagging couches, fantasy camps, Little League, angry wives.* Push a little further, relate such items to personal insights and experiences, and you are likely to discover some of the incongruities and implausibilities at the heart of humor.

Let us stress detail. Abstract humor probably doesn't work for anyone except German philosophers and inebriated graduate students. Look for humor in concrete and proper nouns, in people and places readers will recognize but not expect to encounter. Consider Barry's technique in defending himself against those who might question his attack on sports:

> And before you accuse me of being some kind of sherry-sipping ascot-wearing ballet-attending MacNeil-Lehrer-NewsHour-watching wussy, please note that I am a sports guy myself, having had a legendary athletic career consisting of nearly a third of the 1965 season on the track team at Pleasantville High School ("Where the Leaders of Tomorrow Are Leaving Wads of Gum on the Auditorium Seats of Today").
> –Dave Barry, "A Look at Sports Nuts—And We Do Mean Nuts"

Remove the lively details from the passage and this is what's left:

> And before you accuse me of being some kind of wussy, please note that I am a sports guy myself, having had an athletic career on the track team at Pleasantville High School.

Enough said?

KEY FEATURES OF HUMOROUS ARGUMENTS

Drafting humor and revising humor are yin-yang propositions—opposites that complement each other. Think Democrats and Republicans.

Creating humor is, by nature, a robust, excessive, and egotistical activity. It requires assertiveness, courage, and often a (temporary) suspension of good judgment and taste. Whereas drafting more material than necessary usually makes good sense for writers, you can afford to be downright prodigal with humor. Pile on the examples and illustrations. Take all the risks you can with language. Indulge in puns. Leap into innuendo. Be clever, but not childishly obscene. Push your vocabulary. Play with words and have fun.

Then, when you revise, do the opposite. Recall that Polonius in Shakespeare's *Hamlet* is right about one thing: "Brevity is the soul of wit." Once you have written a humorous passage, whether a tooting horn or a full symphonic parody, you must pare your language to the bone. Every noun must be a thing, every verb an action. Think: less is more. Cut, then cut again.

That's all there is to it.

Finding a Topic

You may use humor in an argument to

- point out flaws in a policy, proposal, or argument
- suggest a policy of your own
- set people in a favorable frame of mind
- admit weaknesses or deflect criticism
- satirize or parody a position, point of view, or style

Opportunities to use humor in daily life are too numerous to catalog, but they are much rarer in academic and professional writing. You can find amusing topics everywhere if you think about the absurdities of your job, home life, or surrounding culture. Try to see things you take for granted from radically different perspectives. Or flip-flop the normal order of affairs: make a small issue cosmic; chop a huge matter to fritters.

Researching Your Topic

You can't exactly research a whimsical argument, but humor does call for some attention to detail. Satires and parodies thrive on actual events, specific facts, telling allusions, or memorable images that can be located in sources or recorded in discussions and conversations. Timeliness is a factor, too; you need to know whom or what your readers will recognize and how they might respond. Seek inspiration for humor in these sources:

- popular magazines, especially weekly journals (for current events)
- TV, including commercials (especially for material about people)
- classic books, music, films, artwork (as inspiration for parodies)
- comedians (to observe how they make a subject funny)

Formulating a Claim

With humorous arguments, satires, and parodies, you won't so much develop a thesis as play upon a theme. But humor of the sort that can grow for several pages does need a focal point, a central claim that requires support and evidence—even if that support strains credulity. (In fact, it probably should.) Here are lines to kick-start a humorous argument:

- What if . . . ?
- What would happen if . . . ?
- Why is it that . . . ?
- How come . . . never happens to . . . ?
- When was the last time you tried to . . . ?
- Why is it that men/women . . . ?
- Can you believe that . . . ?

Preparing a Proposal

If your instructor asks you to prepare a proposal for a satire, parody, or other humorous argument, here's a format you might use (or parody!).

Explain the focus of your project.

Articulate the point of your humor. What is at stake? What do you hope to accomplish?

Specify any models you have for your project. Who or what are you trying to emulate? If you are writing a parody, what is your target or inspiration?

Explain whom you hope to reach by your humor and why this group of readers will be amused.

Briefly discuss the key challenges you anticipate. Defining a point? Finding comic ideas?

Identify the sources you expect to consult. What facts might you have to establish?

Determine the format you expect to use for your project. A conventional paper? A letter to the editor? A Web page?

Thinking about Organization

Humorous arguments can be structured exactly like more serious ones—with claims, supporting reasons, warrants, evidence, qualifiers, and rebuttals. In fact, humor has its own relentless logic. Once you set an argument going, you should press it home with the same vigor you see in serious pieces.

If you write a parody, you need to be thoroughly familiar with the work on which it is based, particularly its organization and distinctive features. In parodying a song, for example, you've got to be sure listeners recognize familiar lines or choruses. In parodying a longer piece, boil it down to essential elements—the most familiar actions in the plot, the most distinctive characters, the best-known passages of dialogue—and then arrange those elements within a compact and rapidly moving design.

Getting and Giving Response

All arguments can benefit from the scrutiny of others. Your instructor may assign you to a peer group for the purpose of reading and responding to each other's drafts; if not, go out of your way to get some careful response. You can use the following questions to evaluate your own draft, to secure response to it from others, or to prepare a response to a colleague's work. If you are evaluating someone else's draft, be sure to supply specific examples to illustrate your points. Most writers respond better to specific comments than to general observations.

Focus

- Is the argument funny? Would another approach to the topic—even a nonhumorous one—be more effective?
- Does the humor make a clear argumentative point? Is its target clear?
- If the piece is a satire, does it suggest a better alternative to the present situation? If not, does it need to?

Logic, Organization, and Format

- Is there logic to the humor? If so, will readers appreciate it?
- Are the points in the argument clearly connected? Are additional or clearer transitions needed?
- Does the humor build toward a climax? If not, would saving the best laughs for last be more effective?
- Is the piece too long, making the humor seem belabored? If so, how might it be cut?

- Does the format of the piece contribute to the humor? Would it be funnier if it were formatted to look like a particular genre—an advertisement, an email message, a sports column, a greeting card? If you've used illustrations, do they enhance the humor? If there are no illustrations, would adding some help?

Style and Detail

- Is the humor too abstract? Does it need more details about specific people, events, and so on?
- If the piece is a parody, does it successfully imitate the language and idioms of whatever is being parodied?
- Are the sentences wordy or too complex for the type of humor being attempted?
- Are there any problems with spelling, grammar, punctuation, or mechanics?

RESPOND.

1. For each of the following items, list particular details that might contribute to a humorous look at the subject. (For an example, see Dave Barry's essay about sports fanatics at the end of this chapter.)

   zealous environmentalists

   clueless builders and developers

   aggressive drivers

   violent Hollywood films

   hemp activists

   drivers of big sport utility vehicles

   Martha Stewart

   high school coaches

   college instructors

   malls and the people who visit them

2. Spend some time listening to a friend who you think is funny. What kind of humor does he or she use? What sorts of details crop up in it? Once you've put in a few days of careful listening, try to write down some of the jokes and stories just as your friend told them. Writing humor may be excruciating at first, but you might find it easier with practice.

   After you've written a few humorous selections, think about how well they translate from the spoken word to the written. What's different? Do they work better in one medium than in another? Show your written efforts to your funny friend and ask for comments. How would he or she revise your written efforts?

3. Using Internet search tools, find a transcript of a funny television or radio show. Read the transcript a few times, paying attention to the places where you laugh the most. Then analyze the humor, trying to understand what makes it funny. This chapter suggests several possible avenues for analysis, including normality, incongruity, simplicity, and details. How does the transcript reflect these principles? Or does it operate by a completely different set of principles? (Some of the best humor is funny because it breaks all the rules.)

The Road to Acme Looniversity

KIRSTEN DOCKENDORFF

With a "click," the television set goes on. You hear that familiar music and see the Warner Brothers logo indicating it's time for *Looney Toons*. We've all watched them, including the many episodes of Wyle E. Coyote and his never-ending quest to catch the Road Runner. Secretly, we've all wanted Wyle E. to succeed, although long before the end of every episode we know that his hard work will only be rewarded by his being dropped from a cliff, smashed by a falling rock, *and* run over by a truck. As if that's not bad enough, Wyle E.'s defeat is also made more miserable by the Road Runner driving over him with his tongue stuck out and a shrill "Beep! Beep!" One thing is clear: Wyle E. has a problem, and it is time for him to solve it.

Like a typical proposal argument, the parody opens with a problem.

One of the easiest ways to get rid of the bird would be for Wyle E. to hire an assassin. This way, he could rest easily knowing a professional was at work. Wyle E. could use the money usually spent on Acme products to cover the assassin's fee. This would also save additional money because Wyle E. would no longer have to buy Acme equipment or pay all of those expensive hospital bills that result when the Acme equipment fails. A professional would be a quick, easy, and cost-effective solution. The major drawback is that Wyle E. would miss the satisfaction of doing the job himself. After so many years of working so hard to catch the Road Runner, he might want to be part of the event.

The parody suggests, assesses, then rejects various solutions to Wyle E. Coyote's problem — just like a real *essay.*

Kirsten Dockendorff wrote this essay while she was a student at Bowling Green State University in Bowling Green, Ohio. In the essay, Dockendorff parodies the structure of conventional proposal arguments (see Chapter 12) by applying it to the dilemma of cartoon character Wyle E. Coyote.

A better way for Wyle E. to kill the Road Runner and still participate might be to get some help from his friends. Wyle E. could call on Elmer Fudd, Yosemite Sam, Sylvester the Cat, and Taz, the Tasmanian Devil. By constructing a plan in which he and his friends combine their natural talents, Wyle E. would have the satisfaction of being part of the bird's demise. Taz, with speed equal to the Road Runner's, could chase the bird into a trap designed by Yosemite Sam: a small mound of birdseed in the Road Runner's path. When the bird stops to eat, a cage would drop. Then Sylvester's natural bird-catching instincts could be of use in disabling the bird to prevent escape, perhaps by breaking its legs. After that, Elmer could use his extraordinary hunting skills to finish him off. The only flaw in this plan might be that his friends don't have much of a record of success: Elmer, Sam, and Taz have never caught Bugs Bunny; Sylvester has never caught Tweety; and you know the results of all Wyle E.'s plans. The chance would thus seem infinitesimal at best that even together they might catch the Road Runner.

To appreciate the humor, a reader has to recognize a host of cartoon characters.

Wyle E.'s major problem in his pursuit of the Road Runner never seems to be the plan itself, but the products he uses to carry out the plan. None of the equipment he buys from Acme ever works correctly. It may work fine in a test run, but when the Road Runner actually falls into the trap, everything goes crazy or fails completely. In one recurring episode, Wyle E. buys a rocket and a pair of roller skates. His plan is to strap the rocket to his back and the skates to his feet, and thus overtake his speedy prey. The test run is fine. Then the bird runs by, and Wyle E. starts the rocket, which immediately runs out of fuel, blows up, or does not go off. If Wyle E. used a company other than Acme, he might avoid the injuries he suffers from faulty Acme equipment. Of course, one obstacle to this plan is the cost of doing business with a new company. Since Wyle E. probably receives a sizable discount from Acme because of his preferred customer status, he perhaps would not get the same treatment from a new company, at least for a while. On his cartoon-character salary, Wyle E. may not be able to afford higher prices.

The humor also depends on readers going along with the joke, regarding Wyle E. Coyote as a person and Acme as a company.

Given the range of possibilities for catching the Road Runner, the best solution to the problem might be for Wyle E. to use his superior intellect. Wyle E. could undoubtedly convince the Road Runner that a dramatic death scene on the show might win him an Emmy. Since roadrunners are known for their vanity, this Road Runner would seem likely to leap at the prospect of winning fame and fortune for his fine acting skills. With such a prestigious award, the Road Runner could do what every actor dreams of doing: direct. He would win not only fame and fortune, but the respect of his hero, Big Bird.

Now the parody mocks actors, too.

If and when Wyle E. catches the Road Runner, the cartoon, of course, would end. Although this might at first seem tragic, the consequences are really not tragic at all. Wyle E. would have more time to pursue his movie career and perhaps even teach at Acme Looniversity. He would have more time to devote to his family, friends, and fans. And he could finally stop paying a therapist since his psychological issues would be resolved. Wyle E. would gain self-confidence and no longer doubt his ability as he did when the birdbrain outsmarted him. He would finally recognize his own genius and realize his lifelong dream of opening a theme restaurant.

Real proposal arguments ponder the feasibility of their solutions — and so does this one.

After years and years of torment and humiliation, it is time for Wyle E. Coyote to catch the Road Runner. Although it is feasible for Wyle E. to pay an assassin to kill the bird, to enlist his friends for help, or to stop using Acme products, the best solution is for Wyle E. to use the immeasurable power of his brain to trick the imbecilic bird. Regardless of the method Wyle E. chooses, one thing is clear: the bird must *die!*

Even the conclusion follows a formula.

A Look at Sports Nuts—And We Do Mean Nuts

DAVE BARRY

Today in our continuing series on How Guys Think, we explore the question: How come guys care so much about sports?

This is a tough one, because caring about sports is, let's face it, silly. I mean, suppose you have a friend who, for no apparent reason, suddenly becomes obsessed with Amtrak. He babbles about Amtrak constantly, citing obscure railroad statistics from 1978; he puts Amtrak bumper stickers on his car; and when something bad happens to Amtrak, such as a train crashes and investigators find that the engineer was drinking and wearing a bunny suit, your friend becomes depressed for weeks. You'd think he was crazy, right? "Bob," you'd say to him as a loving and caring friend, "you're a moron. Amtrak has NOTHING TO DO WITH YOU."

But if Bob is behaving exactly the same deranged way about, say, the Pittsburgh Penguins, it's considered normal guy behavior. He could name his child "Pittsburgh Penguin Johnson" and be considered only mildly eccentric.

There is something wrong with this. And before you accuse me of being some kind of sherry-sipping ascot-wearing ballet-attending MacNeil-Lehrer-NewsHour-watching wussy, please note that I am a sports guy myself, having had a legendary athletic career consisting of nearly a third of the 1965 season on the track team at Pleasantville High School ("Where the Leaders of Tomorrow Are Leaving Wads of Gum on the Auditorium Seats of Today"). I competed in the long jump, because it seemed to be the only event where afterward you didn't fall down and throw up. I probably would have become an Olympic-caliber long-jumper except that, through one of those "bad breaks" so common in sports, I turned out to have the raw leaping ability of a convenience store.

So, okay, I was not Jim Thorpe, but I care as much about sports as the next guy. If you were to put me in the middle of a room, and in one corner was Albert Einstein, in another corner was Abraham Lincoln, in another corner was Plato, in another corner was William Shakespeare, and in another corner (this room is a pentagon) was a TV set showing a football game between

Dave Barry is a syndicated columnist and the author of numerous books, including *Dave Barry's Complete Guide to Guys: A Fairly Short Book* (1995), *Dave Barry Is from Mars and Venus* (1997), and *Dave Barry Talks Back* (1991), from which this piece is taken. In it, Barry offers a not entirely serious answer to an age-old question: "How come guys care so much about sports?"

235

teams that have no connection whatsoever with my life, such as the Green Bay Packers and the Indianapolis Colts, I would ignore the greatest minds in Western thought, gravitate toward the TV, and become far more concerned about the game than I am about my child's education. And SO WOULD THE OTHER GUYS. I guarantee it. Within minutes, Plato would be pounding Lincoln on the shoulder and shouting in ancient Greek that the receiver did NOT have both feet in bounds.

Obviously, sports connect with something deeply rooted in the male psyche, dating back to prehistoric times, when guys survived by hunting and fighting, and they needed many of the skills exhibited by modern athletes—running, throwing, spitting, renegotiating their contracts, adjusting their private parts on nationwide television, etc. So that would explain how come guys like to PARTICIPATE in sports. But how come they care so much about games played by OTHER guys? Does this also date back to prehistoric times? When the hunters were out hurling spears into mastodons, were there also prehistoric guys watching from the hills, drinking prehistoric beer, eating really bad prehistoric hot dogs and shouting "We're No. 1!" but not understanding what it meant because this was before the development of mathematics?

There must have been, because there is no other explanation for such bizarre phenomena as:

- Sports-talk radio, where guys who have never sent get-well cards to their own mothers will express heartfelt, near-suicidal anguish over the hamstring problems of strangers.
- A guy in my office who appears to be a normal middle-age husband and father until you realize that he spends most of his waking hours managing a PRETEND BASEBALL TEAM. This is true. He and some other guys have formed a league where they pay actual money to "draft" major league players, and then they have their pretend teams play a whole pretend season, complete with trades, legalistic memorandums, and heated disputes over the rules. This is crazy, right? If these guys said they were managing herds of pretend caribou, the authorities would be squirting lithium down their throats with turkey basters, right? And yet we all act like it's PERFECTLY NORMAL. In fact, eavesdropping from my office, I find myself getting involved in the discussions. That's how pathetic I am: I'm capable of caring about a pretend sports team that's not even my OWN pretend sports team.

So I don't know about the rest of you guys, but I'm thinking it's time I got some perspective in my life. First thing after the Super Bowl, I'm going to start paying more attention to the things that should matter to me, like my work, my friends, and, above all, my family, especially my little boy, Philadelphia Phillies Barry.

PART 4

STYLISH argument

chapter fourteen

Figurative Language and Argument

Open any magazine or newspaper and you will see figurative language working on behalf of arguments. When the writer of a letter to the editor complains that "Donna Haraway's supposition that because we rely on cell phones and laptops we are cyborgs is [like] saying the Plains Indians were centaurs because they relied on horses," he is using an analogy to rebut (and perhaps ridicule) Haraway's claim. When another writer says that "the digital revolution is whipping through our lives like a Bengali typhoon," she is making an implicit argument about the speed and strength of the digital revolution. When still another writer calls Disney World a "smile factory," she begins a stinging critique of the way pleasure is "manufactured" there.

Just what is figurative language? Traditionally, the terms *figurative language* and *figures of speech* refer to language that differs from the ordinary — that calls up, or "figures," something else. But in fact, all language could be said to call up or figure something else. The word *table,* for example, is not itself a table; rather, it calls up a table in our imaginations. Thus, just as all language is by nature argumentative, so too is it all figurative. Far from being mere decorations or embellishments (something like icing on the cake of thought), figures of speech are indispensable to language use.

More specifically, figurative language brings two major strengths to arguments. First, it often aids understanding by likening something unknown to something known. For example, in arguing for the existence of DNA as they had identified and described it, scientists Watson and Crick used two familiar examples — a helix (spiral) and a zipper — to make their point. Today, arguments about new computer technologies are filled with similar uses of figurative language. Indeed, Microsoft's entire word-processing system depends on likening items to those in an office (as in Microsoft Office) to make them more understandable and familiar to users. Second, figurative language can be helpful in arguments because it is often extremely memorable. Someone arguing that slang should be used in formal writing turns to this memorable definition for support: "Slang is language that takes off its coat, spits on its hands, and gets to work." In a brief poem that carries a powerful argument, Langston Hughes uses figurative language to explore the consequences of unfulfilled dreams:

What happens to a dream deferred?

Does it dry up
Like a raisin in the sun?
Or fester like a sore—
And then run?
Does it stink like rotten meat?
Or crust and sugar over—
Like a syrupy sweet?

Maybe it just sags
Like a heavy load.

Or does it explode?
     –Langston Hughes, "Harlem—A Dream Deferred"

In a famous speech in 1963, Martin Luther King Jr. used figurative language to make his argument unmistakably clear as well as memorable:

> In a sense we have come to our nation's capital to cash a check. When the architects of our republic wrote the magnificent words of the Constitution and the Declaration of Independence, they were signing a promissory note to which every American was to fall heir. This note was a promise that all men would be guaranteed the unalienable rights of life, liberty, and the pursuit of happiness.
>
> It is obvious today that America has defaulted on this promissory note insofar as her citizens of color are concerned. Instead of honoring this sacred obligation, America has given the Negro people a bad check; a check which has come back marked "insufficient funds." But we refuse to believe that the bank of justice is bankrupt. We refuse to believe that there are insufficient funds in the great vaults of opportunity in this nation. So we have come to cash this check—a check that will give us upon demand the riches of freedom and the security of justice.
>
> —Martin Luther King Jr., "I Have a Dream"

The figures of the promissory note and the bad check are especially effective in this passage because they suggest financial exploitation, which fits in well with the overall theme of King's speech.

You may be surprised to learn that during the European Renaissance, schoolchildren sometimes learned and practiced using as many as 180 figures of speech. Such practice seems more than a little excessive today, especially since figures of speech come so naturally to native speakers of the English language; you hear of "nipping a plot in the bud," "getting our act together," "blowing your cover," "marching to a different drummer," "seeing red," "smelling a rat," "being on cloud nine," "throwing in the towel," "tightening our belts," "rolling in the aisles," "turning the screws," "turning over a new leaf"—you get the picture. We don't aim for a complete catalog of figures of speech here, much less for a thorough analysis of the power of figurative language. What we can offer, however, is a brief listing—with examples—of some of the most familiar kinds of figures, along with a reminder that they can be used to extremely good effect in the arguments you write.

Figures have traditionally been classified into two main types: tropes, which involve a change in the ordinary signification, or meaning, of a word or phrase; and schemes, which involve a special arrangement of words. Here we will exemplify the most frequently used figures in each category, beginning with the familiar tropes of metaphor, simile, and analogy.

TROPES

Metaphor

One of the most pervasive uses of figurative language, metaphor offers an implied comparison between two things and thereby clarifies and enlivens many arguments. In the following passage, bell hooks uses the metaphor of the hope chest to enhance her argument that autobiography involves a special kind of treasure hunt:

> **Conceptually, the autobiography was framed in the manner of a hope chest. I remembered my mother's hope chest, with its wonderful odor of cedar, and thought about her taking the most precious items and placing them there for safekeeping. Certain memories were for me a similar treasure. I wanted to place them somewhere for safekeeping. An autobiographical narrative seemed an appropriate place.**
> **—bell hooks, *Bone Black***

In another argument, lawyer Gerry Spence opens "Easy in the Harness: The Tyranny of Freedom" with a question—"What is freedom?"—to which he shortly replies with a metaphor: "Freedom is . . . a blank, white canvas where no commitments, no relationships, no plans, no values, no moral restraints have been painted on the free soul." (As Spence makes clear in his discussion, his title calls on another metaphor—one used by poet Robert Frost, who likened freedom to "being easy in the harness.")

English language use is so filled with metaphors that these powerful, persuasive tools often zip by native speakers unnoticed, so be on the look-out for effective metaphors in everything you read. For example, when a reviewer of new software that promises complete filtering of advertisements on the World Wide Web refers to the product as "a weedwhacker for the Web," he is using a metaphor to advance an argument about the nature and function of that product.

Simile

A direct comparison between two things, simile is pervasive in written and spoken language. You may even have your own favorites: someone's hair is "plastered to him like white on rice," for instance, or, as one of our grandmothers used to say, "prices are high as a cat's back," or, as a special compliment, "you look as pretty as red shoes." Similes are also at work in many arguments, as you can see in this excerpt from a brief *Wired* magazine review of a new magazine for women:

> **Women's magazines occupy a special niche in the cluttered infoscape of modern media. Ask any *Vogue* junkie: no girl-themed Web site or CNN segment on women's health can replace the guilty pleasure of slipping a glossy fashion rag into your shopping cart. Smooth as a pint of chocolate Häagen-Dazs, feckless as a thousand-dollar slip dress, women's magazines wrap culture, trends, health, and trash in a single, decadent package.**
>
> **But like the diet dessert recipes they print, these slick publications can leave a bad taste in your mouth.**
>
> –Tiffany Lee Brown, "En Vogue"

Here three similes are in prominent display: "smooth as a pint of chocolate Häagen-Dazs" and "feckless as a thousand-dollar slip dress" in the third sentence, and "like the diet dessert recipes" in the fourth. Together, the similes add to the image the writer is trying to create of mass-market women's magazines as a mishmash of "trash" and "trends."

Analogy

Analogies compare two different or dissimilar things for special effect, arguing that if two things are alike in one way they are probably alike in other ways as well. Often extended to several sentences, paragraphs, or even whole essays, analogies can help clarify and emphasize points of comparison. Here Maya Angelou uses an analogy to begin an exploration of one area of Harlem:

> **One Hundred and Twenty-fifth Street was to Harlem what the Mississippi was to the South, a long traveling river always going somewhere, carrying something.**
>
> –Maya Angelou, "The Heart of a Woman"

And in an argument about the failures of the aircraft industry, another writer uses an analogy for potent contrast:

> **If the aircraft industry had evolved as spectacularly as the computer industry over the past twenty-five years, a Boeing 767 would cost five hundred dollars today, and it would circle the globe in twenty minutes on five gallons of fuel.**

Other Tropes

Several other tropes deserve special mention.

Hyperbole is the use of overstatement for special effect, a kind of pyrotechnics in prose. The tabloid papers whose headlines scream at shoppers in the grocery checkout line probably qualify as the all-time champions of hyperbole (journalist Tom Wolfe once wrote a satirical review of a *National Enquirer* writers' convention that he titled "Keeps His Mom-in-Law in Chains *meets* Kills Son and Feeds Corpse to Pigs"). Everyone has seen these overstated arguments and, perhaps, marveled at the way they seem to sell.

Hyperbole is also the trademark of more serious writers. In a column arguing that men's magazines fuel the same kind of neurotic anxieties about appearance that have plagued women for so long, Michelle Cottle uses hyperbole and humor to make her point:

> **What self-respecting '90s woman could embrace a publication that runs such enlightened articles as "Turn Your Good Girl Bad" and "How to Wake Up Next to a One-Night Stand"? Or maybe you'll smile and wink knowingly: What red-blooded hetero chick *wouldn't* love all those glossy photo spreads of buff young beefcake in various states of undress, ripped abs and glutes flexed so tightly you could bounce a check on them? Either way you've got the wrong idea. My affection for *Men's Health* is driven by pure gender politics. . . . With page after page of bulging biceps and Gillette jaws, robust hairlines and silken skin, *Men's Health* is peddling a standard of male beauty as unforgiving and unrealistic as the female version sold by those dewy-eyed pre-teen waifs draped across covers of *Glamour* and *Elle.***
> –Michelle Cottle, "Turning Boys into Girls"

As you can well imagine, hyperbole of this sort can easily backfire, so it pays to use it sparingly and for an audience whose reactions you believe you can effectively predict.

Understatement, on the other hand, requires a quiet, muted message to make its point effectively. In her memoir, Rosa Parks—an African American civil rights activist who made history in 1955 by refusing to give up her bus seat to a white passenger—uses understatement so often that it might be said to be characteristic of her writing, a mark of her ethos. She refers to Martin Luther King Jr. simply as "a true leader," to Malcolm X as a person of "strong conviction," and to her own lifelong efforts as simply a small way of "carrying on."

Quiet understatement can be particularly effective in arguments. When Watson and Crick published their first article on the structure of DNA, they felt that they had done nothing less than discover the secret of life. (Imagine what the *National Enquirer* headlines might have been for this story!) Yet in an atmosphere of extreme scientific competitiveness they chose to close their article with a vast understatement, using it purposely to gain emphasis: "It has not escaped our notice," they wrote, "that the specific pairing we have postulated immediately suggests a possible copying mechanism for the genetic material." Forty-some years later, considering the profound developments that have taken place in genetics, the power of this understatement resonates even more strongly.

Rhetorical questions don't really require answers. Rather, they are used to help assert or deny something about an argument. In a review of a book-length argument about the use and misuse of power in the Disney dynasty, the reviewer uses a series of rhetorical questions to sketch in part of the book's argument:

> **If you have ever visited one of the Disney theme parks, though, you have likely wondered at the labor — both seen and unseen — necessary to maintain these fanciful environments. How and when are the grounds tended so painstakingly? How are the signs of high traffic erased from public facilities? What keeps employees so poised, meticulously groomed, and endlessly cheerful?**
>
> –Linda S. Watts, Review of *Inside the Mouse*

Antonomasia is probably most familiar to you from the sports pages: "His Airness" means Michael Jordan; "The Great One," Wayne Gretzky; "The Sultan of Swat," Babe Ruth; and "Fraulein Forehand," Steffi Graf. Such shorthand substitutions of a descriptive word or phrase for a proper name can pack arguments into just one phrase. What does calling Jordan "His Airness" argue about him?

Irony, the use of words to convey a meaning in tension with or opposite to their literal meanings, also works powerfully in arguments. One of the most famous sustained uses of irony in literature occurs in Shakespeare's *Julius Caesar*, as Mark Antony punctuates his condemnation of Brutus with the repeated ironic phrase "But Brutus is an honourable man." In an argument about the inadequacies and dangers of nursing homes, Jill Frawley uses irony in describing herself as "just one little nurse, in one little care facility"; the statement is ironic since as "one little nurse" she has actually made very big differences in nursing home care.

SCHEMES

Schemes, figures that depend on word order, can add quite a bit of syntactic "zing" to arguments. Here we present the ones you are likely to see most often at work.

Parallelism uses grammatically similar words, phrases, or clauses for special effect:

> The Wild Man process involves five basic phases: Sweating, Yelling, Crying, Drum-Beating, and Ripping Your Shirt off Even If It's Expensive.
>> –Joe Bob Briggs, "Get in Touch with Your Ancient Spear"

> We die. That may be the meaning of life. But we *do* language. That may be the measure of our lives.
>> –Toni Morrison, Nobel Prize acceptance speech

> The laws of our land are said to be "by the people, of the people, and for the people."

Antithesis is the use of parallel structures to mark contrast or opposition:

> That's one small step for a man, one giant leap for mankind.
>> –Neil Armstrong

> Those who kill people are called murderers; those who kill animals, sportsmen.

> Love is an ideal thing; marriage a real thing.

Inverted word order, in which the parts of a sentence or clause are not in the usual subject-verb-object order, can help make arguments particularly memorable:

> Into this grey lake plopped the thought, I know this man, don't I?
>> –Doris Lessing

> One game does not a championship make.

> Good looking he was not; wealthy he was not; but brilliant—he was.

As with anything else, however, too much of such a figure can quickly become, well, too much.

Anaphora, or effective repetition, can act like a drumbeat in an argument, bringing the point home. In an argument about the true meaning of freedom, June Jordan uses repetition to focus on students and the ideals in which they want to believe:

CULTURAL CONTEXTS FOR ARGUMENT

Style is always affected by language, culture, and rhetorical tradition. What constitutes effective style, therefore, varies broadly across cultures and depends on the rhetorical situation—purpose, audience, and so on. There is at least one important style question to consider when arguing across cultures: what *level of formality* is most appropriate? In the United States a fairly informal style is often acceptable, even appreciated. Many cultures, however, tend to value more formality. If in doubt, therefore, it is probably wise to err on the side of formality, especially in communicating with elders or with those in authority.

- Take care to use proper titles as appropriate—Ms., Mr., Dr., and so on.
- Do not use first names unless invited to do so.
- Steer clear of slang. Especially when you're communicating with members of other cultures, slang may be seen as disrespectful— and it may not even be understood.

Beyond formality, stylistic preferences vary widely, and when arguing across cultures, the most important stylistic issue might be clarity, especially when you're communicating with people whose native languages are different from your own. In such situations, analogies and similes almost always aid in understanding and can be especially helpful when you're communicating across cultures. Likening something unknown to something familiar can help make your argument forceful—and understandable.

They believe that there is a mainstream majority America that will try to be fair, and that will respect their courage, and admire the intelligence of their defense. They believe that there is a mainstream majority America that will overwhelm the enemies of public and democratic education. They believe that most of us, out here, will despise and resist every assault on freedom in the United States.
                                                    –June Jordan, "Freedom Time"

Reversed structures for special effect have been used widely in political argumentation since President John F. Kennedy's Inaugural Address in 1961 charged citizens, "Ask not what your country can do for you; ask what you can do for your country." Like the other figures we have listed here, this one can help make arguments memorable:

The Democrats won't get elected unless things get worse, and things won't get worse until the Democrats get elected.

–Jeanne Kirkpatrick

The Negro needs the white man to free him from his fears. The white man needs the Negro to free him from his guilt.

–Martin Luther King Jr.

When the going gets tough, the tough get going.

DANGERS OF UNDULY SLANTED LANGUAGE

Although all arguments depend on figurative language to some degree, if the words used call attention to themselves as "stacking the deck" in unfair ways, they will not be particularly helpful in achieving the goals of the argument. In preparing your own arguments, you will want to pay special attention to the connotations of the words you choose—those associations that words and phrases always carry with them. The choices you make will always depend on the purpose you have in mind and those to whom you wish to speak. Should you choose *skinny* or *slender* in describing someone? Should you label a group *left-wing agitators, student demonstrators,* or *supporters of human rights?*

A good example of the power of such choices came in an exchange between Jesse Jackson and Michael Dukakis at the 1988 Democratic National Convention. Jackson was offended that Dukakis, who had defeated Jackson for the Democratic presidential nomination, had asserted his leadership of the party by describing himself as "the quarterback on this team," a phrase that reminded many African Americans of an old stereotype that African Americans were not intelligent enough to play quarterback on football teams. For his part, Dukakis was upset when Jackson told the new voters he had brought into the party that they were being used to "carry bales of cotton" up to "the big house," because the connotations of that language were intended to suggest that Dukakis was like a white plantation owner profiting from the labor of African American slaves. Both speakers later voiced second thoughts about their choice of figurative language in such an important public setting.

The lesson for writers of arguments is a simple one that can be devilishly hard to follow: know your audience and be respectful of them, even as you argue strenuously to make your case.

RESPOND●

1. Identify the types of figurative language used in the following advertising slogans — metaphor, simile, analogy, hyperbole, understatement, rhetorical question, antonomasia, irony, parallelism, antithesis, inverted word order, anaphora, or reversed structure.

   "Good to the last drop." (Maxwell House coffee)

   "It's the real thing." (Coca-Cola)

   "Melts in your mouth, not in your hands." (M&M's)

   "Be all that you can be." (U.S. Army)

   "Does she . . . or doesn't she?" (Clairol)

   "Breakfast of champions." (Wheaties)

   "Double your pleasure; double your fun." (Doublemint gum)

   "Let your fingers do the walking." (the Yellow Pages)

   "Think small." (Volkswagen)

   "We try harder." (Avis)

2. We mentioned in this chapter that during the Renaissance, students would memorize and practice more than a hundred figures of speech. As part of their lessons, these students would be asked to write whole paragraphs using each of the figures in *order,* in what might be called "connected discourse": the paragraph makes sense, and each sentence builds on the one that precedes it. Use the following list of figures to write a paragraph of connected discourse on a topic of your choice. Each sentence should use a different figure, starting with metaphor and ending with reversed structure.

metaphor	irony
simile	parallelism
analogy	antithesis
hyperbole	inverted word order
understatement	anaphora
rhetorical question	reversed structure
antonomasia	

   Now rewrite the paragraph, still on the same topic but using the list of figures in *reverse order.* The first sentence should use reversed structure and the last should use metaphor.

3. Some public speakers are well known for their use of tropes and schemes. (Jesse Jackson comes to mind, as does Ross Perot, who

employs folksy sayings to achieve a certain effect.) Using the Internet, find the text of a recent speech by a speaker who uses figures liberally. Pick a paragraph that seems particularly rich in figures, and rewrite it, eliminating every trace of figurative language. Read the two paragraphs—the original and your revised version—aloud to your class. With the class's help, try to imagine rhetorical situations in which the figure-free version would be most appropriate.

Now find some prose that seems dry and completely unfigurative. (A technical manual, instructions for operating appliances, or a legal document might serve.) Rewrite a part of the piece in the most figurative language you can muster. Then try to list rhetorical situations in which this newly figured language might be most appropriate.

chapter fifteen

Visual Arguments

You know you shouldn't buy camping gear just because you see it advertised in a magazine. But what's the harm in imagining yourself on that Arizona mesa, the sun setting, the camp stove open, the tent up and ready? That could be you reminiscing about the rugged trek that got you there, just like the tanned campers in the ad. Now what's that brand name again, and what's its URL?

A student government committee is meeting to talk about campus safety. One member has prepared a series of graphs showing the steady increase in the number of on-campus attacks over the last five years, along with several photographs that really bring these crimes to life.

It turns out that the governor and now presidential candidate who claims to be against taxes actually raised taxes in his home state—according to his opponent, who is running thirty-second TV spots to make that point. The ads feature a plainly dressed woman who sure looks credible; she's got to be a real person, not an actor, and she says he raised taxes. She wouldn't lie—would she?

You've never heard of the trading firm. But the letter, printed on thick bond with smart color graphics, is impressive and, hey, the company CEO is offering you $75 just to open an online account. The $75 check is right at the top of the letter, and it sure looks real. The company's Web site seems quite professional—quick-loading and easy to navigate. Somebody's on the ball. Perhaps you should sign up?

A glittering silver coupe passes you effortlessly on a steep slope along a curving mountain interstate. It's moving too fast for you to read the nameplate, but on the trunk lid you see a three-pointed star. Hmmmm . . . Maybe after you graduate from law school and your student loans are paid off . . .

You've always thought that the jams on the supermarket shelves taste pretty much alike. But those preserves stocked at eye level—the ones from France—look especially appetizing in their squat little jars with the fancy labels and golden lids. They're probably worth the extra dollar.

■ ■ ■

THE POWER OF VISUAL ARGUMENTS

We need not be reminded that visual images have clout. We see the evidence everywhere, from T-shirts to billboards to computer screens. Everyone is trying to get our attention and they are doing it with images as well as words. Technology is also making it easier for people to create and transmit images. And those images are more compelling than ever, brought to us via DVD and HDTV on our computers, on our walls, in our pockets, even in our cars.

But let's put this in perspective. Visual arguments weren't invented by Bill Gates, and they've always had power. The Pharaohs of Egypt lined the Nile with statues of themselves to assert their authority, and Roman emperors stamped their portraits on coins for the same reason.

In our own era, two events marked turning points in the importance of media images. The first occurred in 1960, when presidential candidates John F. Kennedy and Richard M. Nixon met in a nationally televised debate. (See Figure 15.1.) Kennedy, robust and confident in a dark suit, faced a pale and haggard Nixon barely recovered from an illness. Kennedy looked cool and "presidential"; Nixon did not. Many believe that the contrasting images Kennedy and Nixon presented on that evening radically changed the direction of the 1960 election campaign, leading to Kennedy's narrow victory. For better or worse, the debate also established television as the chief medium for political communication in the United States.

FIGURE 15.1   RICHARD NIXON AND JOHN KENNEDY BEFORE A TELEVISED DEBATE, 1960

The second event is more recent—the introduction in the early 1980s of personal computers with graphic interfaces. These machines, which initially seemed strange and toylike, operated with icons and pictures rather than through arcane commands. Subtly at first, and then with the smack of a tsunami, graphic computers (the only kind we use now) moved people away from an age of print into an era of electronic, image-saturated communications.

So that's where we are at the start of a new millennium. People today are adjusting rapidly to a world of seamless, multichannel communications. Our prophet is Marshall McLuhan, the guru of *Wired* magazine who proclaimed some forty years ago that "the medium is the message." Is the medium also the massage—an artful manipulator of how we think and feel? Anyone reading and writing today has to be prepared to deal with arguments that shuffle more than words.

SHAPING THE MESSAGE

Images make arguments of their own. A photograph, for example, isn't a faithful representation of reality; it's reality shaped by the photographer's point of view. Photographic and video arguments can be seen at work everywhere, but perhaps particularly so during political campaigns. Staff photographers and handlers work to place candidates in settings that will show them in the best possible light—shirtsleeves rolled up, surrounded by smiling children and red-white-and-blue bunting—while their opponents look for opportunities to present them in a bad light. Closer to home, perhaps, you may well have chosen photographs that showed you at your best to include in your college applications. Employers often judge potential employees by the image their clothing helps to create, and universities hire special consultants to help them create attractive "brand" images.

If those producing images shape the messages these images convey—and they certainly do—those "reading" them are by no means passive. Human vision is selective: to some extent, we actively shape what we see. Much of what we see is laden with cultural meanings, too, and we must have "learned" to see them in certain ways. Consider the Statue of Liberty welcoming immigrants to America's shores—and then imagine her instead as Bellona, the goddess of war, guarding New York Harbor with a blazing torch. For a moment at least, she's a different statue.

Of course, we don't always see things the same way, which is one reason eyewitnesses to the same event often report it differently. Or why even instant replays don't always solve disputed calls on football fields.

The visual images that surround us today—and that argue forcefully for our attention and often for our time and money—are constructed to invite, perhaps even coerce, us into seeing them just one way. But each of us has our own powers of vision, our own frames of reference. So visual arguments might best be described as a give-and-take, a dialogue, or even a tussle.

ACHIEVING VISUAL LITERACY

Why take images so seriously? Because they matter. Images change lives and shape behavior. When advertisements for sneakers are powerful enough to lead some kids to kill for the coveted footwear, when five- and ten-second images and sound bites are deciding factors in presidential elections, when the image of Joe Camel is credibly accused of enticing youngsters to smoke, or when a cultural icon like Oprah Winfrey can sell more books in one TV show than a hundred writers might do— it's high time to start paying careful attention to visual elements of argument.

How text is presented affects how it is read—whether it is set in fancy type, plain type, or handwritten; whether it has illustrations or not; whether it looks serious, fanciful, scholarly, or commercial. Figure 15.2 shows one short passage from Martin Luther King Jr.'s "I Have a Dream" speech presented four different ways—as poetry, as an excerpt in newspaper coverage of the speech, as part of a poster, and as it appears in plain text off the Web. Look at the four different versions of this text and consider in each case how the presentation affects the way you perceive and read King's argument. Do the photographs, for example, make King's words seem more—or less—powerful? Does the version set as poetry have more—or less— impact on you? The point, of course, is that as you read any text, you need to consider its presentation—a crucial element in any written argument.

FIGURE 15.2 FOUR DIFFER-
ENT PRESENTATIONS OF THE
SAME TEXT FROM "I HAVE A
DREAM" (A) AS POETRY; (B)
AS NEWSPAPER TEXT; (C) AS
A POSTER; (D) AS WEB TEXT

from "I Have a Dream"

*I say to you today, my friends,
That in spite of the difficulties
And frustrations of the moment,*

*I still have a dream. It is a dream
Deeply rooted in the American dream.*

*I have a dream that one day
This nation will rise up and live
out the true meaning of its creed:*

*"We hold these truths to be self-evident:
that all men are created equal."*

a

I say to you today, my friends, that in spite of the difficulties and frustrations of the moment, I still have a dream. It is a dream deeply rooted in the American dream. I have a dream that one day this nation will rise up and live out the true meaning of its creed: "We hold these truths to be self-evident: that all men are created equal."

b

I say to you today, my friends, that in spite of the difficulties and frustrations of the moment, I still have a dream. It is a dream deeply rooted in the American dream.

I have a dream that one day this nation will rise up and live out the true meaning of its creed: "We hold these truths to be self-evident: that all men are created equal."

c

I say to you today, my friends, that in spite of the difficulties and frustrations of the moment, I still have a dream. It is a dream deeply rooted in the American dream.

I have a dream that one day this nation will rise up and live out the true meaning of its creed: "We hold these truths to be self-evident: that all men are created equal."

d

ANALYZING VISUAL ELEMENTS OF ARGUMENTS

We've probably said enough to suggest that analyzing the visual elements of argument is a challenge, one that's even greater as we begin to encounter multimedia appeals as well, especially on the Web. Here are some questions that can help you recognize—and analyze—visual and multimedia arguments:

ABOUT CONTENT

- What argumentative purpose does the visual convey? What do its creators intend for its effects to be? What is it designed to convey?
- What media does the visual use—print, screen, photographs, drawings, video clips, graphs, charts? Is there sound as well? What are the strengths (or limits) of the media chosen?
- What cultural values or ideals does the visual evoke or suggest? The good life? Love and harmony? Sex appeal? Youth? Adventure? Economic power or dominance? Freedom? Does the visual reinforce these values or question them? What do the visuals do to strengthen the argument?
- What emotions does the visual evoke? Which ones do you think it intends to evoke? Desire? Envy? Empathy? Shame or guilt? Pride? Nostalgia? Something else?

ABOUT DESIGN

- What is your eye drawn to first? Why? How do other media come into play?
- What is in the foreground? In the background? What is in or out of focus? What is moving? What is placed high, and what is placed low? What is to the left, in the center, and to the right? What effect do these placements have on the message?
- Is any particular information highlighted (such as a name, face, or scene) to attract your attention?
- How are light and color used? What effect(s) are they intended to have on you? What about video? Sound?
- What details are included or emphasized? What details are omitted or deemphasized? To what effect? Is anything downplayed, ambiguous, confusing, distracting, or obviously omitted? To what ends?
- Does the visual evoke positive—or negative—feelings about individuals, scenes, or ideas?

- Is anything in the visual repeated, intensified, or exaggerated? Is anything presented as "supernormal" or idealistic? What effects are intended by these strategies, and what effects do they have on you as a viewer?

- What is the role of any words that accompany the visual? How do they clarify or reinforce (or blur or contradict) the message?

- How are you directed to move within the argument? Are you encouraged to read further? Click on a link? Scroll down? Fill out a form? Provide your email address? Place an order?

Take a look at the Web page in Figure 15.3, the 1999–2000 home page of United Colors of Benetton, a company that sells sportswear, handbags,

FIGURE **15.3** BENETTON HOME PAGE, JANUARY 2000 <**http://benetton.com**>

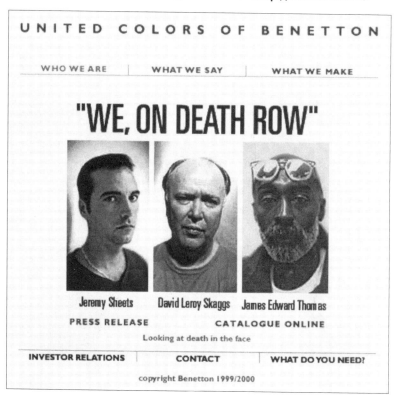

shoes, and more. You might expect a company that sells eighty million items of clothing and accessories annually to feature garments on its home page or to make a pitch to sell you something. And you would find many of those items if you probed the Benetton site more deeply. But here on the company's main page, you see three death-row inmates staring out from under the bold headline, "WE, ON DEATH ROW." The phrase suggests a kind of community, an odd recasting of "We, the people . . ." The convicts are all men—two white, one black—and they seem calm, resigned. The photographs present the men, carefully lighted, framed by soft but potent colors. Clearly, these aren't prison snapshots, but the art of a skilled professional working to make a point with these images.

The portraits so dominate the Web page that it might take you a few moments to notice the actual heading of the page—the name of the company poised above three helpful links: "Who We Are," "What We Say," and "What We Make." Clicking "What We Say" takes you to a page headed by this claim: "ALL HUMAN BEINGS ARE BORN FREE AND EQUAL IN DIGNITY AND RIGHTS." It seems that Benetton wants you to think of the company as one concerned with issues beyond commerce and fashion. Commerce is there on the Benetton home page as well. Beneath the photographs of the convicts are links to "Investor Relations" and "What Do You Need?" But it's hard to ignore those faces or to escape the nagging question—what exactly have the convicts to do with Benetton's core mission? Maybe then you notice a small gray line of type: "Looking at death in the face." You click it for more information. Nothing happens: it is not a link. It's a thought: these men are going to die.

That's what Benetton wants you to ponder as it creates for itself an aura of involvement and concern for social issues. Or, to use the company's own words, available under its "Press Release" link (hard to miss in red): "Benetton has once again chosen to look reality in the face by tackling a social issue, as it did in previous campaigns that focused on war, AIDS, discrimination and racism." So the manufacturer of clothing and accessories promotes its wares through an involvement in social activism. And so its images challenge you to judge the character of the company by looking reality in the face. Do you admire its concerns and its willingness to take controversial stands? Do you consider what's not on the Web page —images of the convicts' victims—which could boldly challenge the statement Benetton is making? Or do you do some of both as you begin to weigh the various perspectives on this argument?

USING VISUALS IN YOUR OWN ARGUMENTS

You too can, and perhaps must, use visuals in your writing. Many college classes now call for projects to be posted on the Web, which almost always involves the use of images. Many courses also require students to make multimedia presentations using software such as PowerPoint, or even good, old-fashioned overhead projectors with transparencies.

Here we sketch out some basic principles of visual rhetoric. To help you appreciate the argumentative character of visual texts, we examine them under some of the same categories we use for written and oral arguments earlier in this book (Chapters 4, 6, and 7), though in a different order. You may be surprised by some of the similarities you will see in visual and verbal arguments.

Visual Arguments Based on Character

What does character have to do with visual argument? Consider two argumentative essays submitted to an instructor. One is scrawled in thick pencil on pages ripped from a spiral notebook, little curls of paper still dangling from the left margin. The other is neatly typed on bond and in a form the professor likely regards as "professional." Is there much doubt about which argument will (at least initially) get the more sympathetic reading? You might object that appearances *shouldn't* count for so much, and you would have a point. The argument scratched in pencil could be the stronger piece, but it faces an uphill battle because its author has sent the wrong signals. Visually, the writer seems to be saying "I don't much care about this message or the people to whom I am sending it."

There may be times when you want to send exactly such a signal to an audience. Some TV advertisements aimed at young people are deliberately designed to antagonize older audiences with their noisy soundtracks, MTV-style quick cuts, and in-your-face style. The point is that the visual rhetoric of any piece you create ought to be a deliberate choice, not an accident. Also keep control of your own visual image. In most cases, when you present an argument, you want to appear authoritative and credible.

Look for images that reinforce your authority and credibility.
For a brochure about your new small business, for instance, you would need to consider images that prove your company has the resources to do its job. Consumers might feel better seeing that you have an actual office,

up-to-date equipment, and a competent staff. Similarly, for a Web site about a company or organization you represent, you would consider including its logo or emblem. Such emblems have authority and weight. That's why university Web sites so often include the seal of the institution somewhere on the home page, or why the president of the United States always travels with a presidential seal to hang upon the speaker's podium. The emblem or logo, like the hood ornament on a car, can convey a wealth of cultural and historical implications. (See Figure 15.4.)

Consider how design reflects your character.

Almost every design element sends signals about character and ethos, so be sure you control them. For example, the type fonts you select for a document can mark you as warm and inviting or efficient and contemporary. The warm and readable fonts often belong to a family called *serif*. The serifs are those little flourishes at the ends of their strokes that make the fonts seem handcrafted and artful:

warm and readable (New York)

warm and readable (Times New Roman)

warm and readable (Bookman)

Cleaner and modern are fonts without the flourishes, rather predictably called *sans serif*. These fonts are colder and simpler — and, some argue, more readable on a computer screen (depending on screen resolution):

efficient and contemporary (Helvetica)

efficient and contemporary (Arial Black)

efficient and contemporary (Geneva)

FIGURE **15.4** THREE IMAGES: THE U.S. PRESIDENTIAL SEAL, THE MCDONALD'S LOGO, AND THE BMW ORNAMENT

You may also be able to use decorative fonts. These are appropriate for special uses, but not for extended texts:

decorative and special uses (Zapf Chancery)

decorative and special uses (Chicago)

Other typographic elements shape your ethos as well. The size of type, for one, can make a difference. You'll seem to be shouting if your headings or text is boldfaced and too large. Tiny type might make you seem evasive.

Lose weight! Pay nothing!*

*Excludes the costs of enrollment and required meal purchases. Minimum contract: 12 months.

Similarly, your choice of color—especially for backgrounds—can make a statement about your taste, personality, and common sense. For instance, you'll make a bad impression with a Web page whose background colors or patterns make reading difficult. If you want to be noticed, you might use bright colors—the same sort that would make an impression in clothing or cars. But more discrete shades might be a better choice in many situations.

Don't ignore the impact of illustrations and photographs. What you picture can send powerful signals about your preferences, sensitivities, and inclusiveness—and it's not always easy. A few years ago, the organizers of a national meeting of writing teachers created a convention program alive with images of women and minorities. But it had more pictures of elephants than of white men—a laughable gaffe in this case, but one that illustrates the problem of reaching all audiences.

Even your choice of medium says something about you. If you decide to make an appeal on a Web site, you send signals about your technical skills and contemporary orientation. A presentation that relies on an overhead projector gives a different impression than one presented on an LCD projector with software. Even the way you dress can affect a spoken argument, enhancing your appeal—or distracting viewers from your message.

Follow required design conventions.

Many kinds of writing have required design conventions. When that's the case, follow them to the letter. It's no accident that lab reports for science courses are sober and unembellished. Visually, they reinforce the serious character of scientific work. The same is true of a college research paper. You might resent the tediousness of placing page numbers in the right place or aligning long quotations just so, but these visual details help convey your competence. So whether you are composing a term paper, résumé, screen-play, or Web site, look for authoritative models and follow them.

Visual Arguments Based on Facts and Reason

We tend to associate facts and reason with verbal arguments, but here too visual elements play an essential role. Indeed, it is hard to imagine a compelling presentation these days that does not rely, to some degree, on visual elements to enhance or even make the argument.

Many readers and listeners now expect ideas to be represented graphically. Not long ago, media critics ridiculed the colorful charts and graphs in newspapers like *USA Today*. Today, comparable features appear in even the most traditional publications *because they work*. They convey information efficiently.

Organize information visually.

A design works well when readers can look at an item and understand what it does. A brilliant, much-copied example of such an intuitive design is a seat adjuster invented many years ago by Mercedes-Benz. It is shaped like a tiny seat. Push any element of the control and the real seat moves the same way—back and forth, up and down. No instructions are necessary.

Good visual design can work the same way in an argument, conveying information without elaborate instructions. Titles, headings, subheadings, pull quotes, running heads, boxes, and so on are some common visual signals. When you present parallel headings in a similar type font, size, and color, you make it clear that the information under these headings is in some way related. So in a conventional term paper, you should use headings and subheadings to group information that is connected or parallel. Similarly, on a Web site, you might create two or three types of headings for groups of related information.

You should also make comparable inferences about the way text should be arranged on a page: look for relationships among items that should look alike. In this book, for example, bulleted lists are used to offer specific guidelines. You might use a list or a box to set off information that should be treated differently from the rest of the presentation, or you might visually mark it in other ways—by shading, color, or typography.

An item presented in large type or under a larger headline should be more important than one that gets less visual attention. Place illustrations carefully: what you position front and center will appear more important than items in less conspicuous places. On a Web site, key headings should usually lead to subsequent pages on the site.

Needless to say, you take a risk if you violate the expectations of your audience or if you present a visual text without coherent signals. Particularly for Web-based materials that may be accessible to people around the world, you can't make many assumptions about what will count as "coherent" across cultures. So you need to think about the roadmap you are giving viewers whenever you present them with a visual text. But design principles do evolve and change from medium to medium. A printed text or an overhead slide, for example, ordinarily works best when its elements are easy to read, simply organized, and surrounded by restful white space. But some types of Web pages seem to thrive on visual clutter, attracting and holding audiences by the variety of information they can pack onto a relatively limited screen. Check out the way the opening screens of most search engines assault a viewer with enticements (Google is a notable exception). Yet, look closely, and you will also see logic in these designs.

Use visuals to convey information efficiently.

Words are immensely powerful and capable of enormous precision and subtlety. But the simple fact is that some information is conveyed more efficiently by charts, graphs, drawings, maps, or photos than by words. When making an argument, especially to a large group, consider what information should be delivered in nonverbal form.

A pie chart is an effective way of comparing a part to the whole. You might use a pie chart to illustrate the ethnic composition of your school, the percentage of taxes paid by people at different income levels, or the consumption of energy by different nations. Pie charts depict such information memorably. (See Figure 15.5.)

FIGURE 15.5 PIE CHART SHOWING RACIAL AND ETHNIC ORIGIN IN THE UNITED STATES, 1990. *SOURCE:* U.S. BUREAU OF THE CENSUS, 1991.

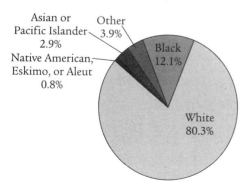

A graph is an efficient device for comparing items over time or other variables. You could use a graph to trace the rise and fall of test scores over several decades, or to show the growth of churches, as in Figure 15.6.

Diagrams or drawings are useful for drawing attention to details. You can use drawings to illustrate complex physical processes or designs of all sort. Indeed, it might have been the artful renderings of President Reagan's proposed Star Wars missile shield in the 1980s that helped to sell the country on the project. Defense Department films showed incoming missiles being destroyed by lasers and smart projectiles—even though no hardware had been built.

You can use maps to illustrate location and spatial relationships— something as simple as the distribution of office space in your student union or as complex as the topography of Utah. Such information might be far more difficult to explain using words alone.

Follow professional guidelines for presenting visuals.

Charts, graphs, tables, and illustrations play such an important role in many fields that professional groups have come up with specific guide-lines for labeling and formatting these items. You need to become famil-

FIGURE 15.6 CHURCH GROWTH BY DENOMINATION, 1700–1780. *SOURCE:* JAMES HENRETTA ET AL., *AMERICA'S HISTORY.* NY: WORTH, 1997.

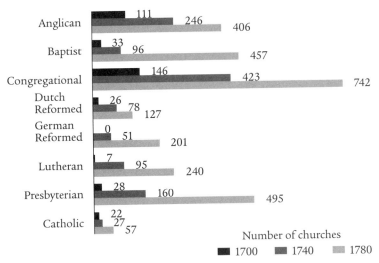

iar with those conventions as you advance in a field. A guide such as the *Publication Manual of the American Psychological Association* (4th edition) or the *MLA Style Manual and Guide to Scholarly Publishing* (2nd edition) describes these rules in detail.

You also must be careful to respect copyright rules when you use visual items created by someone else. It is relatively easy now to download visual texts of all kinds from the Web. Some of these items—like clip art—may be in the public domain, meaning that you are free to use them without paying a royalty. But other visual texts may require permission, especially if you intend to publish your work or use the item commercially. And remember: anything you place on a Web site is considered "published."

Visual Arguments That Appeal to Emotion

To some extent, we tend to be suspicious of arguments supported by visual and multimedia elements because they can seem to manipulate our senses. And many advertisements, political documentaries, rallies, marches, and even church services do in fact use visuals to trigger our emotions. Who has not teared up at a funeral when members of a veteran's family are presented with the flag, a bugler blowing Taps in the distance? Who doesn't recall the public service announcement that featured a fried egg ("This is your brain on drugs")? You might also have seen or heard about *Triumph of the Will*, a Nazi propaganda film from the 1930s that powerfully depicts Hitler as the benign savior of the German people, a hero of Wagnerian dimensions. It is a chilling reminder of how images can be manipulated and abused.

Yet you cannot flip through a magazine without being cajoled or seduced by images of all kinds—most of them designed in some way to attract your eye and mind. Not all such seductions are illicit, nor should you avoid them when emotions can support the legitimate claims you hope to advance.

Appreciate the emotional power of images.

Images can bring a text or presentation to life. Sometimes the images have power in and of themselves to persuade. This was the case with images in the 1960s that showed civil rights demonstrators being assaulted by police dogs and water hoses. Images of starving children in Somalia in the early 1990s had similar power, leading to relief efforts. (See Figure 15.7.)

FIGURE **15.7** SOMALI CHILD, 1992

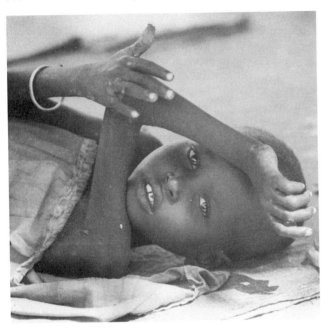

Images you select for a presentation may be equally effective if the visual text works well with other components of the argument. Indeed, a given image might support many different kinds of arguments. Take, for example, the famous *Apollo 8* photograph of our planet as a big blue marble hanging above the horizon of the moon (Figure 15.8). You might use this image to introduce an argument about the need for additional investment in the space program. Or it might become part of an argument about the need to preserve our frail natural environment, or part of an argument against nationalism: *from space, we are one world.* You could, of course, make any of these claims without the image. But the photograph—like most images—may touch members of your audience more powerfully than words alone could.

Appreciate the emotional power of color.

Consider the color red. It attracts hummingbirds—and cops. It excites the human eye in ways that other colors don't. You can make a powerful

FIGURE **15.8** EARTH SHINING OVER THE MOON

statement with a red dress or a red car—or red shoes. In short, red evokes emotions. But so do black, green, pink, and even brown. That we respond to color is part of our biological and cultural makeup. So it makes sense to consider carefully what colors are compatible with the kind of argument you are making. You might find that the best choice is black on a white background.

In most situations, you can be guided in your selection of colors by your own good taste (guys—check your ties), by designs you admire, or by the advice of friends or helpful professionals. Some design and presentation software will even help you choose colors by offering you dependable "default" shades or by offering an array of preexisting designs and compatible colors—for example, of presentation slides.

The colors you choose for a design should follow certain commonsense principles. If you are using background colors on a poster, Web site, or slide, the contrast between words and background should be vivid enough to make reading easy. For example, white letters on a yellow background will likely prove illegible. Any bright background color should be avoided for a long document. Indeed, reading seems easiest with dark letters against a light or white background. Avoid complex patterns, even though they might look interesting and be easy to create. Quite often, they interfere with other, more important elements of your presentation.

As you use visuals in your college projects, test them on prospective readers. That's what professionals do because they appreciate how delicate the choices about visual and multimedia texts can be. These responses will help you analyze your own arguments as well as improve your success with them.

RESPOND ●

1. Find an advertisement with both verbal and visual elements. Analyze the ad's visual argument by answering some of the questions on pp. 258–59, taking care to "reread" its visual elements just as carefully as you would its words. After you've answered each question as thoroughly as possible, switch ads with a classmate and analyze the new argument in the same way. Then compare your own and your classmate's responses to the two advertisements. If they are different— and there is every reason to expect they will be—how do you account for the differences? What is the effect of audience on the argument's reception? What are the differences between your own active reading and your classmate's?

2. Criticism of Camel cigarettes "spokesman" Joe Camel has led Camel's manufacturer to agree to severe restrictions on its ad campaign. Obviously, the image of an ultra-cool, pool-playing camel has great power over children, enticing them to begin smoking at ever-younger ages. Or does it? Debates about Joe's persuasive power are far from settled, with reasonable people weighing in on both sides.

    Write a letter to the editor of a general-circulation newspaper arguing that visual images like Joe Camel do not influence viewers to the degree that antismoking advocates claim. As an alternative, write a one-paragraph topic proposal—a plan for a longer paper—for an English class, in which you argue that such visual arguments do carry great weight and should be regulated. To write either of these documents, you'll need to do some research on the current conversation about advertising images and regulation. You'll also need to provide compelling reasons to support your claim. Remember that you should use this process as a form of inquiry, and not just to find information; develop your own arguments as a result of listening to others'.

3. If you have used the World Wide Web, you have no doubt noticed the relationships between visual design and textual material. In the best Web pages, the elements work together rather than simply competing for space. In fact, even if you have not used the Web, you still know a great deal about graphic design: newspapers, magazines, and your own college papers make use of design principles to create effective texts.

   Find three or four Web or magazine pages that you think exemplify good visual design — and then find just as many that do not. When you've picked the good and bad designs, draw a rough sketch of their physical layout. Where are the graphics? Where is the text? What are the relative size and relationship of text blocks to graphics? How is color used? Can you discern common principles among the pages, or does each good page work well in its own way? Write a brief explanation of what you find, focusing on the way the visual arguments influence audiences.

4. If you have access to the Internet, go to the Pulitzer Prize Archives at <http://www.pulitzer.org/archive/>. Pick a year to review and then study the images of the winners in three categories: editorial cartooning, spot news photography, and feature photography. (Click on "Works" to see the images.) From among the images you review, choose one you believe makes a strong argument. Then, in a paragraph, describe that image and the argument it makes.

chapter sixteen

Arguments in Electronic Environments

A student who's just loaded a new Web browser goes looking for online sources to develop a research assignment about a contemporary political issue. Looking for newsgroups, she notices that the default service on the browser offers many discussion groups sponsored by a big software company. But many of the groups she ordinarily consults don't seem to be available. She contemplates writing her research paper on the way commercial interests can shape and limit political discussion on the Web.

You send email to a friend questioning the integrity of your state's high school competency examinations. You mention irregularities you yourself have witnessed in testing procedures. A week later, you find passages from your original email circulating in a listserv. The remarks aren't attributed to you, but they are sure stirring up a ruckus.

One of the news-talk channels is exploring the issue of genetically engineered foods. Unfortunately, the experts being interviewed have to squeeze in their opinions among interruptions from two aggressive hosts, questions from generally hostile callers, and commercials for Viagra. Meanwhile, the hosts are urging viewers to participate in an online poll on the subject posted on the network's Web site. The results, they admit, are unscientific.

Browsing the <humanities.lit.authors.Shakespeare> newsgroup, you are annoyed to read a flurry of postings arguing that someone other than William Shakespeare of Stratford-upon-Avon wrote the plays. You join the fray by suggesting that these anti-Stratfordians "get a life." Your insult provokes an angry discussion that settles down only when a writer from California offers a much more detailed defense of Shakespeare's authorship than you did. You are relieved to be off the hook.

You've been discussing gender roles on a MOO with a woman who calls herself Sue. She sure seems to have your number, almost anticipating the arguments you make. Even though you find her positions untenable, you admire her intuition and perception. Then you discover that Sue is really your roommate Mike! He says he has enjoyed playing with your mind.

■ ■ ■

If ancient Greece provided classical Western models for oral arguments, and the European Renaissance gave birth to the printed book, the current era will surely be remembered for the electronic expression of ideas. Within the last decade or so, computers have fostered new environments where ideas can be examined, discussed, and debated in configurations many might never have imagined—some beautifully suited to the give-and-take of argument. Is there a special rhetoric of argument for such environments, a way of making effective and honest claims in this brave new world? Clearly there is, but it's a work in progress, evolving gradually as people learn to cross boundaries among written, aural, and visual texts.

It's an exciting time for extending the reach of the human mind. What follows are some observations and speculations about the play of argument online, including email and discussion groups, synchronous communications, and the World Wide Web.

EMAIL AND DISCUSSION GROUPS

Email, Usenet groups, and listservs all transmit electronic messages via the Internet from person to person. Sometimes the messages go from one individual to another; in other cases, they are distributed to groups or to anyone with Internet access. (But this rapid communication has changed more than the speed by which individuals can share ideas.)

Email

Like the telephone, microwave, and VCR, email has earned its place as an essential technology, supporting instant and reliable communication around the globe. An email message can be a private communication to one person or a message distributed among groups, large and small, creating communities linked by information. Unlike regular ("snail") mail, email makes back-and-forth discussions easy and quick: people can speak their minds, survey opinion, or set agendas for face-to-face meetings. And they can meet at all hours, since electronic messages arrive whenever a server routes them. Increasingly, email communication will be wireless, available via cell phone or other mobile devices.

An email message has a character of its own, halfway between the formality of a letter and the intimacy of a telephone conversation. It can feel less intrusive than a phone call, yet at the same time be more insistent—the person too shy to say something in person or on the phone may speak up boldly in email. Like a letter, email preserves a textual record of all thoughts and comments, an advantage in many situations. Yet because it is less formal than a business letter, readers tend to ignore or forgive slips in email (misspellings, irregular punctuation and capitalization) that might disturb them in another type of message.

Arguments in email operate by some new conventions. First, they tend to be "dialogic," with a rapid back-and-forth of voices in conversation. When you send an email, you can usually anticipate a quick reply. In fact, "reply" is an automatic function in email; select it, and your response to a message is attached to the original communication. Second, the very ease and speed of response in email invite rebuttals that may be less carefully considered than those sent by snail mail. Third, because email can be easily forwarded, your arguments may travel well beyond your intended audience, a factor to consider before clicking on "send."

Much advice about email is obvious once you've used it for a while. For one thing, although email messages can be quite lengthy, most people won't tolerate an argument that requires them to scroll through page after page of unrelieved print. You'll likely make a stronger impression with a concise claim, one that fits on a single screen if possible. If you are replying to an email message, send back just enough of the original posting so that your reader knows what you are responding to; this will set your claim within a context.

Remember, too, that your email messages need to be verbally powerful, since the medium may not support some of the formatting options you might otherwise use to enhance your authority. Not all email software supports boldface, italics, multiple fonts, or graphics. But you can highlight your ideas by skipping lines between paragraphs to open some white space, bulleting key ideas or short lists, drawing lines, and following the email convention of using asterisks before and after text you want to emphasize: "Do *not* delete this message before printing it out." In general, don't use all capital letters, LIKE THIS, for emphasis. The online equivalent of shouting, it will alienate many readers — as will using all lowercase letters, which makes text harder to read.

Your email signature, known as a .sig file, can influence readers, too. Automatically attached to the bottom of every email you send (unless you switch this function off), your .sig file might include your address, phone numbers, fax numbers, and professional credentials. You can use the signature as a way to reinforce your credibility by explaining who you are and what you do. Here is an example:

Celia Garcia
Executive Secretary
Students for Responsive Government
University of Texas at San Antonio

Usenet Newsgroups and Listservs

Usenet is an electronic network that provides access to thousands of newsgroups, interactive discussion forums classified by subject and open to anyone with email access to the network. Listservs also use the

Internet to bring together people with common interests, but they are more specialized: you have to subscribe to a particular listserv to receive its messages. In both newsgroups and listservs, messages consist of email-like postings that can be linked topically to form threads exploring particular subjects.

Newsgroups and listservs would seem to be a natural environment for productive argument—where knowledgeable people worldwide can bring and exchange their perspectives and work toward consensus. Unfortunately, not all group discussions live up to this potential. The relative anonymity of online communication removes an important rhetorical component from some debates—the respectable ethos. The result has often been a dumbing down of discussions, especially in newsgroups with the less-regulated "alt." designation. And because postings are so easy in either type of forum, even more responsible groups can be inundated or spammed with pointless messages, unwanted advertisements, and irrational diatribes.

Nevertheless, newsgroups and listservs can be stimulating places for interchanges, particularly where the subject matter is specialized enough to attract informed and interested participants. Before posting, you owe it to the group to learn something about it, either by reading some messages already posted in a newsgroup or by subscribing to a listserv and lurking for enough time to gain a feel for the way issues are introduced, discussed, and debated. If a group offers a file of frequently asked questions (known as FAQs), read what it has to say about the group's rules of discourse and print it out for later reference.

When you decide to join in a conversation, be sure your posting contains enough information to make a smooth transition between the message to which you are responding and your own contribution to the group. If you have little to contribute, don't bother posting. A comment such as "I agree" wastes the time of everyone in the group who bothers to download your item—as some of the members may tell you in none-too-polite terms. In fact, if you are new to the Internet, you may be surprised at the temper of some online conversation participants. You can get *flamed*—bombarded with email—for asking a question that has already been asked and answered repeatedly by other members, for veering too far from the topic of discussion, or just for sending a message someone doesn't like. Flaming is unfortunate, but it is also a reality of newsgroups and listservs.

As sources for academic work, listservs are probably more reliable than newsgroups, though both forums can help you grasp the range of opinion on an issue. In fact, the range expressed in some groups may be startling. You'll likely discover much information too, including the names of reputable authorities, the titles of useful books and articles, and guidance to other groups or Web sites concerned with related topics. But don't quote facts, figures, statistics, or specific claims from newsgroups or list-servs unless you cross-check them with more conventional sources, such as library reference material. Remember, too, that you can usually query individual members of a group by going "off list" to find out more information. In effect you have an email exchange with one person rather than with the whole group.

You can use Internet search engines such as Tile <http://tile.net> and Deja <http://www.deja.com> to locate newsgroups and read newsgroups' archives.

REAL-TIME COMMUNICATION: IRCs AND MOOs

Newsgroups and listservs operate like email, with a delay between the time a message is typed and the time it is received. The senders and receivers of email messages need not even be at their computers at the same time; in fact, the mailbox metaphor common to email systems assumes they are not. Now imagine an electronic conversation in which multiple participants are all online at the same time, although in different places, all receiving messages almost instantaneously as others are typing them—just like a conference call, except that the communication is in words that appear on computer screens. That's the basic shape of Internet relay chat (IRC) and MUD object-oriented (MOO) environments, examples of synchronous communication—communication in real time—on the Internet.

IRCs

IRCs are chatrooms that allow for relatively straightforward online conversations among people gathered together electronically to discuss particular subjects or topics. Typically, IRCs involve people in different and distant locations, but some schools provide local IRC networks to encourage students to participate in online class discussions. Once a topic is established, members of the IRC group begin typing in their comments and responding to one another.

As you might guess, an IRC environment can create a conversational free-for-all as opinions come rolling in. Their sequence can feel frustratingly random, especially to outsiders reading a transcript of such exchanges. After all, by the time a participant responds to a particular message, a dozen more may have appeared on the screen. In such an environment it is difficult to build or sustain complex arguments, especially since the speed of the conversation favors witty or sharp remarks. A chatroom working at its best keeps writers on their toes. Indeed, it can be a form of dialogic freewriting, with writers pouring out their thoughts and watching as they receive almost instantaneous feedback. Since participants can be spread all over the world, IRCs also can support diverse conversations. So IRCs might work well as tools of invention for other, more conventional forms of argument. A good exercise is to print out an IRC transcript and to highlight its best comments or exchanges for future reference.

MOOs

MOOs (and such variants as MUDs and MUSHs) resemble IRCs in that participants communicate online in real time. But MOOs, unlike IRCs, have a spatial dimension: participants enter an imaginary place, take on assumed characters, and follow specified routines. If this sounds a bit like Dungeons and Dragons, you've got the idea. Imagine Dungeons and Dragons played by people who locate their experiences in places as common as libraries and writing centers or as challenging as courtrooms or the pitching deck of the *Santa Maria*.

Arguments in MOOs can involve powerful stretches of the imagination because a participant can be anyone he or she wants to be. Thus, the environment encourages writers to create an ethos self-consciously and to experience what it is like to be someone else — rich rather than poor, powerful rather than powerless, female rather than male. Imaginary situations are crafted, too, making participants unusually sensitive to the contexts in which their words and ideas exist. Indeed, MOOs reflect the power of words to shape one's reality. As such, they raise interesting and powerful questions about the nature of the world "outside."

Not everyone takes MOOs seriously. There's a learning curve for those entering such environments, and to some they remain games — hardly worth serious attention. But game or no, MOOs are an environment for argument that is out there, open for anyone willing to experiment with something new.

WEB SITES

Web sites make arguments of a different sort. These sites consist of electronic pages of information (which may include any combination of words, images, sounds, and film clips) that are linked hypertextually, meaning that you can move from one page to another by clicking your computer's mouse button on parts of a page that are identified as links. Generally, there's no prescribed sequence to those links; you browse through the pages of a site or the entire World Wide Web according to your interests. Therefore, someone coming to a site that you create may not follow the links you provide in the order you had imagined. Readers become participants in your site, with critical agendas of their own.

What are the implications for argument? The Web would seem to suit many traditional components of argument and then to complicate them. Web pages might include conventional claims supported in traditional ways with evidence and good reasons. But instead of merely summarizing or paraphrasing evidence and providing a source citation, a Web author might furnish links to the primary evidence itself—to statistics borrowed directly from a government Web site or to online documents at a university library. Indeed, links within a Web page can be a version of documentation, leading to the very material the original author examined, full and complete.

A site might also provide links to other sites dealing with the same issue, usher readers to discussion groups about it, or (if it's a sophisticated site like those operated by the national political parties) even support chatrooms of its own where anyone can offer an opinion in real time. Perhaps most revolutionary of all, a Web site can incorporate visual and aural elements of diverse kinds into its argument, not as embellishments but as actual persuasive devices. Indeed, writers today need to learn these new techniques of document design if they expect to communicate in this complex medium.

How do arguments actually get made on the Web? The fact is that people are still learning. Already, almost every political group, interest group, academic institution, corporation, and government entity has a Web presence. The home page or full Web site is the "face" an institution uses to present its ethos to readers, a version of what we have called "arguments based on character." Here we can find intriguing differences in the ways arguments may be offered. In 1997, an "off year" in election cycles, the home pages for both the Republican and Democratic National Committees featured many soft-sell elements, crafted to make people feel good about the political parties. The Republicans displayed an image of a Republican Main Street that included, for instance, a red brick schoolhouse topped by a huge American flag. The Democratic Party site unfolded in bold red, white, and blue hues and featured an eye-catching photograph of President Clinton and the first lady sharing a picture book with a group of children. By 2000, however, a presidential election year, the character of both sites had evolved and the arguments presented had harder edges. Most of the inviting graphics were gone, replaced by links that made direct attacks on opposition candidates: "Bush Lite"; Al Gore as Flipper. Whereas the earlier sites seemed to welcome everyone, the election-year pages looked as if they were aimed at true believers.

Beyond home pages of this kind, Web sites typically contain more substantive information. Many sites include extended prose arguments supported by the same kinds of charts, statistics, and graphs you might find in books or newsmagazines. For instance, in 1998 a site sponsored by Common Cause, a progressive citizens' group <http://www.common cause.org/laundromat/index.htm>, provided a series of studies of what it called "the money trail in politics," which were designed to direct readers to information about financial influence in national politics. As shown in Figure 16.1, the page used a simple layout and clever graphics to make its points.

When crafting a Web site designed to present an argument of your own, you will want not only to take full advantage of the electronic medium but also to meet its distinctive challenges. Your pages need to be graphically interesting to persuade readers to enter your site and to encourage them to read your lengthier arguments. If you just post a traditional argument, thick with prose paragraphs that have to be scrolled endlessly, readers might ignore it. Check out the way the online periodical *Slate* <http://www.slate.com> arranges its articles to make them Web readable, or examine the design of other sites you find especially effective in presenting an argument.

Since the Web encourages browsing and surfing, you also need to consider how to cluster ideas so that they retain their appeal. In a traditional print argument, though you can't prevent readers from skipping around and looking ahead, you can largely control the direction they take through your material, from claim to warrant to evidence. On a Web page, however, readers usually want to choose their own paths. Inevitably that means they will play a larger role in constructing *your* argument. You lose an element of control, but your argument gains a new dimension, particularly if you provide links that help readers understand how you came to

FIGURE 16.1   COMMON CAUSE WEB PAGE

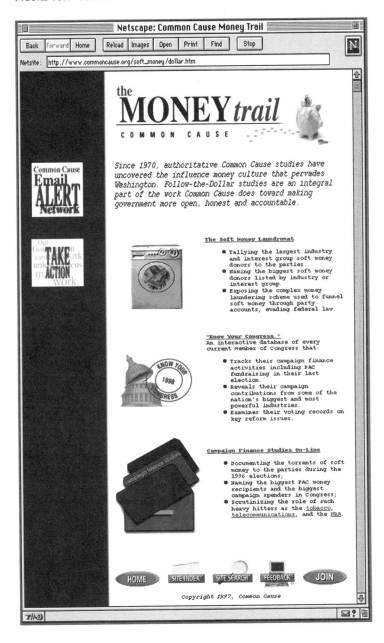

your own conclusions. Sometimes that may mean including links to sites that don't necessarily support your views. But you enhance your credibility by recognizing a full range of ideas, hoping that on their own, readers will reach the same conclusions you have reached.

KEY POINTS TO REMEMBER IN ARGUING ELECTRONICALLY

EMAIL

- Keep your remarks short and pertinent.
- Think twice before replying immediately to an argumentative message. Don't lose your cool.
- Remember that email is easily forwarded. Your actual audience may prove to be much larger than you initially intended.

NEWSGROUPS, LISTSERVS, IRCS, AND MOOS

- Get a feel for groups before posting to them.
- Post concise messages directly related to the interests of the group.
- Consider whether your posting should go to everyone on the list. Would an individual email message be more appropriate?
- Resist the temptation to flame or be impolite, especially when an argument heats up.

WEB SITES

- Plan your site carefully. Use your home page to direct readers to more detailed information within the site.
- Think of design in terms of pages. When you can, chunk a claim to fit within a single page. If your argument is highly readable, readers won't mind some scrolling, but don't expect them to advance through more than four or five screens' worth of material.
- Shape pages according to their purpose. A page of useful links will differ in arrangement from a page of prose argument.
- When your argument requires a lot of text, break it up with helpful headings and white space.
- At the bottom of the home page, include your name, your email address, and the date you created or last updated the site. This information will help other readers cite your work or reach you one-on-one to continue a discussion.

GRAPHICS

- Use graphics purposefully to support an argument. Images should make points you can't convey as effectively in prose.

- Keep graphics to a minimum. It takes time to download pages heavy in graphics — time readers might not have.

- Avoid images that pulse, rotate, or blink. Such glitz will likely distract readers from your argument.

- Graphics taken from the Web may be copyrighted items. Be sure to request permission from and to credit the source for any materials you import into your own pages.

LINKS

- Use links to guide readers to evidence that explains your ideas.

- Be sure your links are diverse. You'll gain credibility by acknowledging alternative views.

- Be sure readers can understand from the context what the links you create will do or where they will lead.

RESPOND ●

1. Newcomers to a newsgroup or listserv normally lurk for a while, reading postings and getting to know the people who participate in the group, before entering the conversation themselves. Over the next several days, pick a group that interests you — there are thousands to choose from — and read as many of its postings as you can. For some groups, this might entail a tremendous amount of work, so limit your reading to those threads (topics within a group) that interest you.

   When you have a sense of the direction of the group, pick a single thread and follow the postings on that topic. Read all the postings that you can, making special note of quoting techniques — how writers refer to previous postings — and other interplay between writers. On the basis of the small evidence that you have (the group may have existed for several years), try to reconstruct the "conversation" on this thread that went on before you arrived. Who were the most common writers? What did they claim? How did others respond to those claims? What is the current state of the conversation? Are people in general agreement or disagreement?

2. FAQs can tell a careful reader a lot about a particular newsgroup or listserv and its contributors. Find the FAQs of three different groups

and read them carefully. What suppositions about audience are inherent in these texts? Write an audience analysis of each FAQ, based on the kinds of questions and answers you see there, their tone, and their length. Who are the FAQ's intended readers? What kinds of rules about argument does each FAQ offer?

3. Find several Web sites that make explicit argumentative claims, and evaluate them on the basis of a set of criteria you develop. What constitutes a good Web-based argument? What are the characteristics of effective Web rhetoric? Do these sites exhibit those characteristics? How does the nonlinear nature of the site affect your reading, or its persuasiveness? If your instructor requests, make a presentation to the class, showing printouts of the site (or directing the class to look at it if you are in a networked classroom) and explaining why the Web-based arguments are effective or ineffective.

4. Take an argumentative paper you've written for any class—it should be longer than two pages—and literally cut it up into separate paragraphs. Shuffle the stack of paragraphs so that they are completely reordered. Then read the paragraphs in their new order, from top to bottom. How is the argument affected? Is your claim still clear? Is your evidence powerful?

   Now imagine that those paragraphs were separate pages on a Web site that readers could browse through in any order. Would the site's argument be effective? If not, how could you rearrange the argument so that readers could move among its sections without being confused? Try to make an arrangement that could translate well to the Web's hypertextual environment. You might need to create headings that point readers in appropriate directions, or you might write transitions that help readers make decisions about what to read next.

chapter seventeen

Spoken Arguments

In the wake of a devastating hurricane, local ministers search for just the right words to offer comfort and inspire hope in their congregations.

At a campus rally, student leaders call for the administration to provide increased access for students with handicaps.

A customer looking for a good buy on a new car settles in for some tough negotiations with the salesperson and manager.

At the half, the team is down by ten. In the locker room, the captain calls on all her persuasive powers to rebuild morale and help seize the momentum.

For a course in psychology, a student gives a multimedia presentation on the work of neuroscientist Constance Pert.

During their wedding, a couple exchanges the special vows they have worked together to create.

■ ■ ■

As these examples suggest, people are called on every day to present spoken arguments of one kind or another. Successful speakers point to several crucial elements in that success: whenever possible, they have thorough knowledge of their subjects; they pay very careful attention to the values, ideas, and needs of their listeners; and they use structures and styles that make their spoken arguments easy to follow. Equally important, they keep in mind the interactive nature of spoken arguments (live audiences can argue back!) and, whenever possible, they practice, practice—and then practice some more.

CONTEXTS FOR SPOKEN ARGUMENTS

Perhaps the most common context for spoken argument takes place in ordinary discussions, whether you're trying to persuade your parents that you need a new computer for your college work, to explore the meaning of a poem in class, or to make a decision about a new company health plan. In such everyday contexts, many people automatically choose the tone of voice, kind of evidence, and length of speaking time to suit the situation. You can improve your own performance in such contexts by observing closely other speakers you find effective and by joining in on conversations whenever you possibly can: the more you participate in lively discussions, the more comfortable you will be doing so.

Formal Presentations

You may well be asked to make more formal spoken arguments. In such cases, you need to consider the full context carefully. Note how much time you have to prepare and how long the presentation should be. You want to use the allotted time effectively, while not infringing on the time of others. Consider also what visual aids, handouts, or other materials might help make the presentation successful. Will you have an overhead projector? Can you use PowerPoint or other computer presentation tools? A statistical pie chart may carry a lot of weight in one argument while photographs will make your point better in another. (See Chapter 15.)

Think about whether you are to make the presentation alone or as part of a group—and plan and practice accordingly. Especially with a group, turn-taking will need to be worked out carefully. Check out where your presentation will take place—in a classroom with fixed chairs? A lecture or assembly hall? An informal sitting area? Will you have a lectern? An overhead projector? Will you sit or stand? Remain in one place or move around? What will the lighting be, and can you adjust it? Finally, note any criteria for evaluation: how will your spoken argument be assessed?

Whenever you make a formal presentation, you need to consider several key elements:

- Determine your major argumentative *purpose*. Is it to inform? Convince or persuade? Explore? Make a decision? Something else?

- Who is your *audience*? Your instructor may be one important member, in addition to other class members. Think carefully about what they will know about your topic and what opinions they are likely to hold.

- Consider your own *stance* toward your topic and audience. Are you an expert? Novice? Fairly well informed? Interested observer? Peer?

- *Structure* your presentation to make it easy to follow, and remember to take special care to plan an introduction that gets the audience's attention and a conclusion that makes your argument memorable.

ARGUMENTS TO BE HEARD

Even if you rely on a printed text, that text must be written to be *heard* rather than *read*. Such a text—whether in the form of an overhead list, note cards, or a full written-out text—should feature a strong introduction and conclusion, a clear structure with helpful signposts, straightforward syntax, and concrete diction.

Introductions and Conclusions

Like readers, listeners tend to remember beginnings and endings most readily. Work hard, therefore, to make these elements of your spoken argument especially memorable. Consider including a provocative or puzzling statement, opinion, or question; a vivid anecdote; a powerful quotation; or a vivid visual image. If you can refer to the interests or experiences of your listeners in the introduction or conclusion, do so.

Amy Tan used some of these techniques in the opening of a talk she gave in 1989 to the Language Symposium in San Francisco. In addressing this group of language experts, Tan began with a puzzling statement—given that she was speaking to a group of language scholars—and then related that statement to the interests of her audience:

> **I am not a scholar of English or literature. I cannot give you much more than personal opinions on the English language and its variations in this country or others.**
>
> —Amy Tan, "Mother Tongue"

Structures and Signposts

For a spoken argument, you want your organizational structure to be crystal clear. Offer an overview of your main points toward the beginning of your presentation and make sure that you have a clearly delineated beginning, middle, and end to the presentation. Throughout, remember to pause between major points and to use helpful signposts to mark your movement from one topic to the next. Such signposts act as explicit transitions in your spoken argument and thus should be clear and concrete: *The second crisis point in the breakup of the Soviet Union occurred hard on the heels of the first* rather than *The breakup of the Soviet Union came to another crisis. . . .* In addition to such explicit transitions as *next, on the contrary*, or *finally*, you can offer signposts to your listeners by carefully repeating key words and ideas as well as by carefully introducing each new idea with concrete topic sentences.

Diction and Syntax

Avoid long, complicated sentences, and use straightforward syntax (subject-verb-object, for instance, rather than an inversion) as much as possible. Remember, too, that listeners can hold onto concrete verbs and nouns more easily than they can grasp a steady stream of abstractions. So when you need to deal with abstract ideas, try to illustrate them with concrete examples.

Take a look at the following paragraph from Ben McCorkle's essay on the Simpsons in Chapter 10, first as he wrote it for his essay and then for an oral presentation:

Written Version

The Simpson family has occasionally been described as a "nuclear" family, which obviously has a double meaning: first, the family consists of two parents and three children, and, second, Homer works at a nuclear power plant with very relaxed safety codes. The overused label *dysfunctional*, when applied to the Simpsons, suddenly takes on new meaning. Every episode seems to include a scene in which son Bart is being choked by his father, the baby is being neglected, or Homer is sitting in a drunken stupor transfixed by the television screen. The comedy in these scenes comes from the exaggeration of commonplace household events (although some talk shows and news programs would have us believe that these exaggerations are not confined to the madcap world of cartoons).

—Ben McCorkle, "*The Simpsons:* A Mirror of Society"

Spoken Version

What does it mean to describe the Simpsons as a *nuclear* family? Clearly, a double meaning is at work. First, the Simpsons fit the dictionary meaning—a family unit consisting of two parents and some children. The second meaning, however, packs more of a punch. You see, Homer works at a nuclear power plant [pause here] with *very* relaxed safety codes!

Still another overused family label describes the Simpsons. Did everyone guess I was going to say *dysfunctional?* And like "nuclear," when it comes to the Simpsons, "dysfunctional" takes on a whole new meaning.

Remember the scene when Bart is being choked by his father?

How about the many times the baby is being neglected?

Or the classic view—Homer sitting in a stupor transfixed by the TV screen!

My point here is that the comedy in these scenes often comes from double meanings—and from a lot of exaggeration of everyday household events.

Note that the revised paragraph presents the same information, but this time it is written to be heard. See how the revision uses helpful signposts, some repetition, a list, italicized words to prompt the speaker to give special emphasis, and simple syntax to help make it easy to listen to.

ARGUMENTS TO BE REMEMBERED

You can probably think of spoken arguments that still stick in your memory—a song like Bruce Springsteen's "Born in the USA," for instance, or a political call to arms like Martin Luther King Jr.'s "I Have a Dream." These arguments are memorable in part because they call on the power of figures of speech and other devices of language. In addition, careful repetition can make spoken arguments memorable, especially when linked with parallelism and climactic order. (See Chapter 14 for more on using figurative language to make arguments more vivid and memorable.)

Repetition, Parallelism, and Climactic Order

Whether they are used alone or in combination, repetition, parallelism, and climactic order are especially appropriate for spoken arguments that sound a call to arms or that seek passionate engagement from the audience. Perhaps no person in this century has used them more effectively than Martin Luther King Jr., whose sermons and speeches helped to spearhead the civil rights movement. Standing on the steps of the Lincoln Memorial in Washington, D.C., on August 28, 1963, with hundreds of thousands of marchers before him, King called on the nation to make good on the promissory note represented by the Emancipation Proclamation. Look at the way he uses repetition, parallelism, and climactic order in the following paragraph to invoke a nation to action:

> It is obvious today that America has defaulted on this promissory note insofar as her citizens of color are concerned. Instead of honoring this sacred obligation, America has given the Negro people a bad check which has come back marked "insufficient funds." But *we refuse* to believe that the bank of justice is bankrupt. *We refuse* to believe that there are insufficient funds in the great vaults of opportunity of this nation. So *we have come* to cash this check—a check that will give us upon demand the riches of freedom and the security of justice. *We have also come* to this hallowed spot to remind America of the fierce urgency of now. This is *no time* to engage in the luxury of cooling off or to take the tranquilizing drug of gradualism. *Now is the time* to rise from the dark and desolate valley of segregation to the sunlit path of racial justice. *Now is the time* to open the doors of opportunity to all of God's children. *Now is the time* to lift our nation from the quicksands of racial injustice to the solid rock of brotherhood. (emphasis added)
> —Martin Luther King Jr., "I Have a Dream"

The italicized words highlight the way King uses repetition to drum home his theme. But along with that repetition, King sets up a powerful set of parallel verb phrases, calling on all "to rise" from the "dark and desolate valley of segregation" to the "sunlit path of racial justice" and "to open the doors of opportunity" for all. The final verb phrase ("to lift") leads to a strong climax, as King moves from what each individual should do to what the entire nation should do: "to lift our nation from the quicksands of racial injustice to the solid rock of brotherhood." These stylistic choices, together with the vivid image of the "bad check" help to make King's speech powerful, persuasive—and memorable.

Thank goodness you don't have to be as highly skilled as Dr. King, however, to take advantage of the power of repetition and parallelism: simply repeating a key word in your argument can help impress it on your audience, as can arranging parts of sentences or items in a list in parallel order.

THE ROLE OF VISUALS

Visuals often play an important part in spoken arguments and they should be prepared with great care. Don't think of them as add-ons but rather as a major means of getting across your message and supporting the claims you are making. In this regard, a visual—like a picture—can be worth a thousand words, helping your audience *see* examples or illustrations or other data that make your argument compelling. Test the effectiveness of your visuals on classmates, friends, or family members, asking them specifically to judge whether the visuals help advance your argument.

Whatever visuals you use—charts, graphs, photographs, summary statements, sample quotations, lists—must be large enough to be readily seen by your audience. If you use PowerPoint or other overhead projections, be sure that the information on each frame is simple, clear, and easy to read and process. The same rule holds true for posters, flip charts, or a chalkboard. And remember not to turn your back on your audience while you refer to any of these visuals. Finally, if you prepare supplementary materials for your audience—bibliographies or other texts—distribute these at the end of the presentation so that they will not distract the audience from your spoken argument.

For a talk about how best to make an effective oral presentation, one writer used the PowerPoint slide shown in Figure 17.1. Note how easy this visual is to read: uncluttered, plenty of white space pulling readers from

FIGURE 17.1 SAMPLE POWERPOINT SLIDE

the top—where the main topic is announced—through a series of supporting points and then to an eye-catching photograph that demonstrates these points.

THE IMPORTANCE OF DELIVERY

When an orator in ancient times was asked to rank the most important parts of effective rhetoric, he said, "Delivery, delivery, delivery." Indeed, most effective spoken arguments are *performances* that call on you to pay very careful attention to the persuasive effects your clothing, body language, voice, and so on will have on the audience. Many practiced speakers say that they learned to improve the performance of spoken arguments through extensive practice. To make this advice work for you, get a draft of your spoken argument, including all visuals, together enough in advance to allow for several run-throughs. Some speakers audiotape or videotape these rehearsals and then revise the argument and the performance based on a study of the tapes. Others practice in front of a mirror, watching every movement with a critical eye. Still others practice in front of friends. Any of these techniques can work; the main thing is to practice.

One point of all that practice is to make sure you can be heard clearly. Especially if you are at all soft-spoken, you will need to concentrate on projecting your voice. Or you may need to practice lowering the pitch or speaking more slowly or enunciating each word more clearly. Tone of voice can dispose audiences for—or against—speakers. Those who sound sarcastic, for instance, usually win few friends. For most spoken arguments, you want to develop a tone that conveys interest and commitment to your position as well as respect for your audience.

The way you dress, the way you move, as well as the sound of your voice make arguments of their own that can either add to or detract from the main one you are trying to make. How to dress for an effective presentation, of course, depends on what is appropriate for your topic, audience, and setting, but most experienced speakers like to wear clothes that are simple and comfortable and that allow for easy movement—but that are not overly casual: "dressing up" a little indicates that you take pride in your appearance, that you have confidence in your argument, and that you respect your audience.

Most speakers make a stronger impression standing than sitting. Stand with your hands resting lightly on the lectern or at your side (don't fidget with anything!) and with both feet solidly on the floor—and move about a little, even if you are using a lectern. Moving a bit may also help you make good eye contact with members of your audience. And according to several studies, making eye contact is especially important for spoken arguments, since audiences perceive those who look at them directly to be more honest, friendly, and informed than others who do not.

Last but not at all least: time your presentation carefully to make sure you will stay within the allotted time. If you are working from a written text, a good rule of thumb is to allow roughly two and a half minutes for every double-spaced 8-1/2 x 11-inch page of text (or one and a half minutes for every 5 x 7-inch card). The only way to make sure of your time, however, is to set a clock and time the presentation precisely. Knowing that you will not intrude on the time allotted to other speakers not only signals your respect for their presentations but will also help you relax and gain self-confidence; and when your audience senses your self-confidence, they will become increasingly receptive to your message.

Some Helpful Presentation Strategies

In spite of your best preparation, you may feel some anxiety before your presentation. (According to the Gallup Poll, Americans often identify public speaking as a major fear, scarier than attacks from outer space!) Experienced speakers say they have strategies for dealing with anxiety—and even that a little anxiety (and accompanying adrenalin) can act to a speaker's advantage.

The most effective strategy seems to be knowing your topic and material through and through. Confidence in your own knowledge goes a long way toward making you a confident speaker. In addition to being well prepared, you may wish to try some of the following strategies:

- Visualize your presentation. Go over the scene of the presentation in your mind, and think it through completely.
- Get some rest before the presentation, and avoid consuming excessive amounts of caffeine.
- Concentrate on relaxing. Consider doing some deep-breathing exercises right before you begin.
- Pause before you begin, concentrating on your opening lines.
- Remember to interact with the audience whenever possible; doing so will often help you relax and even have some fun.

Finally, remember to allow time for audience members to respond and ask questions. Try to keep your answers brief so that others may get in on the conversation. And at the very end of your presentation, thank your audience for attending so generously to your arguments.

RESPOND●

1. Take a brief passage—one or two paragraphs—from an essay you've written. Then, following the guidelines in this chapter, rewrite the passage to be heard. Finally, make a list of every change you made.

2. Look in the TV listings for a speech or oral presentation you'd like to hear. Check out C-SPAN or Sunday morning news shows such as *Meet the Press*. Watch and listen to the presentation, making notes of the strategies the speaker uses to good effect—signpost language, repetition, figurative language, and so on.

PART 5

CONVENTIONS OF **argument**

chapter eighteen

What Counts
as Evidence

A downtown office worker who can never find a space in the company lot to park her motorcycle decides to argue for a designated motorcycle parking area. In building her argument, she decides to conduct a survey to find out exactly how many employees drive cars to work and how many ride motorcycles.

A business consultant wants to identify characteristics of effective teamwork so that he can convince his partners to adopt these characteristics as part of their training program. To begin gathering evidence for this argument, the consultant decides to conduct on-site observations of three effective teams, followed by in-depth interviews with each member.

For an argument aimed at showing that occupations are often unconsciously thought of as masculine or feminine, a student decides to carry out an experiment: she will ask fifty people chosen at random to draw pictures of a doctor, a police officer, a nurse, a CEO, a lawyer, and a secretary — and see which are depicted as men, which as women. The results of this experiment will become evidence for (or against) the argument.

Trying to convince her own family not to put their elderly grandmother into a "home," a former nursing home administrator offers her twelve years of personal experience in three different nursing homes as part of the evidence in support of her contention.

In arguing that virtual reality technology may lead people to ignore or disregard the most serious of "real" world problems, a student writer cites sixteen library sources that review and critique cyberspace and virtual reality as one way of providing evidence for his claim.

■ ■ ■

EVIDENCE AND THE RHETORICAL SITUATION

As the examples above demonstrate, people use all kinds of evidence in making and supporting claims. But the evidence they use does not exist in a vacuum; instead, it becomes part of the larger context of the argument and the argument's situation: when, where, and to whom it is made. Remembering the rhetorical situation into which evidence enters suggests an important point regarding argumentative evidence: it may be persuasive in one time and place but not in another; it may convince one kind of audience but not another; it may work with one genre of discourse but not another.

To be most persuasive, then, evidence should match the time in which the argument takes place. For example, arguing that a military leader should employ a certain tactic because that very tactic worked effectively for George Washington is likely to fail if Washington's use of the tactic is the only evidence provided. After all, a military tactic that was effective in 1776 is more than likely an *ineffective* one today. In the same way, a writer may achieve excellent results by using her own experience as well as an extensive survey of local leaders and teenagers as evidence to support a proposal for a new teen center in her small-town community—but she may have far less success in arguing for the same thing in a distant, large inner-city area.

Careful writers also need to consider the disciplinary context in which they plan to use evidence, since some disciplines privilege certain kinds of evidence and others do not. Observable, quantifiable data may constitute the best evidence in, say, experimental psychology, but the same kind of data may be less appropriate—or impossible to come by—in a historical study. As you become more familiar with a particular discipline or area of study, you will gain a sense of just what it takes to prove a point or support a claim in that field. The following questions will help you begin understanding the rhetorical situation of a particular discipline:

- How do other writers in the field use precedence and authority as evidence? What or who counts as an authority in this field? How are the credentials of authorities established?

- What kinds of data seem to be preferred as evidence? How are such data gathered and presented?

- How are statistics or other numerical information used and presented as evidence? Are tables, charts, or graphs commonly used? How much weight do they carry?

- How are definitions, causal analyses, evaluations, analogies, and examples used as evidence?

- How does the field use firsthand and secondhand sources as evidence?

- How is personal experience used as evidence?

- How are quotations used as part of evidence?

As these questions suggest, evidence may not always travel well from one field to another. As you consider the kinds of evidence surveyed in the rest of this chapter, consider in which contexts—in which rhetorical situations—each kind of evidence would be most (or least) effective.

FIRSTHAND EVIDENCE

Firsthand evidence comes from research you have carried out or been closely involved with, and much of this kind of research requires you to collect and examine data. Here we will discuss the kinds of firsthand research most commonly conducted by student writers.

Observations

"What," you may wonder, "could be any easier than observing something?" You just choose a subject, look at it closely, and record what you see and hear. If observing were so easy, eyewitnesses would all provide reliable accounts. Yet experience shows that several people who have observed the same phenomenon generally offer contradictory evidence on the basis of those observations. Trained observers say that getting down a faithful record of an observation requires intense concentration and mental agility.

Before you begin an observation, then, decide exactly what you want to find out and anticipate what you are likely to see. Do you want to observe an action repeated by many people (such as pedestrians crossing a street, in relation to an argument for putting in a new stoplight), a sequence of actions (such as the stages involved in student registration, which you want to argue is far too complicated), or the interactions of a group (such as meetings of the campus Young Republicans, which you want to see adhere to strict parliamentary procedures)? Once you have a clear sense of what you will observe and what questions you wish to answer through the observation, use the following guidelines to achieve the best results:

- Make sure the observation relates directly to your claim.
- Brainstorm about what you are looking for, but don't be rigidly bound to your expectations.
- Develop an appropriate system for collecting data. Consider using a split notebook or page: on one side, record the minute details of your observations directly; on the other, record your thoughts or impressions.
- Be aware that the way you record data will affect the outcome, if only in respect to what you decide to include in your observational notes and what you leave out.
- Record the precise date, time, and place of the observation.

In the following brief excerpt, editor Nell Bernstein uses information drawn from careful observation to introduce an argument about why some teenagers are drawn to taking on a new identity:

> Her lipstick is dark, the lip liner even darker, nearly black. In baggy pants, a blue plaid Pendleton, her bangs pulled back tight off her forehead, 15-year-old April is a perfect cholita, a Mexican gangsta girl.
> But April Miller is Anglo. "And I don't like it!" she complains. "I'd rather be Mexican."
>
> —Nell Bernstein, "Goin' Gangsta, Choosin' Cholita"

Interviews

Some evidence is best obtained through direct interviews. If you can talk with an expert—in person, on the phone, or online—you might get information you could not have obtained through any other type of research. In addition to getting expert opinion, you might ask for first-hand accounts, biographical information, or suggestions of other places to look or other people to consult. The following guidelines will help you conduct effective interviews:

- Determine the exact purpose of the interview, and be sure it is directly related to your claim.
- Set up the interview well in advance. Specify how long it will take, and if you wish to tape-record the session, ask permission to do so.
- Prepare a written list of both factual and open-ended questions. (Brainstorming with friends can help you come up with good questions.) Leave plenty of space for notes after each question. If the interview proceeds in a direction that you had not expected but that seems promising, don't feel you have to cover every one of your questions.
- Record the subject's full name and title, as well as the date, time, and place of the interview.
- Be sure to thank those you interview, either in person or with a follow-up letter or email message.

In arguing that alternative athletic venues such as the Gay Games do not pose a major challenge to the dominant structure of sports, Michael Messner uses data drawn from extensive interviews with participants in the Gay Games, including the following remarks from one of his subjects, Mike T:

> "You don't win by beating someone else. We defined winning as doing your very best. That way, everyone is a winner. And we have age-group competition, so all ages are involved. We have parity: if there's a men's sport, there's a women's sport to complement it. And we go out and recruit in Third World and minority areas. All these people are gonna get together for a week, they're gonna march in protest together, they're gonna hold hands."
>
> –Michael Messner, "In Living Color"

Messner uses this quotation from an interview subject to illustrate his contention that the Gay Games focus on bridging differences and overcoming prejudices of all kinds.

Surveys and Questionnaires

Surveys usually require the use of questionnaires. On any questionnaire, the questions should be clear, easy to understand, and designed so that respondents' answers can be analyzed easily. Questions that ask respondents to say "yes" or "no" or to rank items on a scale (1 to 5, for example, or "most helpful" to "least helpful") are particularly easy to tabulate. Here are some guidelines to help you prepare for and carry out a survey:

- Write out your purpose in conducting the survey, and make sure its results will be directly related to your claim.

- Brainstorm potential questions to include in the survey, and ask how each relates to your purpose and claim.

- Figure out how many people you want to contact, what the demographics of your sample should be (men in their twenties, or an equal number of men and women?), and how you plan to reach these people.

- Draft questions, making sure that each calls for a short, specific answer.

- Test the questions on several people, and revise those that are ambiguous, hard to answer, or too time-consuming to answer.

- If your questionnaire is to be sent by mail or email, draft a cover letter explaining your purpose and giving a clear deadline. For mail, provide an addressed, stamped return envelope.

- On the final draft of the questionnaire, leave plenty of space for answers.

- Proofread the final draft carefully; typos will make a bad impression on those whose help you are seeking.

In an argument about the way computers are misused in schools, LynNell Hancock uses information drawn from several surveys, including the one she mentions in the following paragraph:

> **Having enough terminals to go around is one problem. But another important question is what the equipment is used for. Not much beyond rote drills and word processing, according to Linda Roberts, a technology consultant for the U.S. Department of Education. A 1992 National Assessment of Educational Progress survey found that most fourth-grade math students were using computers to play games "like Donkey Kong." By the eighth grade, most math students weren't using them at all.**
>
> **—LynNell Hancock, "The Haves and the Have-Nots"**

Experiments

Some arguments may be supported by evidence gathered through experiments. In the sciences, experimental data are highly valued—if the experiment is conducted in a rigorously controlled situation. For other kinds of writing, "looser" and more informal experiments can be acceptable, especially if they are intended to provide only part of the support for an argument. If you want to argue that the recipes in *Gourmand* magazine are impossibly tedious to follow and take far more time than the average person wishes to spend, you might ask five or six people to conduct a little experiment with you: following two recipes apiece from a recent issue and recording and timing every step. The evidence you gather from this informal experiment could provide some concrete support—by way of specific examples—for your contention. But such experiments should be taken with a grain of salt; they may not be effective with certain audiences, and if they can easily be attacked as skewed or sloppily done ("The people you asked to make these recipes couldn't cook their way out of paper bags!"), then they may do more harm than good.

In an essay about computer hackers and the threats they pose to various individuals and systems, Winn Schwartau reports on an experiment performed by an ex-hacker he knows:

> One afternoon in Newport Beach, Jesse [the ex-hacker] put on a demonstration to show how easy it was to rob a bank.
>
> Jesse took his audience to a trash bin behind Pacific Bell, the Southern California Baby Bell service provider. Dumpster diving proved to be an effective means of social engineering because within minutes, an internal telephone company employee list was dredged out of the garbage. On it, predictably, were handwritten notes with computer passwords.
>
> In the neighborhood was a bank, which shall go nameless. After some more dumpster diving, financial and personal profiles of wealthy bank customers surfaced. That was all Jesse said he needed to commit the crime.
>
> At a nearby phone booth, Jesse used a portable computer with an acoustic modem to dial into the telephone company's computer. Jesse knew a lot about the telephone company's computers, so he made a few changes. He gave the pay phone a new number, that of one of the wealthy clients about whom he now knew almost everything. He also turned off the victim's phone with that same number. Jesse then called the bank and identified himself as Mr. Rich, an alias.
>
> "How can we help you, Mr. Rich?"

"I would like to transfer $100,000 to this bank account number."
"I will need certain information."
"Of course."
"What is your balance?"
"About _____," he supplied the number accurately.
"What is your address?"
Jesse gave the address.
"Are you at home, Mr. Rich?"
"Yes."
"We'll need to call you back for positive identification."
"I understand. Thank you for providing such good security."
In less than a minute the phone rang.
"Hello, Rich here."
The money was transferred, then transferred back to Mr. Rich's account again, to the surprise and embarrassment of the bank. The money was returned and the point was made.

–Winn Schwartau, "Hackers: The First Information Warriors"

Personal Experience

Personal experience can serve as powerful evidence when it is appropriate to the subject, to your purpose, and to the audience. Remember that if it is your *only* evidence, however, personal experience probably will not be sufficient to carry the argument. Nevertheless, it can be especially effective for drawing listeners or readers into an argument, as Sam Fulwood III demonstrates in the opening of an essay about the black middle class:

Race awareness displaced my blissful childhood in 1969.

I was then in the sixth grade at Oaklawn Elementary, a three-year-old school built on the edge of my neighborhood in Charlotte, N.C. Everybody knew that one day little white boys and girls would attend classes there, but at the time, the sparkling new rooms contained only black students and teachers. . . .

Mrs. Cunningham, a proper and proud black woman, knew that my father was a Presbyterian minister and my mother was an elementary school teacher, the perfect pair of parents for unchallenged credentials into black society's elite. She was convinced, on the advice of my teachers, that I should be among the first students from her elementary school to attend the nearest white junior high school the following year. This was an honor, she declared. Mrs. Cunningham countered any arguments I attempted about staying at the neighborhood school. As I needed additional persuading, she stated: "I am

CULTURAL CONTEXTS FOR ARGUMENT

Personal experience counts in making academic arguments in some but not all cultures. Showing that you have personal experience with a topic can carry strong persuasive appeal with many English-speaking audiences, however, so it will probably be a useful way to argue a point in the United States. As with all evidence used to make a point, evidence based on your own experience must be pertinent to the topic, understandable to the audience, and clearly related to your purpose and claim.

absolutely certain that you can hold your own with the best [white students] at Ransom Junior High." . . .

I evolved that day into a race-child, one who believed that he would illuminate the magnificent social changes wrought by racial progress. Overt racial barriers were falling, and I, among the favored in Charlotte's black middle class, thought my future would be free of racism, free of oppression. I believed I was standing on the portico of the Promised Land.

–Sam Fulwood III, "The Rage of the Black Middle Class"

SECONDHAND EVIDENCE

Secondhand evidence comes from sources beyond yourself—books, articles, films, online sources, and so on.

Library Sources

Your college library has not only a great number of print materials (books, periodicals, reference works) but also computer terminals that provide access to electronic catalogs and indexes as well as to other libraries' catalogs via the Internet. Although this book isn't designed to give a complete overview of library resources, we can offer a few key questions that can help you use the library most efficiently:

- What kinds of sources do you need to consult? Check your assignment to see whether you are required to consult different kinds of sources. If you must use print sources, find out whether they are readily available in your library or whether you must make special arrangements (such as an interlibrary loan) to use them. If you need to locate nonprint sources, find out where those are kept and whether you need special permission to examine them.

- How current do your sources need to be? If you must investigate the very latest findings about a new treatment for Alzheimer's, you will probably want to check periodicals, medical journals, or the Web. If you want broader, more detailed coverage and background information, you may need to depend more on books. If your argument deals with a specific time period, you may need to examine newspapers, magazines, or books written during that period.

- How many sources should you consult? Expect to look over many more sources than you will end up using. The best guideline is to make sure you have enough sources to support your claim.

- Do you know your way around the library? If not, ask a librarian for help in locating the following resources in the library: general and specialized encyclopedias; biographical resources; almanacs, yearbooks, and atlases; book and periodical indexes; specialized indexes and abstracts; the circulation computer or library catalog; special collections; audio, video, and art collections; the interlibrary loan office.

- Do you know how to conduct subject heading searches about your topic? Consult the *Library of Congress Subject Headings* (LCSH) for a list of standard subject headings related to your topic. This reference work is a helpful starting point because it lists the subject headings used in most library catalogs and indexes.

Online Sources

Today, most students have fairly easy access to online sources from the college library or from a campus computer center. In addition, some dormitory rooms are now wired for immediate Internet connections to your own computer. But in many instances in dorms, and almost certainly at home, you will need a modem and a software package (usually available at the campus bookstore at low cost) to get access to the Internet. With a modem connection, you can link to the college computer system and thus get access. Or you may need to subscribe to an Internet service provider (ISP), such as America Online, CompuServe, or Prodigy. These companies often offer bonus features in addition to access to the Internet, such as encyclopedias and various kinds of software. However, commercial services can be expensive, so you may want to check local sources, such as a Freenet.

Many important resources for argument are now available in databases, either online or on CD-ROM. To search such databases, you must provide a list of authors, titles, or keywords (sometimes called "descriptors"). Especially if you have to pay a fee for such searches, limit the search as much as you can. To be most efficient, choose keywords very carefully. Sometimes you can search just by author or title; then the keywords are obvious. More often, however, you will search with subject headings. For an argument about the fate of the hero in contemporary films, for example, you might find that *film* and *hero* produce far too many possible matches or "hits." You might further narrow the search by adding a third keyword, say, *American* or *current*.

In doing such searches, you will need to observe the search logic for a particular database. Using *and* between keywords (*movies and heroes*) usually indicates that both terms must appear in a file for it to be called up. Using *or* between keywords usually instructs the computer to locate every file in which either one word or the other shows up, whereas using *not* tells the computer to exclude files containing a particular word from the search results (*movies not heroes*).

Software programs called browsers allow you to navigate the contents of the Web and to move from one Web site to another. Today, most browsers—such as Netscape Navigator, Mosaic, and Microsoft Internet Explorer—are graphics browsers that display both text and visual images.

Web-based search engines can be used to carry out keyword searches or view a list of contents available in a series of directories. Here are a few of the most popular search engines:

AltaVista	<http://www.altavista.digital.com>
Ask Jeeves	<http://www.askjeeves.com>
Dogpile	<http://www.dogpile.com>
Google	<http://www.google.com>
Infoseek	<http://www.infoseek.com>
Lycos	<http://www.lycos.com>
WebCrawler	<http://webcrawler.com>
Yahoo!	<http://www.yahoo.com>

USING EVIDENCE EFFECTIVELY

You may gather an impressive amount of evidence on your topic—from firsthand interviews, from careful observations, and from intensive library and online research. But until that evidence is woven into the fabric of your own argument, it is just a pile of data. Using your evidence effectively calls for turning data into information that will be persuasive to your intended audience.

Considering Audiences

The ethos you bring to an argument is crucial to your success in connecting with your audience. You want to present yourself as reliable and credible, naturally, but you also need to think carefully about the way your evidence relates to your audience. Is it appropriate to this particular group of readers or listeners? Does it speak to them in ways they will understand and respond to? Does it acknowledge and appeal to where they are "coming from"? It's hard to give any definite advice for making sure that your evidence is appropriate to the audience. But in general, timeliness is important to audiences: the more up-to-date your evidence, the better. In addition, evidence that is representative is usually more persuasive than evidence that is extreme or unusual. For example, in arguing for a campus-wide escort service after 10 P.M., a writer who cites numbers of students frightened, threatened, or attacked on their way across campus after dark and numbers of calls for help from campus phone boxes will probably be in a stronger position than one who cites only an attack that occurred four years ago.

Building a Critical Mass

Throughout this chapter we have stressed the need to discover as much evidence as possible in support of your claim. If you can find only one or two pieces of evidence, only one or two reasons to back up your contention, then you may be on weak ground. Although there is no magic number, no definite way of saying how much is "enough" evidence, you should build toward a critical mass, a number of pieces of evidence all pulling in the direction of your claim. Especially if your evidence relies heavily on personal experience or on one major example, you should stretch your search for additional sources and good reasons to back up your claim.

Arranging Evidence

You can begin to devise a plan for arranging your evidence effectively by producing a rough outline or diagram of your argument, a series of hand-written or computer note cards that can be grouped into categories, or

---

CULTURAL CONTEXTS FOR ARGUMENT

How do you decide what evidence will best support your claims? The answer depends, in large part, on how you define evidence. Differing notions of what counts as evidence can lead to arguments that go nowhere fast.

One example of such a failed argument occurred in 1979, when Oriana Fallaci, an Italian journalist, was interviewing the Ayatollah Khomeini. Fallaci argued in a way common in North American and Western European cultures: she presented what she considered strong assertions backed up with facts ("Iran denies freedom to people. . . . Many people have been put in prison and even executed, just for speaking out in opposition."). In response, Khomeini relied on very different kinds of evidence: analogies ("Just as a finger with gangrene should be cut off so that it will not destroy the whole body, so should people who corrupt others be pulled out like weeds so they will not infect the whole field.") and, above all, the authority of the Q'uran. Partly because of these differing beliefs about what counts as evidence, the interview ended in a shouting match.

People in the United States tend to give great weight to factual evidence, but as this example shows, the same is not true in some other parts of the world. In arguing across cultures, you need to think carefully about how you are accustomed to using evidence—and to pay attention to what counts as evidence to members of other cultures.

- Do you rely on facts? Examples? Firsthand experience?
- Do you include testimony from experts—and which experts are valued most (and why)?
- Do you cite religious or philosophical texts? Proverbs or everyday wisdom?
- Do you use analogies as evidence? How much do they count?

Once you determine what counts as evidence in your own arguments, ask these same questions about the use of evidence by members of other cultures.

anything else that makes the major points of the argument very clear. Then review your evidence, deciding which pieces support which points in the argument. In general, try to position your strongest pieces of evidence in key places—near the beginning of paragraphs, at the end of the introduction, or where you build toward a powerful conclusion. In addition, try to achieve a balance between your own argument and your own words, and the sources you use or quote in support of the argument. The sources of evidence are important props in the structure, but they should not overpower the structure (your argument) itself.

RESPOND●

1. What counts as evidence depends in large part on the rhetorical situation. One audience might find personal testimony compelling in a given case, whereas another might require data that only experimental studies can provide. The Christine Hoff Sommers excerpt in Chapter 7 (see p. 75) offers a good example of audience-specific responses to evidence. Lynda Gorov, the author of the *Boston Globe* piece Sommers quotes, believed the evidence she found in "one study of women's shelters out West" that pointed toward a rise in spousal abuse on the day of the Super Bowl. Another writer Sommers mentions, Ken Ringle, did not accept that evidence and went looking for expert testimony.

   Imagine that you want to argue for a national anti-abuse educational campaign composed of television ads to air before and during the Super Bowl—and you want the National Football League to pay for those ads. Make a list of reasons and evidence to support your claim, aimed at NFL executives. What kind of evidence would be most compelling to that group? How would you rethink your use of evidence if you were writing for the newsletter of a local women's shelter? This is not an exercise in pulling the wool over anyone's eyes; your goal is simply to anticipate the kind of evidence that different audiences would find persuasive given the same case.

2. Finding, evaluating, and arranging evidence in an argument is often a *discovery* process: sometimes you're concerned not only with digging up support for an already established claim but also with creating and revising tentative claims. Surveys and interviews can help you figure out what to argue, as well as provide evidence for a claim.

   Interview a classmate with the goal of writing a brief proposal argument about his or her career goals. The claim should be "My classmate should be doing X five years from now." Limit yourself to ten questions; write them ahead of time and do not deviate from them. Record the results of the interview (written notes are fine—you don't need a tape recorder).

Then interview another classmate, with the same goal in mind. Ask the same first question, but this time let the answer dictate the rest of the questions. You still get only ten questions.

Which interview gave you more information? Which one helped you learn more about your classmate's goals? Which one better helped you develop claims about his or her future?

3. Imagine that you're trying to decide whether to take a class with a particular professor, but you don't know if he or she is a good teacher. You might already have an opinion, based on some vaguely defined criteria and dormitory gossip, but you're not sure if that evidence is reliable. You decide to observe a class to inform your decision.

Visit a class in which you are not a student, and make notes on your observations following the guidelines in this chapter (p. 300). You probably only need a single day's visit to get a sense of the note-taking process, though you would, of course, need much more time to write an honest evaluation of the professor.

Write a short evaluation of the professor's teaching abilities on the basis of your observations. Then write an analysis of your evaluation. Is it honest? Fair? What other kinds of evidence might you need if you wanted to make an informed decision about the class and the teacher?

chapter nineteen

Fallacies
of Argument

"Either you eat your broccoli or you don't get dessert!"

"But if you don't give me an "A," I won't get into medical school."

"You would if you loved me."

"Make love, not war."

"All my friends have AOL. I'm the only one who can't get instant messages!"

■ ■ ■

Fallacies are arguments supposedly flawed by their very nature or structure; as such, you should avoid them in your own writing and question them in arguments you read. That said, it's important to appreciate that one person's fallacy may well be another person's stroke of genius.

How can that be, if fallacies are faulty arguments? Remember that arguments ordinarily work in complex social, political, and cultural environments where people are far more likely to detect the mote in someone else's eye than the beam in their own.

Consider, for example, the fallacy termed *ad hominem* argument — "to the man." It describes a strategy of attacking the character of those with whom one disagrees rather than the substance of their arguments: *So you think government entitlement programs are growing out of control? Well, you're an idiot.* It's an argument of a kind everyone has blurted out at some time in their lives.

But there are also situations when an issue of character is germane to an argument. If that weren't so, appeals based on character would be pointless. The problem arises in deciding when such arguments are legitimate and when they are fallacious. You are much more likely to regard attacks on people you admire as *ad hominem,* and attacks on those you disagree with as warranted. Moreover, debates about character can become quite ugly and polarizing; consider Anita Hill and Clarence Thomas, Paula Jones and Bill Clinton, Pete Rose and major league baseball. (For more on arguments based on character, see Chapter 6.)

It might be wise to think of fallacies not in terms of errors you can detect and expose in someone else's work, but as strategies hurtful to everyone (including the person advancing them) because they make civil argument more difficult. Fallacies are impediments to the kind of rich conversations experienced writers ought to cultivate — regardless of their differences.

To help you understand fallacies of argument, we've classified them according to three rhetorical appeals discussed in earlier chapters: emotional arguments, arguments based on character, and logical arguments. (See Chapters 4, 6, and 7.)

FALLACIES OF EMOTIONAL ARGUMENT

In Western tradition, emotional arguments have long been dismissed as "womanish" and, therefore, weak and suspect. But such views are not only close-minded and sexist; they're flat-out wrong. Emotional arguments can be both powerful and appropriate in many circumstances, and most writers use them as a matter of course. However, writers who attempt to evoke either excessive or inappropriate feelings on the part of their audiences violate the good faith on which legitimate argument depends. The essential connection between writers and readers won't last if it is built on deception or manipulation.

Scare Tactics

Corrupters of children, the New Testament warns, would be better off dropped into the sea with millstones around their necks. Would that the same fate awaited politicians, advertisers, and public figures who peddle ideas by scaring people. It is the essence of demagoguery to reduce complicated issues to threats or to exaggerate a possible danger well beyond its statistical likelihood. Yet scare tactics, which do just that, are remarkably common in everything ranging from ads for life insurance to threats of audits by the Internal Revenue Service. Such tactics work because it is usually easier to imagine a dire consequence than to appreciate its remote probability. That may be why so many people fear flying, despite the fine safety record of commercial aviation.

Scare tactics can also be used to magnify existing, sometimes legitimate fears into panic or prejudice. People who genuinely fear losing their jobs can be persuaded, easily enough, to mistrust all immigrants as people who might work for less money; people living on fixed incomes can be convinced that even minor modifications of entitlement programs represent dire threats to their standard of living. Such tactics have the effect of closing off thinking because people who are scared seldom act rationally.

Even well-intended fear campaigns—like those directed against drugs or HIV infection—can misfire if their warnings prove too shrill. When AIDS failed to occur within the heterosexual population at the rate health professionals originally predicted, many people became suspicious of the establishment's warnings and grew unduly careless about their own sexual behavior, thereby greatly increasing their risk of exposure to infection.

Either-Or Choices

Presenting arguments that require people to choose one of only two alternatives can be a kind of scare tactic. The preferred option is drawn in the warmest light, whereas the alternative is cast as an ominous shadow. Sometimes *either-or* choices are benign strategies to get something accomplished: *Either you eat your broccoli or you don't get dessert.* Such arguments become fallacious when they reduce a complicated issue to excessively simple terms or when they deliberately obscure other alternatives.

To suggest that Social Security must be privatized or the system will go broke may have rhetorical power, but the choice is too simple. The fiscal problems of Social Security can be addressed in any number of ways, including privatization. To defend privatization, fallaciously, as the only possible course of action is to lose the support of people who know better.

But then *either-or* arguments—like most scare tactics—are often purposefully designed to seduce those who aren't well informed about a subject. And that cynical rationale is yet another reason the tactic violates principles of civil discourse. Argument should enlighten people, making them more knowledgeable and more capable of acting intelligently and independently.

Slippery Slope

The slippery slope fallacy is well named, describing an argument that casts a tiny misstep today as tomorrow's avalanche. Of course, not all arguments aimed at preventing dire consequences are slippery slope fallacies: the parent who corrects a child for misbehavior now is acting sensibly to prevent more serious problems as the child grows older. And like the homeowner who repairs a loose shingle to prevent an entire roof from rotting, businesses and institutions that worry about little problems often prevent bigger ones. The city of New York learned an important lesson in the 1990s about controlling crime by applying what had become known as "the broken window theory": after the mayor directed police to crack down on petty crimes that make urban life especially unpleasant, major crimes declined as well.

The slippery slope fallacy arises when a writer exaggerates the future consequences of an action, usually with the intention of frightening readers. As such, slippery slope arguments are also scare tactics. But people encounter them so often that they come to seem almost reasonable. For instance, defenders of free speech typically regard even mild attempts to govern behavior as constitutional matters: for example, a school board's request that a school pupil cut his ponytail becomes a direct assault on the child's First Amendment rights, litigated through the courts. Similarly, opponents of gun control warn that any legislation regulating firearms is just a first step toward the government knocking down citizens' doors and seizing all their weapons. Ideas and actions do have consequences, but they aren't always as dire as writers fond of slippery slope tactics would have you believe.

Sentimental Appeals

Sentimental appeals are arguments that use emotions excessively to distract readers from facts. Quite often, such appeals are highly personal and individual—focusing attention on heart-warming or heart-wrenching situations that make readers feel guilty about raising legitimate objections to related proposals or policies. Emotions become an impediment to civil discourse when they keep people from thinking clearly.

Yet, sentimental appeals are a major vehicle of television news, where it is customary to convey ideas through personal tales that tug at viewers' heartstrings. For example, a camera might document the day-to-day life of a single mother on welfare whose on-screen generosity, kindness, and tears come to represent the spirit of an entire welfare clientele under attack by callous legislators; or the welfare recipient might be shown driving a Cadillac and trading food stamps for money while a lower-middle-class family struggles to meet its grocery budget. In either case, the conclusion the reporter wants you to reach is supported by powerful images that evoke emotions in support of that conclusion. But though the individual stories presented may be genuinely moving, they seldom give a complete picture of a complex social or economic issue.

Bandwagon Appeals

Bandwagon appeals are arguments that urge people to follow the same path everyone else is taking. Curiously, many American parents seem endowed with the ability to refute bandwagon appeals. When their kids whine that *Everyone else is going camping overnight without chaperones,* the parents reply instinctively, *And if everyone else jumps off a cliff (or a railroad bridge, or the Empire State Building), you will too?* The children stomp and groan—and then try a different line of argument.

Unfortunately, not all bandwagon approaches are so transparent. Though Americans like to imagine themselves as rugged individualists, they're easily seduced by ideas endorsed by the mass media and popular culture. Such trends are often little more than harmless fashion statements. At other times, however, Americans become obsessed by issues selected for their attention by politicians or by media or cultural elites. In recent years, issues of this kind have included the "war on drugs," health care reform, AIDS prevention, gun control, tax reform, welfare reform, teen smoking, and campaign finance reform. Everyone must be concerned by this issue-of-the-day, and something—*anything*—must be done! More often than not, enough people jump on the bandwagon to achieve a measure of reform. And when changes occur because people have become sufficiently informed to exercise good judgment, then one can speak of "achieving consensus," a rational goal for civil argument.

But sometimes bandwagons run downhill and out of control, as they did in the 1950s when many careers were destroyed by "witch hunts" for suspected communists during the McCarthy era and in the late 1980s when concerns over child abuse mushroomed into indiscriminate prosecutions of parents and child care workers. In a democratic society, the bandwagon appeal is among the most potentially serious and permanently damaging fallacies of argument.

FALLACIES OF ETHICAL ARGUMENT

The presence of an author in an argument is called ethos. To build connections with readers, writers typically seek an ethos that casts themselves as honest, well informed, and sympathetic. Not surprisingly, readers pay closer attention to authors whom they respect. But *trust me* is a scary warrant. People usually need more than promises to move them to action—and they don't like to be intimidated by writers who exploit issues of character to limit how readers can respond to complex problems. When choice is constricted, civil discourse usually ends. (For more on ethos, see Chapter 6.)

Appeals to False Authority

One of the best strategies a writer can employ to support an idea is to draw on the authority of widely respected people, texts, or institutions. Relying on respected voices, past and present, is a mainstay of civil discourse; in fact, some academic research papers are essentially exercises in finding and reflecting on the work of reputable authorities. Writers may introduce these authorities into their arguments through allusions, citations, or direct quotations. (See Chapter 21 for more on assessing the reliability of sources.)

False authority occurs chiefly when writers offer themselves, or other authorities they cite, as *sufficient* warrant for believing a claim:

Claim	X is true because I say so.
Warrant	What I say must be true.
Claim	X is true because Y says so.
Warrant	What Y says must be true.

Rarely will you see authority asserted quite so baldly as in these examples, because few readers would accept a claim stated in either of these ways. Nonetheless, claims of authority drive many persuasive campaigns. American pundits and politicians are fond of citing the U.S. Constitution or Bill of Rights, a reasonable practice when the documents are interpreted respectfully. However, as often as not, the constitutional rights claimed aren't in the texts themselves or don't mean what the speakers think they do. And most constitutional issues are self-evidently debatable.

Likewise, the claims of religion are often based on texts or teachings of great authority within a community of believers. However, the power of these texts is usually more limited outside that group and, hence, less capable of persuading solely on the grounds of their authority—though arguments of faith often have power on other grounds.

Institutions can be cited as authorities within their proper spheres. Certainly, serious attention should be paid to claims supported by authorities one respects or recognizes—the White House, the FBI, the FDA, the National Science Foundation, the *New York Times,* the *Wall Street Journal,* and so on. But one ought not to accept facts or information *simply* because they have the imprimatur of such agencies. To quote a Russian proverb made famous by Ronald Reagan, "Trust, but verify."

Dogmatism

A writer who attempts to persuade by asserting or assuming that a particular position is the only one conceivably acceptable within a community is trying to enforce dogmatism. Dogmatism is a fallacy of ethos because the tactic undermines the trust that must exist between those who would make and those who would receive arguments. In effect, arbiters of dogmatic opinion imply that there are no arguments to be made: the truth is self-evident to those who know better.

Doubtless, there are arguments beyond the pale of civil discourse—positions and claims so outrageous or absurd that they are unworthy of serious attention. Attacks on the historical reality of the Holocaust fall into this category. But relatively few subjects in a free society ought to be off the table—certainly none that can be defended with facts, testimony, and good reasons. In general, therefore, the suggestion that merely raising an issue for debate is somehow "politically incorrect"—whether racist or sexist, unpatriotic or sacrilegious, or insensitive or offensive in some other way—may well represent a fallacy of argument deployed to constrict the range of acceptable opinion.

Moral Equivalence

A fallacy of argument perhaps more common today than a decade ago is moral equivalence—that is, suggesting that serious wrongdoings don't differ in kind from more minor offenses. A warning sign that this fallacy is likely to come into play is the retort of the politician or bureaucrat accused of wrongdoing: *But everyone else does it too!* Richard Nixon insisted that the crimes that led to his resignation did not differ in kind from the activities of previous presidents; Bill Clinton made similar claims about the fund-raising and other scandals of his administration. Regardless of the validity of these particular defenses, there is a point at which the scale of a morally questionable act overwhelms even its shady precedents.

Moral equivalence can work both ways. It is not uncommon to read arguments in which relatively innocuous activities are raised to the level of major crimes. Some would say that the national campaign against smoking falls into this category—a common and legally sanctioned behavior now given the social stigma of serious drug abuse. And if smoking is almost criminal, should one not be equally concerned with people who use and abuse chocolate—a sweet and fatty food responsible for a host of health problems? You see how easy it is to make an equivalence argument. Yet suggesting that all behaviors of a particular kind—in this case, abuses of substances—are equally wrong (whether they involve cigarettes, alcohol, drugs, or fatty foods) blurs the subtle distinctions people need to make in weighing claims.

Ad Hominem Arguments

One obviously gendered term that feminists have not been eager to neuter—probably with good reason—is the argument *ad hominem,* "to the man." *Ad hominem* arguments are attacks directed at the character of a person rather than at the claims he or she makes. The theory is simple: destroy the credibility of your opponents, and you either destroy their ability to present reasonable appeals or you distract from the successful arguments they may be offering. Critics of Rush Limbaugh's conservative stances rarely fail to note his heft; opponents of Bill Clinton's military policies just as reliably mention "draft dodging."

In such cases, *ad hominem* tactics turn arguments into ham-fisted, two-sided affairs with good guys and bad guys. Civil argument resists this destructive nastiness, though the temptation to use such tactics persists even (some would say, especially) in colleges and universities.

Of course, character does matter in argument. People expect the proponent of peace to be civil, the advocate of ecology to respect the environment, the champion of justice to be fair even in private dealings. But it is fallacious to attack an idea by exposing the frailties of its advocates or attacking their motives, backgrounds, or unchangeable traits.

FALLACIES OF LOGICAL ARGUMENT

Logical fallacies are arguments in which the claims, warrants, and/or evidence are invalid, insufficient, or disconnected. In the abstract, such problems seem easy enough to spot; in practice, they can be camouflaged by artful presentations. Indeed, logical fallacies pose a challenge to civil argument because they often seem quite reasonable and natural, especially when they appeal to people's self-interests. Whole industries (such as phone-in psychic networks) depend on one or more of the logical fallacies for their existence; political campaigns, too, rely on them to prop up that current staple of democratic interchange—the fifteen-second TV spot.

Hasty Generalization

Among logical fallacies, only faulty causality might be able to challenge hasty generalization for the crown of most prevalent. A hasty generalization is an inference drawn from insufficient evidence: *Because my Honda broke down, all Hondas must be junk.* It also forms the basis for most stereotypes about people or institutions: because a few people in a large group are observed to act in a certain way, one infers that all members of that group will behave similarly. The resulting conclusions are usually sweeping claims of little merit: *Women are bad drivers; men are boors; Scots are stingy; Italians are romantic; English teachers are tweedy; scientists are nerds.* You could, no doubt, expand this roster of stereotypes by the hundreds.

To draw valid inferences, you must always have sufficient evidence: a random sample of a population, a selection large enough to represent fully the subjects of your study, an objective methodology for sampling the population or evidence, and so on (see Chapter 18). And you must qualify your claims appropriately. After all, people do need generalizations to help make reasonable decisions in life; and such claims can be offered legitimately if placed in context and tagged with appropriate qualifiers: *some, a few, many, most, occasionally, rarely, possibly, in some cases, under certain circumstances, in my experience.*

You should be especially alert to the fallacy of hasty generalization when you read reports and studies of any kind, especially case studies based on carefully selected populations. Be alert for the fallacy, too, in the interpretation of poll numbers. Everything from the number of people selected to the time the poll was taken to the exact wording of the questions may affect its outcome.

Faulty Causality

In Latin, the fallacy of faulty causality is described by the expression *post hoc, ergo propter hoc,* which translates word-for-word as "after this, therefore because of this." Odd as the translation may sound, it accurately describes what faulty causality is — the fallacious assumption that because one event or action follows another, the first necessarily causes the second.

Some actions, of course, do produce reactions. Step on the brake pedal in your car, and you move hydraulic fluid that pushes calipers against disks to create friction that stops the vehicle. Or, if you happen to be chair of the Federal Reserve Board, you raise interest rates to increase the cost of borrowing to slow the growth of the economy in order to curb inflation — you hope. Causal relationships of this kind are reasonably convincing because one can provide evidence of relationships between the events sufficient to convince most people that an initial action did, indeed, cause others.

But as even the Federal Reserve example suggests, causality can be difficult to control when economic, political, or social relationships are involved. That's why suspiciously simple or politically convenient causal claims should always be subject to scrutiny.

Begging the Question

There's probably not a teacher in the country who hasn't heard the following argument from a student: *You can't give me a "C" in this course; I'm an "A" student.* The accused felon's version of the same argument goes this way: *I can't be guilty of embezzlement; I'm an honest person.* In both cases, the problem with the claim is that it is made on grounds that cannot be accepted as true because those grounds are in doubt. How can the student claim to be an "A" student when she just earned a "C"? How can the accused felon defend himself on the grounds of honesty when that honesty is now suspect? Setting such arguments in Toulmin terms helps to expose the fallacy:

Claim + Reason	You can't give me a "C" in this course because I'm an "A" student.
Warrant	An "A" student is someone who can't receive "C"s.
Claim + Reason	I can't be guilty of embezzlement because I'm an honest person.
Warrant	An honest person cannot be guilty of embezzlement.

With the warrants stated, you can see why begging the question — that is, assuming as true the very claim that is disputed — is a form of circular argument, divorced from reality. If you assume that an "A" student can't receive "C"s, then the first argument stands. But no one is an "A" student *by definition*; that standing has to be earned by performance in individual courses. Otherwise, there would be no point for a student who once earned an "A" to be taking additional courses; "A" students can only get "A"s, right?

Likewise, even though someone with an honest record is unlikely to embezzle, a claim of honesty is not an adequate defense against specific charges. An honest person won't embezzle, but merely claiming to be honest does not make it so. (For more on Toulmin argument, see Chapter 8.)

Equivocation

Both the finest definition and the most famous literary examples of equivocation come from Shakespeare's tragedy *Macbeth*. In the drama, three witches, representing the fates, make prophecies that seem advantageous to the ambitious Macbeth, but that prove disastrous when understood more fully. He is told, for example, that he has nothing to fear from his enemies "till Birnam wood / Do come to Dunsinane" (*Mac.* V.v.44–45); but these woods do move when enemy soldiers cut Birnam's boughs for camouflage and march on Macbeth's fortress. Catching on to the game, Macbeth begins "[t]o doubt the equivocation of the fiend / That *lies like truth*" (V.v.43–44, emphasis added). An equivocation, then, is an argument that gives a lie an honest appearance; it is a half-truth.

Equivocations are usually juvenile tricks of language, the kind children relish when claiming "I don't even have a nickel," knowing that they have dimes. Consider the plagiarist who copies a paper word-for-word from a source and then declares—honestly, she thinks—that "I wrote the entire paper myself," meaning that she physically copied the piece on her own. But the plagiarist is using "wrote" equivocally—that is, in a limited sense, knowing that most people would understand "writing" as something more than the mere copying of words.

As you might suspect, equivocations are artful dodges that work only as long as readers or listeners don't catch on. But once they do, the device undermines both the logic of the appeal and the good character of the writer. A writer who equivocates becomes, to use yet another Shakespearean phrase, a "corrupter of words."

Non Sequitur

A *non sequitur* is an argument in which claims, reasons, or warrants fail to connect logically; one point does not follow from another. As with other fallacies, children are notably adept at framing *non sequiturs.* Consider this familiar form: *You don't love me or you'd buy me that bicycle!* It might be more evident to harassed parents that no connection exists between love and Huffys if they were to consider the implied warrant:

Claim	**You must not love me**
Reason	**. . . because you haven't bought me that bicycle.**
Warrant	**Buying bicycles for children is essential to loving them.**

A five-year-old might endorse that warrant, but no responsible adult would because love does not depend on buying things, at least not a particular bicycle. Activities more logically related to love might include feeding and clothing children, taking care of them when they are sick, providing shelter and education, and so on.

In effect, *non sequiturs* occur when writers omit a step in an otherwise logical chain of reasoning, assuming that readers agree with what may be a highly contestable claim. For example, it is a *non sequitur* simply to argue that the comparatively poor performance of American students on international mathematics examinations means the country should spend more money on math education. Such a conclusion *might* be justified if a correlation were known or found to exist between mathematical ability and money spent on education. But the students' performance might be poor for reasons other than education funding, so a writer should first establish the nature of the problem before offering a solution.

Faulty Analogy

Comparisons give ideas greater presence or help clarify concepts. Consider all the comparisons packed into this reference to Jack Kennedy from a tribute to Jacqueline Kennedy by Stanley Crouch:

> The Kennedys had spark and Jack had grown into a handsome man, a male swan rising out of the Billy the Kid version of an Irish duckling he had been when he was a young senator.
>
> —Stanley Crouch, "Blues for Jackie"

When comparisons are extended, they become analogies—ways of understanding unfamiliar ideas by comparing them with something that is already known. Some argue that it is through comparisons, metaphors, and analogies that people come to understand the universe. Neil Postman draws readers' attention to the importance of analogies when he asks them to consider how the brain works:

> Is the human mind, for example, like a dark cavern (needing illumination)? A muscle (needing exercise)? A vessel (needing filling)? A lump of clay (needing shaping)? A garden (needing cultivation)? Or, as some may say today, is it like a computer that processes data?
>
> —Neil Postman, "The Word Weavers/The World Makers"

Useful as such comparisons are, they may prove quite false either on their own or when pushed too far or taken too seriously. At this point they become faulty analogies, inaccurate or inconsequential comparisons between objects or concepts. To think of a human mind as a garden has charm: gardens thrive only if carefully planted, weeded, watered, pruned, and harvested; so too the mind must be cultivated, if it is to bear fruit. But gardens also thrive when spread with manure. Need we follow the analogy down that path? Probably not.

RESPOND●

1. Following is a list of political slogans or phrases that may be examples of logical fallacies. Discuss each item to determine what you may know about the slogan and then decide which, if any, fallacy might be used to describe it.

   "It's the economy, stupid." (sign on the wall at Bill Clinton's campaign headquarters)

   "Nixon's the one." (campaign slogan)

   "Fifty-four forty or fight."

   "Make love, not war." (antiwar slogan during the Vietnam War)

"A chicken in every pot."

"No taxation without representation."

"No Payne, your gain." (aimed at an opponent named Payne)

"Loose lips sink ships."

"Guns don't kill, people do." (NRA slogan)

"If you can't stand the heat, get out of the kitchen."

2. We don't want you to argue fallaciously, but it's fun and good practice to frame argumentative fallacies in your own language. Pick an argumentative topic—maybe even one that you've used for a paper in this class—and write a few paragraphs making nothing but fallacious arguments in each sentence. Try to include all the fallacies of emotional, ethical, and logical argument that are discussed in this chapter. It will be a challenge, since some of the fallacies are difficult to recognize, much less produce. Then rewrite the paragraphs, removing all traces of fallacious reasoning, rewriting for clarity, and improving the quality of the argument. This may be an even greater challenge— sometimes fallacies are hard to fix.

3. Choose a paper you've written for this or another class, and analyze it carefully for signs of fallacious reasoning. Once you've tried analyzing your own prose, find an editorial, a syndicated column, and a political speech and look for the fallacies in them. Which fallacies are most common in the four arguments? How do you account for their prevalence? Which are the least common? How do you account for their absence? What seems to be the role of audience in determining what is a fallacy and what is not? Did you find what seem to be fallacies other than the kinds discussed in this chapter?

4. Arguments on the Web are no more likely to contain fallacies than are arguments in any other text, but the fallacies *can* take on different forms. The hypertextual nature of Web arguments and the ease of including visuals along with text make certain fallacies more likely to occur there. Find a Web site sponsored by an organization, business, government entity, or other group (such as the sites of the Democratic and Republican National Committees that were discussed in Chapter 16), and analyze the site for fallacious reasoning. Among other considerations, look at the relationship between text and graphics, and between individual pages and the pages that surround or are linked to them. How does the technique of separating information into discrete pages affect the argument? Then send an email message to the site's creators, explaining what you found and proposing ways the arguments in the site could be improved.

chapter twenty

Intellectual Property

A student writing an essay about Title IX's effect on college athletic programs finds some powerful supporting evidence for her argument on a Web site. Can she use this information without gaining permission?

Day care centers around the country receive letters arguing that they will be liable to lawsuit if they use representations of Disney characters without explicit permission or show Disney films "outside the home."

In California, one large vintner sues another, claiming that the second "stole" the idea of a wine label from the first, although a judge later found that even though the labels were similar, the second was not "copied" from the first.

Musicians argue against other musicians, saying that the increasingly popular use of "sampling" in songs amounts to a form of musical "plagiarism."

On the electronic frontier, the development of digital "watermarks" makes it possible to trace not only documents printed out but those read online as well; as a result, some lawyers argue that millions of Internet users are probably guilty of copyright infringement.

■ ■ ■

In an age of agriculture and industrialization, products that can provide a livelihood are likely to be concrete things: crops, automobiles, houses. But in an age of information such as the current one, *ideas* (intellectual property) are arguably society's most important products. Hence the growing importance of—and growing controversies surrounding—what counts as "property" in an information age.

Perhaps the framers of the Constitution foresaw such a shift in the bases of the nation's economy. At any rate, they articulated in the Constitution a delicate balance between the public's need for information and the incentives necessary to encourage people to produce work—both material and intellectual. Thus, the Constitution empowers Congress "[t]o promote the progress of Science and useful Arts, by securing for limited Times to Authors and Inventors the exclusive Right to their respective Writings and Discoveries" (Article 1, Section 8, Clause 8). This passage allows for *limited* protection (copyright) of the expression of ideas ("Writings and Discoveries"), and through the years that time limit has been extended to up to lifetime plus seventy-five years (and it may be extended yet again to lifetime plus one hundred years).

Why is this historical information important to student writers? First, because writers need to know that ideas themselves cannot be copyrighted—only the *expression* of those ideas. Second, this information explains why some works fall out of copyright and are available for students to use without paying a fee (as you have to do for copyright-protected material in a coursepack, for instance). Third, this information is crucial to the current debates over who owns online materials—materials that may never take any form of concrete *expression*. The debate will certainly be raging during and after the publication of this book—and the way in which it is resolved will have many direct effects on students and teachers. For up-to-date information about copyright law, see the Digital Future Coalition site at <http://www.dfc.org> or the U.S. Copyright site at <http://lcweb.loc.gov/copyright/>.

RECOGNIZING PLAGIARISM

In a way, it is completely true that there is "nothing new under the sun." Indeed, whatever you think or write or say draws on everything you have ever heard or read or experienced. Trying to recall every influence or source of information you have drawn on, even in one day, would take so long that you would have little time left in which to say anything at all. Luckily, people are seldom if ever called on to list every single influence or source of their ideas and writings.

Certainly, recognizing and avoiding plagiarism is a good deal easier and more practical than that. And avoiding plagiarism is very important, for in Western culture *the use of someone else's words or ideas without acknowledgment and as your own is an act of dishonesty that can bring devastating results.* In some cases, students who plagiarize fail courses or are expelled. Eminent political, business, and scientific leaders have lost positions, appointments, or awards following charges of plagiarism. You might want to check out some sites on the Web that offer further information:

- <http://www.indiana.edu/~wts/wts/plagiarism.html>
- <http://www.guilford.edu/ASC/honor.html>
- <http://www.willamette.edu/wu/policy/cheat.html>

CULTURAL CONTEXTS FOR ARGUMENT

Not all cultures accept Western notions of plagiarism, which rest on a belief that language can be owned by writers. Indeed, in many countries, and in some communities within the United States, using the words of others is considered a sign of deep respect and an indication of knowledge—and attribution is not expected or required. In writing arguments in the United States, however, you should credit all materials but those that are common knowledge, that are available in a wide variety of sources, or that are your own findings from field research.

ACKNOWLEDGING YOUR USE OF SOURCES

The safest way to avoid charges of plagiarism is to acknowledge as many of your sources as possible, with the following three exceptions:

- *common knowledge,* a specific source of information most readers will know (that Bill Clinton won the 1996 presidential election, for instance)
- *facts available from a wide variety of sources* (that the Japanese bombing of Pearl Harbor occurred on December 7, 1941, for example)
- *your own findings from field research* (observations, interviews, experiments, or surveys you have conducted), which should simply be announced as your own

For all other source material you should give credit as fully as possible, placing quotation marks around any quoted material, citing your sources according to the documentation style you are using, and including them in a list of references or works cited. Include in material to be credited all of the following:

- *direct quotations*
- *facts not widely known or arguable statements*
- *judgments, opinions, and claims made by others*
- *statistics, charts, tables, graphs, or other illustrations* from any source
- *collaborations,* the help provided by friends, colleagues, instructors, supervisors, or others

(See Chapters 21 and 22 for more on using and documenting sources.)

ACKNOWLEDGING COLLABORATION

We have already noted the importance of acknowledging the inspirations and ideas you derive from talking with others. Such help counts as one form of collaboration, and you may also be involved in more formal kinds of collaborative work—preparing for a group presentation to a class, for example, or writing a group report. Writers generally acknowledge all participants in collaborative projects at the beginning of the presentation, report, or essay—in print texts, often in a footnote or brief prefatory note. The fifth edition of the *MLA Handbook for Writers of Research Papers* (1999) calls attention to the growing importance of collaborative work and gives the following advice on how to deal with issues of assigning fair credit all around:

> Joint participation in research and writing is common and, in fact, encouraged in many courses and in many professions, and it does not constitute plagiarism provided that credit is given for all contributions. One way to give credit, if roles were clearly demarcated or were unequal, is to state exactly who did what. Another way, especially if roles and contributions were merged and truly shared, is to acknowledge all concerned equally. Ask your instructor for advice if you are not certain how to acknowledge collaboration.

USING COPYRIGHTED INTERNET SOURCES

If you've done any surfing on the Net, you already know that it opens the doors to worldwide collaborations, as you can contact individuals and groups around the globe and have access to whole libraries of information. As a result, writing (most especially, online writing) seems increasingly to be made up of a huge patchwork of materials that you alone or you and many others weave together. (For a fascinating discussion of just how complicated charges and countercharges of plagiarism can be on the Internet, see <http://www.ombuds.org/narrative1.html>, where you can read a description of a mediation involving a Web site that included summaries of other people's work.) But when you use information gathered from Internet sources in your own work, it is subject to the same rules that govern information gathered from other types of sources.

Thus, whether or not the material includes a copyright notice or symbol ("© 2000 by John J. Ruszkiewicz and Andrea A. Lunsford," for example), it is more than likely copyrighted—and you may need to request permission to use part or all of it. Although they are currently in danger, "fair use" laws still allow writers to use brief passages from published works (generally up to 300 words from a book, 150 from a periodical article, or 4 lines from a poem) without permission from the copyright holder *if* the use is for educational or personal, noncommercial reasons *and* full credit is given to the source. For personal communication such as email or for listserv postings, however, you should ask permission of the writer before you include any of his or her material in your own argument. For graphics, photos, or other images you wish to reproduce in your text, you should also request permission from the creator or owner (except when you are using them in work only turned into an instructor, which is "fair use"). And if you are going to disseminate your work beyond your classroom—especially online—you must ask permission for any material you borrow from an Internet source.

Here are some examples of student requests for permission:

To: litman@mindspring.com
CC: lunsford.2@osu.edu
Subject: Request for permission

Dear Professor Litman:

I am writing to request permission to quote from your essay "Copyright, Owners' Rights and Users' Privileges on the Internet: Implied Licences, Caching, Linking, Fair Use, and Sign-on Licences." I want to quote some of your work as part of an essay I am writing for my composition class at Ohio State University to explain the complex debates over ownership on the Internet and to argue that students in my class should be participating in these debates. I will give full credit to you and will cite the URL where I first found your work: <http://www.msen.com/~litman/dayton/htm>.

Thank you very much for considering my request.

Raul Sanchez <sanchez.32@osu.edu>

To: fridanet@aol.com
CC: lunsford.2@osu.edu
Subject: Request for permission

Dear Kimberley Masters:

I am a student at Ohio State University writing to request your permission to download and use a photograph of Frida Kahlo in a three-piece suit <fridanet/suit.htm#top> as an illustration in a project about Kahlo that I and two other students are working on in our composition class. In the report on our project, we will cite <http://members.aol.com/fridanet/kahlo.htm> as the URL, unless you wish for us to use a different source.

Thank you very much for considering our request.

Jennifer Fox <fox.360@osu.edu>

CREDITING SOURCES IN ARGUMENTS

Acknowledging your sources and giving full credit is especially important in argumentative writing because doing so helps establish your ethos as a writer. In the first place, saying "thank you" to those who have been of help to you reflects gratitude and openness, qualities that audiences generally respond to very well. Second, acknowledging your sources demonstrates that you have "done your homework," that you know the conversation surrounding your topic and are familiar with what others have thought and said about it, and that you want to help readers find other contributions to the conversation and perhaps join it themselves. Finally, acknowledging sources reminds you to think very critically about your own stance in your argument and about how well you have used your sources. Are they timely and reliable? Have you used them in a biased or overly selective way? Have you used them accurately, double-checking all quotations and paraphrases? Thinking through these questions will improve your overall argument.

RESPOND.

1. Not everyone agrees with the concept of intellectual material as property, as something to be protected. Lately the slogan "information wants to be free" has been showing up in popular magazines and on the Internet, often along with a call to readers to take action against forms of protection such as data encryption and further extension of copyright.

   Using a Web search engine, look for pages where the phrase "free information" appears. Find several sites that make arguments in favor of free information, and analyze them in terms of their rhetorical appeals. What claims do the authors make? How do they appeal to their audience? What is the site's ethos, and how is it created? Once you have read some arguments in favor of free information, return to this chapter's arguments about intellectual property. Which do you find more persuasive? Why?

2. Although this text is principally concerned with ideas and their written expression, there are other forms of protection available for intellectual property. Scientific and technological developments are protectable under patent law, which differs in some significant ways from copyright law.

Find the standards for protection under U.S. copyright law and U.S. patent law. You might begin by visiting the U.S. copyright Web site at <http://lcweb.loc.gov/copyright/>. Then, imagine that you are the president of a small, high-tech corporation and are trying to inform your employees of the legal protections available to them and their work. Write a paragraph or two explaining the differences between copyright and patent and suggesting a policy that balances employees' rights to intellectual property with the business's needs to develop new products.

3. Using the definitions of *patent* and *copyright* that you found for the previous exercise, write a few paragraphs speculating on the reasons behind the differences in protection granted by each. Be sure to consider the application process, too. How does a person go about getting copyright or patent protection? Why are the processes different?

chapter twenty-one

Assessing and Using Sources

ASSESSING SOURCES

As many examples in this text have shown, the quality of an argument often depends to a large degree on the quality of the sources used to support or prove it. As a result, careful evaluation and assessment of *all* your sources is important, including those you gather in libraries or from other print sources, in online searches, or in field research you conduct yourself.

Print Sources

Since you want the information you glean from sources to be reliable and persuasive, it pays to evaluate thoroughly each potential source. The following principles can help you in conducting such an evaluation for print sources:

- *Relevance.* Is the source closely related to your argumentative claim? For a book, the table of contents and the index may help you decide. For an article, check to see if there is an abstract that summarizes the contents.

- *Credentials and stance of author/publisher.* Is the author an expert on the topic? What is the author's stance on the issue(s) involved, and how does this stance influence the information in the source? Does the author's stance support or challenge your own views? If the source was published by a corporation, government agency, or interest group, what is the publisher's position on the topic? If you are evaluating an article, what kind of periodical published it? Popular? Academic? Alternative? Right- or left-leaning in terms of political perspective? If only *one* perspective is presented, do you need to balance or expand it?

- *Date of publication.* Recent sources are often more useful than older ones, particularly in the sciences. However, in some fields such as history or literature, the most authoritative works can be the older ones.

- *Level of specialization.* General sources can be helpful as you begin your research, but later in the project you may need the authority or currentness of more specialized sources. On the other hand, keep in mind that extremely specialized works on your topic may be too difficult for your audience to understand easily.

- *Audience.* Was the source written for a general readership? For specialists? For advocates or opponents?

- *Cross-referencing.* Is the source cited in other works? If it is, do the citations refer to it as an "authority"?

- *Length.* Is the source long enough to provide adequate detail in support of your claim?

- *Availability.* Do you have access to the source? If it is not readily accessible, your time might be better spent looking elsewhere.

- *Omissions.* What is missing or omitted from the source? Might such exclusions affect whether or how you can use the source as evidence?

Electronic Sources

You will probably find working on the Internet and the World Wide Web both exciting and frustrating, for even though these tools have great potential, they are still in a fairly primitive state. Unlike most library-based sources, much material on the Internet in general and on the Web in particular is still the work of enthusiastic amateurs; sloppy research, commercial advertisements, one-sided statements, even false information all rub elbows with good, reliable evidence in cyberspace. As a result, some scholars refuse to trust anything on the Net and look for corroboration before accepting evidence they find there. In such an environment, you must be the judge of how accurate and trustworthy particular electronic sources are. In making these judgments you should rely on the same kind of careful thinking you would use to assess any source. In addition, you may find some of the following questions helpful in evaluating online sources:

- Who has posted the document or message or created the site? An individual? An interest group? A company? A government agency? Does the URL offer any clues? Note especially the final suffix in a domain name —.com (commercial); .org (nonprofit organization); .edu (educational institution); .gov (government agency) — or the geographical domains that indicate country of origin, as in .ca (Canada) or .ar (Argentina).

- What can you determine about the credibility of the author? Can the information in the document or site be verified in other sources? How accurate and complete is it?

- Who can be held accountable for the information in the document or site? How well and thoroughly does it credit its own sources?

- How current is the document or site? Be especially cautious of undated materials.

- How effectively is the document or site designed? How "friendly" is it? Are its links, if any, helpful? What effects do design, visuals, and/or sound have on the message? (See Chapters 15 and 16.)

- What perspectives are represented? If only one perspective is represented, how can you balance or expand this point of view?

Field Research

If you have conducted experiments, surveys, interviews, observations, or any other field research in developing and supporting an argument, make sure to review your own results with a critical eye. The following questions can help you evaluate your own field research:

- Have you rechecked all data and all conclusions to make sure they are accurate and warranted?

- Have you identified the exact time, place, and participants in all field research?
- Have you made clear what part you played in the research and how, if at all, your role could have influenced the results or findings?
- If your research involved other people, have you gotten their permission to use their words or other material in your argument? Have you asked whether you could use their names or whether the names should be kept confidential?

USING SOURCES

As you locate, examine, and evaluate sources in support of an argument, remember to keep a careful record of where you have found them. For print sources, you may want to keep a working bibliography on your computer—or a list in a notebook you can carry with you. In any case, make sure you take down the *name of the author;* the *title* of the book or periodical and article, if any; the *publisher* and *city of publication;* the *date of publication;* relevant *volume, issue,* and *page numbers;* and any other information you may later need in preparing a works-cited or references list. In addition, for a book, note where you found it—the section of the library, for example, along with the call number for the book.

For electronic sources, you should also keep a careful record of the information you will need in your works-cited or references list—particularly the *name of the database or online source,* the full *electronic address or URL,* and several potentially important dates: (1) the *date the document was first produced;* (2) the *date the document was published on the Web*—this may be a version number or a revision date; and (3) the *date you accessed the document.* In general, the simplest way to ensure that you have this information is to get a printout of the source.

Signal Words and Introductions

Because your sources will probably be extremely important to the success of your arguments, you need to introduce them carefully to your readers. Doing so usually calls for beginning a sentence in which you are going to use a source with a signal phrase of some kind: *According to noted child psychiatrist Robert Coles, children develop complex ethical systems at extremely young ages.* In this sentence, the signal phrase tells readers that you are about to draw on the work of a person named Robert Coles and that this person is a "noted child psychiatrist." Here is an example that uses a quotation from a source in more than one sentence (note that in the MLA style, ellipsis marks are enclosed in brackets):

> In *Job Shift*, consultant William Bridges worries about "dejobbing and about what a future shaped by it is going to be like." Even more worrisome, Bridges argues, is the possibility that "the sense of craft and of professional vocation [. . .] will break down under the need to earn a fee" (228).

"Worries" and "argues" add a sense of urgency to the message Bridges offers and suggest that the writer either agrees with—or is neutral about—these points. Other signal verbs have a more negative slant, indicating that the point being introduced in the quotation is open to debate and that others (including the writer) might disagree with it. If the writer of the passage above had said, for instance, that Bridges "unreasonably contends" or that he "fantasizes," these signal verbs would carry quite different connotations from those associated with "argues." In some cases, a signal verb may require more complex phrasing to get the writer's full meaning across:

> Bridges recognizes the dangers of changes in work yet refuses to be overcome by them: "The real issue is not how to stop the change but how to provide the necessary knowledge and skills to equip people to operate successfully in this New World" (229).

As these examples illustrate, the signal verb is important because it allows you to characterize the author's or source's viewpoint or perspective as well as your own—so choose these verbs with care. Other frequently used signal verbs include *acknowledges, advises, agrees, allows, asserts, believes, charges, claims, concludes, concurs, confirms, criticizes, declares, disagrees, discusses, disputes, emphasizes, expresses, interprets, lists, objects, observes, offers, opposes, remarks, replies, reports, responds, reveals, states, suggests, thinks,* and *writes.*

Quotations

For supporting argumentative claims, you will want to quote—that is, to reproduce an author's precise words—in at least three kinds of situations: when the wording is so memorable or expresses a point so well that you cannot improve it or shorten it without weakening it; when the author is a respected authority whose opinion supports your own ideas particularly well; and when an author challenges or disagrees profoundly with others in the field. The following guidelines can help you make sure that you quote accurately:

- Copy quotations carefully, being sure that punctuation, capitalization, and spelling are exactly as they are in the original.

- Enclose the quotation in quotation marks; don't rely on your memory to distinguish your own words from those of your source. If in doubt, recheck all quotations for accuracy.

- Use square brackets if you introduce words of your own into the quotation or make changes to it. *("And [more] brain research isn't going to define further the matter of 'mind.'")*

- Use ellipsis marks if you omit material and enclose them in brackets. *("And brain research isn't going to define [. . .] the matter of 'mind.'")*

- Make sure you have all the information necessary to create an in-text citation as well as an item in your works-cited or references list.

- If you're quoting a short passage (four lines or less, MLA style; forty words or less, APA style), it should be worked into your text, enclosed by quotation marks. Longer quotations should be set off from the regular text. Begin such a quotation on a new line, indenting every line one inch or ten spaces (MLA) or five to seven spaces (APA). Set-off quotations do not need to be enclosed in quotation marks.

- If the quotation extends over more than one page, indicate page breaks in case you decide to use only part of the quotation in your argument.

- Label the quotation with a note that tells you where and/or how you think you will use it.

Paraphrases

Paraphrases involve putting an author's material (including major and minor points, usually in the order they are presented in the original) into *your own words and sentence structures*. Here are some guidelines that can help you paraphrase accurately:

- Include all main points and any important details from the original source, in the same order in which the author presents them.

- State the meaning in your own words and sentence structures. If you want to include especially memorable or powerful language from the original source, enclose it in quotation marks.

- Make sure you have all the information necessary to create an in-text citation as well as an item in your works-cited or references list.

- If you are paraphrasing material that extends over more than one page, indicate page breaks if possible in case you decide to use only part of the paraphrase in your argument.

- Label the paraphrase with a note suggesting where and/or how you intend to use it in your argument.

Summaries

A summary is a significantly shortened version of a passage—or even a whole chapter of a work—that captures the main ideas *in your own words.* Unlike a paraphrase, a summary uses just enough information to record the points you want to emphasize. Summaries can be extremely valuable in supporting arguments. Here are some guidelines to help you prepare accurate and helpful summaries:

- Include just enough information to recount the main points you want to cite. A summary is usually much shorter than the original.

- Use your own words. If you include any language from the original, enclose it in quotation marks.

- Make sure you have all the information necessary to create an in-text citation as well as an item in your works-cited or references list.

- If you are summarizing material that extends over more than one page, indicate page breaks in case you decide to use only part of the summary in your argument.

- Label the summary with a note that suggests where and/or how you intend to use it in your argument.

RESPOND •

1. Select one of the essays at the end of Chapters 9–13, such as Gretel Ehrlich's "About Men" (Chapter 9) or Larissa MacFarquhar's "Who Cares If Johnny Can't Read?" (Chapter 10). Then write a brief summary

of the essay that includes both direct quotations and paraphrases. Be careful to attribute the ideas properly, even when you paraphrase.

Trade summaries with a partner, and compare the passages you selected to quote and paraphrase, and the signal phrases you used to introduce them. How do your choices create an ethos for the original author that differs from the one your partner has created? How do the signal phrases shape a reader's sense of the author's position? Which summary best represents the author's argument? Why?

2. Imagine that you are in the beginning stages of research for a paper on the history of race relations in the United States. You have an initial bibliography, but you need to shorten the list so that you can begin reading—you need to make some tough decisions about which works to cut.

   Turn to the examples for a list of works cited (MLA style) and a list of references (APA style) in Chapter 22. Use the criteria in this chapter to help you select five of these sources for inclusion in your short list. For each source that you pick, write a few sentences explaining your decision. How relevant is the source? How recent? How specialized?

3. Return to the Internet sites you found in exercise 1 of Chapter 20 that discuss free information. Using the criteria in this chapter for evaluating electronic sources, judge each of those sites. Select three that you believe are most trustworthy, and write a paragraph summarizing their arguments and recommending them to an audience unfamiliar with the debate.

chapter twenty-two

Documenting Sources

What does documenting sources have to do with argument? First, the sources themselves form part of the argument, showing that a writer has done some homework, knows what others have said about the topic, and understands how to use these sources as support for a claim. The list of works cited or references makes an argument, saying, perhaps, "Look at how thoroughly this essay has been researched" or "Note how up-to-date I am!" Even the style of documentation makes an argument, though in a very subtle way. You will note in the instructions that follow, for example, that for a print source the Modern Language Association (MLA) style for a list of works cited requires putting the date of publication at or near the end of an entry, whereas the American Psychological Association (APA) style for a list of references involves putting the date near the beginning. (The exercise at the end of this chapter asks you to consider what argument this difference represents.) And when a documentation style calls for listing only the first author and et al. in citing works by multiple authors, it is subtly arguing that only the first author really matters — or at least that acknowledging the others is less important than keeping citations brief. Pay attention to the fine points of documentation and documentation style, always asking what these elements add (or do not add) to your arguments.

MLA STYLE

Documentation styles vary from discipline to discipline, with different formats favored in the social sciences and the natural sciences, for example. Widely used in fields in the humanities, the MLA style is fully described in the *MLA Handbook for Writers of Research Papers* (5th edition, 1999) and the *MLA Style Manual and Guide to Scholarly Publishing* (2nd edition, 1998). In this discussion, we provide guidelines drawn from the *MLA Handbook* for in-text citations, notes, and entries in the list of works cited.

In-Text Citations

The MLA style calls for in-text citations in the body of an argument to document sources of quotations, paraphrases, summaries, and so on. Keep an in-text citation short, but include enough information for readers to locate the source in the list of works cited. Place the citation as near to the relevant material as possible without disrupting the flow of the sentence, as in the following examples.

1. Author Named in a Signal Phrase

Ordinarily, use the author's name in a signal phrase — to introduce the material — and cite the page number(s) in parentheses.

> Loomba argues that Caliban's "political colour" (emphasis hers) is black, given his stage representations, which have varied from animalistic to a kind of missing link (143).

2. Author Named in Parentheses

When you don't mention the author in a signal phrase, include the author's last name before the page number(s) in the parentheses.

> Renaissance visions of "other" worlds, particularly in plays and travel narratives, often accentuated the differences of the Other even when striking similarities to the English existed (Bartels 434).

3. Two or Three Authors

Use all authors' last names.

> Kiniry and Rose maintain that a curriculum focused on critical thinking and writing strategies will help students improve their academic writing abilities (v).

4. Four or More Authors

The MLA allows you to use all authors' last names, or to use only the first author's name with *et al.* (in regular type, not underlined or italicized). Although either format is acceptable when applied consistently throughout a paper, in an argument it may be better to name all authors who contributed to the work.

> Similarly, as Goldberger, Tarule, Clinchy, and Belenky note, their new book builds on their collaborative experiences (xii).

5. Organization as Author

Give the full name of a corporate author if it is brief or a shortened form if it is long.

> Clements sold Nancy to Henry Waring, another Catholic slaveholder (Montgomery County 77).

6. Unknown Author

Use the full title of the work if it is brief or a shortened form if it is long.

> Hollywood executives insisted that the second kiss between the men be cut from the film ("The New Wave" 53).

7. Author of Two or More Works

When you use two or more works by the same author, include the title of the work or a shortened version of it in the citation.

> Green challenges the conception of blacks that the whites in Wellington want to force on him when he declares "I ain't no w'ite folks' nigger, I ain'. I don' call no man 'marster'" (qtd. in Chesnutt, Marrow of Tradition 304).

8. Authors with the Same Last Name

When you use works by two or more authors with the same last name, include each author's first initial in the citation.

> Father Divine's teachings focused on eternal life, salvation, and socio-economic progress (R. Washington 17).

9. Multivolume Work

Note the volume number first and then the page number(s), with a colon and one space between them.

> Aristotle's "On Plants" is now available in a new translation, edited by Barnes (2: 1252).

10. Literary Work

Because literary works are often available in many different editions, you need to include enough information for readers to locate the passage in any edition. For a prose work such as a novel or play, first cite the page number from the edition you used, followed by a semicolon; then indicate the part or chapter number (114; *ch.* 3) or act or scene in a play (42; *sc.* 2). For verse plays, omit the page number and give instead the act, scene, and line numbers, separated by periods.

> Before he takes his own life, Othello says he is "one that loved not wisely but too well" (5.2.348).

For a poem, cite the stanza and line numbers. If the poem has only line numbers, use the word *line(s)* in the first reference *(lines 33–34)*.

> Looking back, Lenore Keeshig-Tobias recalls growing up on the reserve, "thinking it was the most/beautiful place in the world" (l.2-3).

11. Works in an Anthology

For an essay, short story, or other short work within an anthology, use the name of the author of the work, not the editor of the anthology; but use the page number(s) from the anthology.

> In the end, if the black artist accepts any duties at all, that duty is to express the beauty of blackness (Hughes 1271).

12. Bible

Identify quotations by chapter and verse (*John* 3.16). Spell out the names of books mentioned in your text. In a parenthetical citation, use standard scholarly abbreviations for books of the Bible with five or more letters (*Gen.* for *Genesis*).

13. Indirect Source

Use the abbreviation *qtd. in* to indicate that what you are quoting or paraphrasing is quoted (as part of a conversation, interview, letter, or excerpt) in the source you are using.

> As Catherine Belsey states, "to speak is to have access to the language which defines, delimits and locates power" (qtd. in Bartels 453).

14. Two or More Sources in the Same Citation

Separate the information for each source with a semicolon.

> Adefunmi was able to patch up the subsequent holes left in worship by substituting various Yoruba, Dahomean, or Fon customs made available to him through research (Brandon 115-17; Hunt 27).

15. Entire Work or One-Page Article

Include the citation in the text without any page numbers or parentheses.

> The relationship between revolutionary innocence and the preservation of an oppressive post-revolutionary regime is one theme Milan Kundera explores in The Book of Laughter and Forgetting.

16. Work without Page Numbers

If the work is not paginated, include instead the section (*sec.*), part (*pt.*), or paragraph (*par.*) numbers, if available.

Zora Neale Hurston is one of the great anthropologists of the twentieth century, according to Kip Hinton (par. 2).

17. Other Nonprint Source

Give enough information in a signal phrase or parenthetical citation for readers to locate the source in the list of works cited. Usually give the author or title under which you list the source.

> In his film version of Hamlet, Zefferelli highlights the sexual tension between the prince and his mother.

Explanatory and Bibliographic Notes

The MLA recommends using explanatory notes for information or commentary that does not readily fit into your text but is needed for clarification, further explanation, or justification. In addition, the MLA allows bibliographic notes for information about a source. Use superscript numbers in your text at the end of a sentence to refer readers to the notes, which usually appear as endnotes (with the heading Notes) on a separate page before the list of works cited. Indent the first line of each note five spaces, and double-space all entries.

Text with Superscript Indicating a Note

> Heilbrun describes her decision to choose life over death and notes her affinity to artist Käthe Kollwitz's love of work.[2]

Note

> [2]Kollwitz, like Heilbrun, identified work as the essence of life: "The readiness forms in waves inside myself," and "I need only be on the alert [. . .]" (10).

List of Works Cited

A list of works cited is an alphabetical listing of the sources you cite in your essay. The list appears on a separate page at the end of your argument, after any notes, with the heading Works Cited. (If you are asked to list everything you have read as background, call the list Works Consulted.)

The first line of each entry should align on the left; subsequent lines indent one-half inch or five spaces. Double-space.

Books

The basic information for a book includes three elements, each followed by a period: the author's name, last name first; the title and subtitle, underlined or (if your instructor permits) italicized; and the publication information, including the city, a shortened form of the publisher's name, and the date. For a book with multiple authors, only the first author's name is inverted.

1. One Author

Jacobs, Jane. The Death and Life of Great American Cities. New York: Vintage, 1992.

2. Two or More Authors

Arbib, Michael, and Mary Hesse. The Construction of Reality. Cambridge: Cambridge UP, 1986.

3. Organization as Author

American Cancer Society. The Dangers of Smoking, the Benefits of Quitting. New York: Amer. Cancer Soc., 1972.

4. Unknown Author

The Spanish Republic. London: Eyre, 1933.

5. Two or More Books by the Same Author

List the works alphabetically by title.

Gaines, Ernest. A Gathering of Old Men. New York: Viking, 1984.
---. A Lesson before Dying. New York: Vintage, 1994.

6. Editor

Rorty, Amelie Oksenberg, ed. Essays on Aristotle's Poetics. Princeton: Princeton UP, 1992.

7. Author and Editor

Shakespeare, William. The Tempest. Ed. Frank Kermode. London:
Routledge, 1994.

8. Selection in an Anthology or Chapter in an Edited Book

Brown, Paul. "'This thing of darkness I acknowledge mine': The Tempest
and the Discourse of Colonialism." Political Shakespeare: Essays
in Cultural Materialism. Ed. Jonathan Dillimore and Alan Sinfield.
Ithaca: Cornell UP, 1985. 48-71.

9. Two or More Works from the Same Anthology

Gates, Henry Louis, Jr., and Nellie McKay, eds. The Norton Anthology of
African American Literature. New York: Norton, 1997.
Neal, Larry. "The Black Arts Movement." Gates and McKay 1960-1972.
Karenga, Maulana. "Black Art: Mute Matter Given Force and Function."
Gates and McKay 1973-1977.

10. Translation

Kundera, Milan. The Book of Laughter and Forgetting. Trans. Michael
Henry Haim. New York: Penguin, 1984.

11. Edition Other than the First

Stoessinger, John G. Why Nations Go to War. 6th ed. New York: St.
Martin's, 1993.

12. One Volume of a Multivolume Work

Byron, Lord George. Byron's Letters and Journals. Ed. Leslie A.
Marchand. Vol. 2. London: J. Murray, 1973-1982.

13. Two or More Volumes of a Multivolume Work

Byron, Lord George. Byron's Letters and Journals. Ed. Leslie A.
Marchand. 12 vols. London: J. Murray, 1973-1982.

14. Preface, Foreword, Introduction, or Afterword

Walker, Alexander. Introduction. Film Censorship. By Guy Phelps.
London: Gollancz, 1975. vii-xi.

15. Article in a Reference Work

"Carolina Campaign." The Columbia Encyclopedia. 5th ed. 1993.

16. Book That Is Part of a Series

Shakespeare, William. Othello. Ed. M. R. Ridley. The Arden Shakespeare
Ser. 3. London: Routledge, 1993.

17. Government Document

United States. Cong. House Committee on the Judiciary. Impeachment of
the President. 40th Cong., 1st sess. H. Rept. 7, 1867. Washington:
GPO, 1867.

18. Pamphlet

An Answer to the President's Message to the Fiftieth Congress.
Philadelphia: Manufacturer's Club of Philadelphia, 1887.

19. Published Proceedings of a Conference

Edwards, Ron, ed. Proceedings of the Third National Folklore
Conference. Canberra, Austral.: Australian Folk Trust, 1988.

20. Title within a Title

Tauernier-Courbin, Jacqueline. Ernest Hemingway's A Moveable Feast:
The Making of a Myth. Boston: Northeastern UP, 1991.

Periodicals

The basic entry for a periodical includes the following three elements,
separated by periods: the author's name, last name first; the article title,
in quotation marks; and the publication information, including the periodical title (underlined or italicized), the volume and issue numbers (if
any), the date of publication, and the page number(s). For works with multiple authors, only the first author's name is inverted. Note, too, that the
period following the article title goes *inside* the closing quotation mark.

21. Article in a Journal Paginated by Volume

Wood, Winifred J. "Double Desire: Overlapping Discourses in a Film
Writing Course." College English 60 (1998): 278-300.

22. Article in a Journal Paginated by Issue

Radavich, David. "Man among Men: David Mamet's Homosocial Order."
American Drama 1.1 (1991): 46-66.

23. Article in a Monthly Magazine

Heartney, Eleanor. "Portrait of a Decade." Art in America Oct. 1997:
102-05.

24. Article in a Newspaper

Mitchell, Alison. "Campaign Finance Bill Approaches Deadlock." New
York Times 26 Feb. 1998, late ed.: A16.

25. Editorial or Letter to Editor

Danto, Arthur. "'Elitism' and the N.E.A." Editorial. The Nation 17 Nov.
1997: 6-7.

26. Unsigned Article

"Court Rejects the Sale of Medical Marijuana." New York Times 26 Feb.
1998, late ed.: A21.

27. Review

Partner, Peter. "The Dangers of Divinity." Rev. of The Shape of the Holy:
Early Islamic Jerusalem, by Oleg Grabar. New York Review of
Books 5 Feb. 1998: 27-28.

Electronic Sources

Most of the following models are based on the MLA's guidelines for
citing electronic sources in the MLA Handbook (5th edition, 1999) as well as
on up-to-date information available at <http://www.mla.org/style/
sources.htm>. Formats not covered by the MLA are based on Andrew
Harnack and Eugene Kleppinger, Online! A Reference Guide to Using Internet
Sources (2000 edition).

The MLA requires that URLs be enclosed in angle brackets. Also, if a
URL will not all fit on one line, it should be broken only after the second
slash in the opening protocol http:// or after a slash later in the URL, with
no hyphen at the line break.

The basic MLA entry for most electronic sources should include the following elements:

- name of the author, editor, or compiler
- title of the work, document, or posting
- date of electronic publication or last update, if available
- date of access
- URL in angle brackets

28. *CD-ROM, Diskette, or Magnetic Tape, Single Issue*

McPherson, James M., ed. The American Heritage New History of the Civil War. CD-ROM. New York: Viking, 1996.

29. *Periodically Revised CD-ROM*

Include the author's name; publication information for the print version of the text (including its title and date of publication); the title of the database; the medium (CD-ROM); the name of the company producing it; and the electronic publication date (month and year, if possible).

Heyman, Steven. "The Dangerously Exciting Client." Psychotherapy Patient 9.1 (1994): 37-46. PsycLIT. CD-ROM. SilverPlatter. Nov. 1996.

30. *Scholarly Project or Reference Database*

Include the title of the project or database, underlined or italicized; the name of the editor, if any, preceded by *Ed.*; the version number, if relevant and not part of the title; the date of electronic publication or of the latest update; the name of any sponsoring institution or organization; the date of access; and the URL.

The Orlando Project: An Integrated History of Women's Writing in the British Isles. 1997. U of Alberta. 1 Mar. 2000 <http://www.ualberta.ca/ORLANDO/>.

31. *Professional or Personal Web Site*

Include the name of the person who created the site, if relevant; the title of the site (underlined) or (if there is no title) a description such as *Home page*; the name of any institution or organization associated with the site; the date of access; and the URL.

Classical Myth: The Ancient Sources. 24 June 1999. Dept. of Greek and
Roman Studies, U of Victoria. 1 Mar. 2000 <http://web.uvic.ca/
grs/bowman/myth/index.html>.

Bays, Carter L. Home page. 3 Jan. 1998. 1 Mar. 2000 <http://
www.con.wesleyan.edu/~cbays/homepage.html>.

32. Online Book

Begin with the name of the author—or, if only an editor, a compiler, or a
translator is identified, the name of that person followed by *ed., comp.,* or
trans. Then give the title and the name of any editor, compiler, or translator not listed earlier, preceded by *Ed., Comp.,* or *Trans.* If the online version
of the text has not been published before, give the date of electronic
publication and the name of any sponsoring institution or organization.
Then give any publication information (city, publisher, and/or year) for
the original print version that is given in the source; the date of access;
and the URL.

Maugham, W. Somerset. Of Human Bondage. London: Macmillan, 1972.
1 Mar. 2000 <http://www.bibliomania.com/Fiction/Maugham/
Human/index.html>.

For a poem, an essay, or other short work within an online book, include
its title after the author's name. Give the URL of the short work, not of the
book, if they differ.

Dickinson, Emily, "The Grass." Poems: Emily Dickinson. Boston: Roberts
Brothers, 1891. Humanities Text Initiative American Verse
Collection. Ed. Nancy Kushigian. 1995. U of Michigan.
1 Mar. 2000 <http://www.hti.umich.edu/bin/
amv-idx.pl?type=HTML&rgn=DIV1&byte=9559331>.

33. Article in an Online Periodical

Follow the formats for citing articles in print periodicals, but adapt them
as necessary to the online medium. Include the page numbers of the article or the total number of pages, paragraphs, parts, or other numbered
sections, if any; the date of access; and the URL.

White, Richard B. "The Mahar Movement's Military Component." South
Asia Graduate Research Journal 1.1 (May 1994). 1 Mar. 2000
<http://asnic.utexas.edu/asnic/sagar/spring.1994/
richard.white.art.html>.

Gwande, Atul. "Drowsy Docs." <u>Slate</u> 9 Oct. 1997. 1 Mar. 2000
<http://www.slate.com/MedicalExaminer/97-10-09/
MedicalExaminer.asp>.

34. Listserv Posting

Begin with the author's name, the title of the posting, and the description
Online posting. Then give the date of the posting, the name of the listserv,
the date of access, and either the URL of the listserv or (preferably) the
URL of an archival version of the posting. If a URL is unavailable, give the
email address of the list moderator.

Chagall, Nancy. "Web Publishing and Censorship." Online posting. 2 Feb.
1997. ACW: Alliance for Computers and Writing Discussion List.
10 Oct. 1997 <http://english.ttu.edu/acw-1/archive.htm>.

35. Newsgroup Posting

Give the author's name and the title of the posting followed by *Online posting,* the date of the posting, and the date of access. Then give the name of
the newsgroup with the prefix *news:.*

Martin, Jerry. "The IRA & Sinn Fein." Online posting. 31 Mar. 1998.
31 Mar. 1998 <news:soc.culture.irish>.

36. Email Message

Include the writer's name, the subject line, the description *Email to the
author* or *Email to [the recipient's name],* and the date of the message.

DeLaRosa, Alexis. "Do This." Email to the author. 25 May 1997.

37. Synchronous Communication (MOO, MUD, or IRC)

Include the name of any specific speaker(s) you are citing; a description
of the event; its date; the name of the forum; the date of access; and the
URL of the posting (with the prefix *telnet:*) or (preferably) of an archival
version.

Patuto, Jeremy, Simon Fennel, and James Goss. The Mytilene debate.
9 May 1996. MiamiMOO. 28 Mar. 1998 <http://
moo.cas.muohio.edu/cgi-bin/moo?look+4085>.

38. Online Interview, Work of Art, or Film

Follow the general guidelines for the print version of the source, but also include information on the electronic medium, such as publication information for a CD-ROM or the date of electronic publication, the date of access, and the URL for a Web site.

> Dyson, Esther. Interview. Hotseat. 23 May 1997. 1 Mar. 2000
>   <http://www.hotwired.com/packet/hotseat/97/20/index4a.html>.
> Aleni, Guilio. K'un-yu t'u-shu. ca. 1620. Vatican, Rome. 28 Mar. 1998
>   <http://www.ncsa.uiuc.edu/SDG/Experimental/vatican.exhibit/
>   exhibit/full-images/i-rome-to-china/china02.gif>.
> John Woo, dir. Face Off. 1997. Hollywood.com. 8 Mar. 2000
>   <http://www.hollywood.com/multimedia/movies/faceoff/trailer/
>   mmindex.html>.

39. FTP (File Transfer Protocol), Telnet, or Gopher Site

Substitute FTP, Telnet, or Gopher for http at the beginning of the URL.

> Korn, Peter. "How Much Does Breast Cancer Really Cost?" Self Oct.
>   1994. 5 May 1997 <gopher://nysernet.org:70/00/BCTC/
>   Sources/SELF/94/how-much>.

Other Sources

40. Unpublished Dissertation

> West, Susan. "From Owning to Owning Up: 'Authorial' Rights and
>   Rhetorical Responsibilities." Diss. Ohio State U, 1996.

41. Published Dissertation

> Baum, Bernard. Decentralization of Authority in a Bureaucracy. Diss. U of
>   Chicago. Englewood Cliffs: Prentice-Hall, 1961.

42. Article from a Microform

> Sharpe, Lora. "A Quilter's Tribute." Boston Globe 25 Mar. 1989:
>   13. Newsbank: Social Relations 12 (1989): fiche 6, grids B4-6.

43. Personal Interview

> Harding, Sandra. Telephone interview. 14 May 2000.

44. Letter

Jacobs, Harriet. "Letter to Amy Post." 4 Apr. 1853. Incidents in the Life of a Slave Girl. Ed. Jean Fagan Yellin. Cambridge: Harvard UP, 1987. 234-35.

45. Film

He Got Game. Dir. Spike Lee. Perf. Denzel Washington and Ray Allen. Touchstone, 1998.

46. Television or Radio Program

King of the Hill. Writ. Jim Dauterive. Perf. Mike Judge and Pamela Seagall. FOX, New York. 29 Mar. 1998.

47. Sound Recording

Fugees. "Ready or Not." The Score. Sony, 1996.

48. Lecture or Speech

Higginbotham, Leon. "Baccalaureate Address." Wesleyan U, Middletown. 26 May 1996.

49. Performance

Freak. By John Leguizamo. Dir. David Bar Katz. Cort Theater, New York. 7 Mar. 1998.

50. Map or Chart

The Political and Physical World. Map. Washington: Natl. Geographic, 1975.

51. Cartoon

Cheney, Tom. Cartoon. New Yorker 16 Mar. 1998: 49.

52. Advertisement

Toyota. Advertisement. Discover Mar. 1998: 7.

APA STYLE

The *Publication Manual of the American Psychological Association* (4th edition, 1994) provides comprehensive advice to student and professional writers in the social sciences. Here we draw on the *Publication Manual*'s guidelines to provide an overview of APA style for in-text citations, content notes, and entries in the list of references.

In-Text Citations

The APA style calls for in-text citations in the body of an argument to document sources of quotations, paraphrases, summaries, and so on. These in-text citations correspond to full bibliographic entries in the list of references at the end of the text.

1. Author Named in a Signal Phrase

Generally, use the author's name in a signal phrase to introduce the cited material, and place the date, in parentheses, immediately after the author's name. For a quotation, the page number, preceded by *p.*, appears in parentheses after the quotation. For electronic texts or other works without page numbers, paragraph numbers may be used instead. For a long, set-off quotation, position the page reference in parentheses two spaces after the punctuation at the end of the quotation.

> According to Brandon (1993), Adefunmi opposed all forms of racism and believed that black nationalism should not be a destructive force.

2. Author Named in Parentheses

When you do not mention the author in a signal phrase, give the name and the date, separated by a comma, in parentheses at the end of the cited material.

> Adefunmi opposed all forms of racism and believed that black nationalism should not be a destructive force (Brandon, 1993).

3. Two Authors

Use both names in all citations. Use *and* in a signal phrase, but use an ampersand (&) in parentheses.

Associated with purity and wisdom, Obatala is the creator of human beings, whom he is said to have formed out of clay (Edwards & Mason, 1985).

4. Three to Five Authors

List all the authors' names for the first reference. In subsequent references, use just the first author's name followed by *et al.* (in regular type, not underlined or italicized).

Lenhoff, Wang, Greenberg, and Bellugi (1997) cite tests that indicate that segments of the left brain hemisphere are not affected by Williams syndrome whereas the right hemisphere is significantly affected.

Shackelford drew on the study by Lenhoff et al. (1997).

5. Six or More Authors

Use only the first author's name and *et al.* (in regular type, not underlined or italicized) in *every* citation, including the first.

As Flower et al. (1990) demonstrate, reading and writing involve both cognitive and social processes.

6. Organization as Author

If the name of an organization or a corporation is long, spell it out the first time, followed by an abbreviation in brackets. In later citations, use the abbreviation only.

First Citation.   (Federal Bureau of Investigation [FBI], 1952)
Subsequent Citations.   (FBI, 1952)

7. Unknown Author

Use the title or its first few words in a signal phrase or in parentheses.

These ideas paralleled the tenets of New Thought and provided a bridge for ideological compatibility between the Bishop and the Fairmount Avenue Ministry (New Amsterdam News, 1932).

8. Authors with the Same Last Name

If your list of references includes works by different authors with the same last name, include the authors' initials in each citation.

C. McKay (1935) claimed that no men lived in the household, though at least one man lived in the Brooklyn collective.

9. Two or More Sources in the Same Citation

List sources by the same author chronologically by publication year. List sources by different authors in alphabetical order by the authors' last names, separated by semicolons.

While traditional forms of argument are warlike and agonistic, alternative models do exist (Foss & Foss, 1997; Makau, 1999).

10. Specific Parts of a Source

Use abbreviations (*chap., p.,* and so on) in a parenthetical citation to name the part of a work you are citing.

Bellah (1992, chap. 6) described the birth of New American myths.

11. Personal Communication

Cite any personal letters, email messages, electronic bulletin-board correspondence, telephone conversations, or personal interviews by giving the person's initial(s) and last name, the identification *personal communication,* and the date.

V. Sweete (personal communication, March 7, 1983) supported these claims.

Content Notes

The APA recommends using content notes for material that will expand or supplement your argument but otherwise would interrupt the text. Indicate such notes in your text by inserting superscript numerals. Type the notes themselves on a separate page headed *Footnotes,* centered at the top of the page. Double-space all entries. Indent the first line of each note five to seven spaces, and begin subsequent lines at the left margin:

Text with Superscript Indicating a Note

Data related to children's preferences in books were instrumental in designing the questionnaire.[1]

Note

[1] Rudine Sims Bishop and members of the Reading Readiness Research Group provided helpful data.

List of References

The alphabetical list of sources cited in your text is called *References*. (If your instructor asks you to list everything you have read as background—not just the sources you cite—call the list *Bibliography*.) The list of references appears on a separate page at the end of your paper.

For print sources, the APA style specifies the treatment and placement of four basic elements—author, publication date, title, and publication information.

- List all authors with last name first, and use only initials for first and middle names. Separate the names of multiple authors with commas, and use an ampersand (&) before the last author's name.

- Enclose the publication date in parentheses. Use only the year for books and journals; use the year, a comma, and the month or month and day for magazines. Do not abbreviate.

- Underline or italicize titles and subtitles of books and periodicals. Do not enclose titles of articles in quotation marks. For books and articles, capitalize only the first word of the title and subtitle and any proper nouns or proper adjectives. Capitalize all major words in a periodical title.

- For a book, list the city of publication (and the country or postal abbreviation for the state if the city is unfamiliar) and the publisher's name, dropping *Inc., Co.,* or *Publishers*. For a periodical, follow the periodical title with a comma, the volume number (underlined or italicized), the issue number (if provided) in parentheses and followed by a comma, and the inclusive page numbers of the article. For newspaper articles and for articles or chapters in books, include the abbreviation *p.* ("page") or *pp.* ("pages").

The following APA-style examples appear double-spaced and in a "hanging indent" format, in which the first line aligns on the left and the subsequent lines indent one-half inch or five spaces.

Books

1. One Author

Jung, C. (1968). Analytical psychology: Its theory and practice. London: Routledge and K. Paul.

2. Two or More Authors

Steininger, M., Newell, J. D., & Garcia, L. (1984). Ethical issues in psychology. Homewood, IL: Dow Jones-Irwin.

3. Organization as Author

Use the word *Author* as the publisher when the organization is both the author and the publisher.

Pennsylvania Mental Health, Inc. (1960). Mental health education: A critique. Philadelphia: Author.

4. Unknown Author

National Geographic atlas of the world. (1996). Washington, DC: National Geographic Society.

5. Two or More Works by the Same Author

List the works in chronological order of publication. Repeat the author's name in each entry.

Rose, M. (1984). Writer's block: The cognitive dimension. Carbondale, IL: Southern Illinois University Press.

Rose, M. (1995). Possible lives: The promise of public education in America. Boston: Houghton Mifflin.

6. Editor

Greenbaum, S. (Ed.). (1977). Acceptability in language. The Hague, Netherlands: Mouton.

7. Selection in a Book with an Editor

Ong, W. J. (1988). Literacy and orality in our times. In G. Tate & E. P. J. Corbett (Eds.), The writing teacher's sourcebook (pp. 37-46). New York: Oxford University Press.

8. Translation

Konig, R. (1973). A la mode: On the social psychology of fashion. (F. Bradley, Trans.). New York: Seabury Press.

9. Edition Other than the First

Wrightsman, L. (1992). Assumptions about human nature: Implications for researchers and practitioners (2nd ed.). Newbury Park, CA: Sage.

10. One Volume of a Multivolume Work

Will, J. S. (1921). Protestantism in France (Vol. 2). Toronto: University of Toronto Press.

11. Article in a Reference Work

Chernow, B., & Vattasi, G. (Eds.). (1993). Psychomimetic drug. In The Columbia encyclopedia (5th ed., p. 2238). New York: Columbia University Press.

If no author is listed, begin with the title.

12. Republication

Sharp, C. (1978). History of Hartlepool. Hartlepool, UK: Hartlepool Borough Council. (Original work published 1816)

13. Government Document

U.S. Bureau of the Census. (1976). Census of population and housing 1970. Washington, DC: U.S. Government Printing Office.

Periodicals

14. Article in a Journal Paginated by Volume

Shuy, R. (1981). A holistic view of language. Research in the Teaching of English, 15, 110-111.

15. Article in a Journal Paginated by Issue

Rudavich, D. (1991). Man among men: David Mamet's homosocial order. American Drama, 1(1), 46-66.

16. Article in a Monthly Magazine

Cartmill, M. (1998, March). Oppressed by evolution. Discover, 78-83.

17. Article in a Newspaper

Glasser, R. J. (1998, March 4). As life ebbs, so does time to elect comforts of hospice. The New York Times, pp. A1, A8.

18. Editorial or Letter to the Editor

Seidel, M. C. (1998, January). Frankreich uber alles [Letter to the editor]. Harper's, 4.

19. Unsigned Article

Guidelines issued on assisted suicide. (1998, March 4). The New York Times, p. A15.

20. Review

Richardson, S. (1998, February). [Review of the book The Secret Family]. Discover, 88.

21. Published Interview

Shor, I. (1997). [Interview with A. Greenbaum]. Writing on the Edge, 8(2), 7-20.

Electronic Sources

Most of the following models are based on the APA's updated guidelines for citing electronic sources posted at <http://www.apa.org/journals/webref.html> as well as the APA Publication Manual (4th edition). Formats not covered by the APA guidelines are based on Online! A Reference Guide to Using Internet Sources (2000 edition), by Andrew Harnack and Eugene Kleppinger.

The basic APA entry for most electronic sources should include the following elements:

- name of the author, editor, or compiler
- date of electronic publication or most recent update
- title of the work, document, or posting

- date of access, including a retrieval date statement followed by a colon
- URL, with no angle brackets and no closing punctuation

22. *CD-ROM Abstract*

Natchez, G. (1987). Frida Kahlo and Diego Rivera: The transformation of catastrophe to creativity. Psychotherapy Patient, 8, 153-174. Abstract retrieved from PsycLIT database (SilverPlatter File, CD-ROM 1999 release, Item 76-11344)

23. *Material from an Information Service or Online Database*

Belenky, M. F. (1984). The role of deafness in the moral development of hearing impaired children. In A. Areson & J. De Caro (Eds.), Teaching, learning and development. Rochester, NY: National Institute for the Deaf. Retrieved January 20, 2000 from ERIC online database (No. ED 248 646).

24. *Material from a Database Accessed via the Web*

Pryor, T., & Wiederman, M. W. (1998). Personality features and expressed concerns of adolescents with eating disorders. Adolesence, 33, 291-301. Retrieved February 7, 2000 from Electric Library database on the World Wide Web: http://www.elibrary.com

25. *Software or Computer Program*

Lotus Organizer (Version 2.1) [Computer software]. (1996). Cambridge, MA: Lotus Development Corp.

26. *World Wide Web Site*

After the document title, include the title of the complete work or site, if applicable, underlined or italicized.

The Feminist Majority. (1995). Athletics in the lives of women and girls. Empowering women in sports. Retrieved March 2, 2000 from the World Wide Web: http://www.feminist.org/research/sports2.html

27. FTP Site

Instead of the URL, you can use the abbreviation *ftp://* followed by the address of the FTP site and the full path to follow to find the document, with no closing punctuation.

> Altar, T. W. (1993). Vitamin B_{12} and vegans. Retrieved May 28, 1996
> from the World Wide Web: ftp://wiretap.spies.com/library
> /article/food/b12.txt

28. Telnet Site

After the title of the document, include the title of the full work, if applicable, underlined or italicized and followed by a period. Then include the date of access, the complete telnet address, and directions to access the document.

> Aquatic Conservation Network. (n.d.). About the aquatic conservation
> network. National capital freenet. Retrieved May 28, 1996 from
> Freenet: telnet freenet.carleton.ca login as guest, go acn, press 1

29. Gopher Site

Include any print publication information, underlined or italicized where appropriate. Then give the date of retrieval and the gopher address.

> Korn, P. (1994, October). How much does breast cancer really cost? Self.
> Retrieved May 5, 1997: gopher://nysernet.org:70/00/BCIC/Sources
> /SELF/94/how-much

30. Listserv Posting

Include the author's name, the date and subject line of the posting, the date of access, and the listserv address.

> Gill, D. (1996, January 9). Environmental archaeology in the Aegean.
> Retrieved March 28, 1998 from the listserv: aegeanet@rome
> .classics.lsa.umich.edu

31. Newsgroup Posting

Include the author's name, the date and subject line of the posting, the access date, and the name of the newsgroup.

Sand, P. (1996, April 20). Java disabled by default in Linux Netscape. Retrieved May 10, 1996, from the newsgroup: Keokuk.unh.edu

32. Email Message

The APA discourages including email messages in a list of references and suggests citing them as personal communications in your text.

33. Synchronous Communication (MOO, MUD, and IRC)

Provide the name(s) of the speaker(s), if known, or the name of the site; the date of the event, in parentheses; its title, if appropriate; the date of retrieval; and the URL.

Patuto, J., Fennel, S., & Goss, J. (1996, May 9). The Mytilene debate. Retrieved March 29, 1998 from the World Wide Web: http://moo.cas.muohio.edu/cgi-vin/moo?look+4085

Other Sources

34. Technical or Research Reports and Working Papers

Synott, T. J. (1979). Impact of human activities: IPAL technical reports (Tech. Rep. No. D2a, D2b, and D2c). Nairobi, Kenya: Integrated Project in Arid Lands, University of Nairobi EP.

35. Unpublished Paper Presented at a Meeting or Symposium

Welch, K. (1998, April). Electric rhetoric and screen literacy. Paper presented at the Conference on College Composition and Communication, Chicago.

36. Unpublished Dissertation

Barnett, T. (1997). Communities in conflict: Composition, racial discourse, and the 60s revolution. Unpublished doctoral dissertation, Ohio State University, Columbus.

37. Poster Presentation

Mensching, G. (1992, May). A simple, effective one-shot for disinterested students. Poster session presented at the National LOEX Library Instruction Conference, Ann Arbor, MI.

38. Film or Videotape

Stone, Oliver. (Director). (1995). <u>Natural born killers</u> [Film]. Los Angeles: Warner Brothers.

39. Television Series, Single Episode

Begin with the names of the script writer(s), and give the name of the director, in parentheses, after the episode title.

Nikulina, T. (1998, April 16). Top gun over Moscow (N. Schulz, Director). In P. Apsell (Executive Producer), <u>Nova.</u> New York: WNET.

40. Sound Recording

For recordings by an artist other than the writer, begin with the writer's name, followed by the date of copyright. Give the recording date if it is different from the copyright date.

Ivey, A., Jr., & Sall, R. (1995). Rollin' with my homies [Recorded by Coolio]. On <u>Clueless</u> soundtrack [CD]. Hollywood, CA: Capitol Records.

RESPOND●

1. The MLA and APA styles differ in several important ways, both for in-text citations and for lists of sources. You've probably noticed a few: the APA lowercases most words in titles and lists the publication date right after the author's name, whereas the MLA capitalizes most words and puts the publication date at the end of the works-cited entry. More interesting than the details, though, is the reasoning behind the differences. Placing the publication date near the front of a citation, for instance, reveals a special concern for that information in the APA style. Similarly, the MLA's decision to capitalize titles is not arbitrary: that style is preferred in the humanities for a reason.

   Find as many consistent differences between the MLA and APA styles as you can. Then, for each difference, try to discover the reasons these groups organize or present information in that way. The MLA and APA style manuals themselves may be of help. You might also begin by determining which academic disciplines subscribe to the APA style and which to the MLA.

GLOSSARY

accidental condition in a definition, an element that helps to explain what is being defined but is not essential to it. An accidental condition in defining a bird might be "ability to fly" because most, but not all, birds can fly. (See also *essential condition* and *sufficient condition*.)

***ad hominem* argument** a fallacy of argument in which a writer's claim is answered by irrelevant attacks on his or her character.

analogy an extended comparison between something unfamiliar and something more familiar for the purpose of illuminating or dramatizing the unfamiliar. An analogy might, for example, compare nuclear fission (relatively unfamiliar) to an opening break in pool or billiards (more familiar).

anaphora a figure of speech involving repetition, particularly of the same word at the beginning of several clauses.

antithesis the use of parallel structures to call attention to contrasts or opposites, as in *Some like it hot; some like it cold.*

antonomasia use of a title, epithet, or description in place of a name, as in *Your Honor* for *Judge.*

argument (1) a spoken, written, or visual text that expresses a point of view; (2) the use of evidence and reason to discover some version of the truth, as distinct from *persuasion,* the attempt to change someone else's point of view.

artistic appeal support for an argument that a writer creates based on principles of reason and shared knowledge rather than on facts and evidence. (See also *inartistic appeal*.)

assumption a belief regarded as true, upon which other claims are based.

assumption, cultural a belief regarded as true or commonsensical within a particular culture, such as the belief in individual freedom in American culture.

audience the person or persons to whom an argument is directed.

authority the quality conveyed by a writer who is knowledgeable about his or her subject and confident in that knowledge.

background the information a writer provides to create the context for an argument.

backing in Toulmin argument, the evidence provided to support a *warrant*.

bandwagon appeal a fallacy of argument in which a course of action is recommended on the grounds that everyone else is following it.

begging the question a fallacy of argument in which a claim is based on the very grounds that are in doubt or dispute: *Rita can't be the bicycle thief; she's never stolen anything.*

ceremonial argument an argument that deals with current values and addresses questions of praise and blame. Also called *epideictic,* ceremonial arguments include eulogies and graduation speeches.

character, appeal based on a strategy in which a writer presents an authoritative or credible self-image in order to dispose an audience well toward a claim.

claim a statement that asserts a belief or truth. In arguments, most claims require supporting evidence. The claim is a key component in Toulmin argument.

connecting (1) identifying with a writer or reader; or (2) crafting an argument to emphasize where writers and audiences share interests, concerns, or experiences.

connotation the suggestions or associations that surround most words and extend beyond their literal meaning, creating associational effects. *Slender* and *skinny* have similar meanings, for example, but carry different connotations, the former more positive than the latter.

context the entire situation in which a piece of writing takes place, including the writer's purpose(s) for writing; the intended audience; the time and place of writing; the institutional, social, personal, and other influences on the piece of writing; the material conditions of writing (whether it is, for instance, online or on paper, in handwriting or print); and the writer's attitude toward the subject and the audience.

conviction the belief that a claim or course of action is true or reasonable. In a proposal argument, a writer must move an audience beyond conviction to action.

credibility an impression of integrity, honesty, and trustworthiness conveyed by a writer in an argument.

criterion in evaluative arguments, the standard by which something is measured to determine its quality or value.

definition, argument of an argument in which the claim specifies that something does or does not meet the conditions or features set forth in a definition: *Affirmative action is discrimination.*

deliberative argument an argument that deals with action to be taken in the future, focusing on matters of policy. Deliberative arguments include parliamentary debates and campaign platforms.

dogmatism a fallacy of argument in which a claim is supported on the grounds that it is the only conclusion acceptable within a given community.

either-or **choice** a fallacy of argument in which a complicated issue is represented as offering only two possible courses of action, one of which is made to seem vastly preferable to the other. *Either-or* choices generally misrepresent complicated arguments by oversimplifying them.

emotional appeal a strategy in which a writer tries to generate specific emotions (such as fear, envy, anger, or pity) in an audience to dispose it to accept a claim.

enthymeme in Toulmin argument, a statement that links a claim to a supporting reason: *The bank will fail* (claim) *because it has lost the support of its largest investors* (reason). In classical rhetoric, an enthymeme is a *syllogism* with one term understood but not stated: *Socrates is mortal because he is a human being.* (The understood term is: *All human beings are mortal.*)

epideictic argument see *ceremonial argument.*

equivocation a fallacy of argument in which a lie is given the appearance of truth, or in which the truth is misrepresented in deceptive language.

essential condition in a definition, an element that must be part of the definition but, by itself, isn't enough to define the term. An essential condition in defining a bird might be "winged": all birds have wings, yet wings alone do not define a bird since some insects and mammals also have wings. (See also *accidental condition* and *sufficient condition.*)

ethical appeal see *character, appeal based on,* and *ethos.*

ethnographic observation a form of field research involving close and extended observation of a group, event, or phenomenon; careful and detailed note-taking during the observation; analysis of the notes; and interpretation of that analysis.

ethos the self-image a writer creates to define a relationship with readers. In arguments, most writers try to establish an ethos that suggests honesty and credibility.

evaluation, argument of an argument in which the claim specifies that something does or does not meet established criteria: *The Nikon F5 is the most sophisticated 35mm camera currently available.*

evidence material offered to support an argument. See *artistic appeal* and *inartistic appeal.*

example, definition by a definition that operates by identifying individual examples of what is being defined: *Sports car—Corvette, Viper, Miata, Boxster.*

experimental evidence evidence gathered through experimentation; often evidence that can be quantified (for example, a survey of students before and after an election might yield statistical evidence about changes in their attitudes toward the candidates). Experimental evidence is frequently crucial to scientific arguments.

fact, argument of an argument in which the claim is a statement that can be proved or disproved with specific evidence or testimony: *The winter of 1998 in the United States was probably the warmest on record.*

fallacy of argument a flaw in the structure of an argument that renders its conclusion invalid or suspect. See *ad hominem argument, bandwagon appeal, begging the question, dogmatism, either-or choice, equivocation, false authority, faulty analogy, faulty causality, hasty generalization, moral equivalence, non sequitur, scare tactic, sentimental appeal,* and *slippery slope.*

false authority a fallacy of argument in which a claim is based on the expertise of someone who lacks appropriate credentials.

faulty analogy a fallacy of argument in which a comparison between two objects or concepts is inaccurate or inconsequential.

faulty causality a fallacy of argument in which an unwarranted assumption is made that because one event follows another, the first event causes the second. Faulty causality forms the basis of many superstitions.

forensic argument an argument that deals with actions that have occurred in the past. Sometimes called judicial arguments, forensic arguments include legal cases involving judgments of guilt or innocence.

formal definition a definition that identifies something first by the general class to which it belongs (*genus*) and then by the characteristics that distinguish it from other members of that class (*species*): *Baseball is a game* (genus) *played on a diamond by opposing teams of nine players who score runs by circling bases after striking a ball with a bat* (species).

genus in a definition, the general class to which an object or concept belongs: *baseball is a sport; green is a color.*

grounds in Toulmin argument, the evidence provided to support a claim or reason, or *enthymeme.*

hasty generalization a fallacy of argument in which an inference is drawn from insufficient data.

hyperbole use of overstatement for special effect.

hypothesis an assumption about what the findings of one's research or the conclusion to one's argument may be. A hypothesis must always be tested against evidence, counterarguments, and so on.

immediate reason the cause that leads directly to an effect, such as an automobile accident that results in an injury to the driver. (See also *necessary reason* and *sufficient reason.*)

inartistic appeal support for an argument using facts, statistics, eyewitness testimony, or other evidence the writer finds. (See also *artistic appeal.*)

intended readers the actual, real-life people whom a writer consciously wants to address in a piece of writing.

invention the process of finding and creating arguments to support a claim.

inverted word order moving grammatical elements of a sentence out of their usual order (subject-verb-object/complement) for special effect, as in *Tired I was; sleepy I was not.*

invitational argument a term used by Sonja Foss to describe arguments that are aimed not at vanquishing an opponent but at inviting others to collaborate in exploring mutually satisfying ways to solve problems.

invoked readers the readers directly addressed or implied in a text, which may include some that the writer did not consciously intend to reach. An argument that refers to *those who have experienced a major trauma*, for example, invokes all readers who have undergone this experience.

irony use of language that suggests a meaning in contrast to the literal meaning of the words.

line of argument a strategy or approach used in an argument. Argumentative strategies include appeals to the heart (emotional appeals), to values, to character (ethical appeals), and to facts and reason (logical appeals).

logical appeal a strategy in which a writer uses facts, evidence, and reason to make audience members accept a claim.

metaphor a figure of speech that makes a comparison, as in *The ship was a beacon of hope*.

moral equivalence a fallacy of argument in which no distinction is made between serious issues, problems, or failings and much less important ones.

necessary reason a cause that must be present for an effect to occur; for example, infection with a particular virus is a necessary reason for the development of AIDS. (See also *immediate reason* and *sufficient reason*.)

non sequitur a fallacy of argument in which claims, reasons, or warrants fail to connect logically; one point does not follow from another. *If you're really my friend, you'll lend me five hundred dollars.*

operational definition a definition that identifies an object by what it does or by the conditions that create it: *A line is the shortest distance between two points*.

parallelism use of similar grammatical structures or forms to create pleasing rhythms and other effects, as in *in the classroom, on the playground, and at the mall*.

parody a form of humor in which a writer transforms something familiar into a different form to make a comic point.

pathetic appeal see *emotional appeal*.

persuasion the act of seeking to change someone else's point of view.

precedents actions or decisions in the past that have established a pattern or model for subsequent actions. Precedents are particularly important in legal cases.

prejudices irrational beliefs, usually based on inadequate or outdated information.

premise a statement or position regarded as true and upon which other claims are based.

propaganda an argument that seeks to advance a point of view without regard to reason, fairness, or truth.

proposal argument an argument in which a claim is made in favor of or opposing a specific course of action: *Sport utility vehicles should have to meet the same fuel economy standards as passenger cars.*

qualifiers words or phrases that limit the scope of a claim: *usually; in a few cases; under these circumstances.*

qualitative argument an argument of evaluation that relies on non-numerical criteria supported by reason, tradition, precedent, or logic.

quantitative argument an argument of evaluation that relies on criteria that can be measured, counted, or demonstrated objectively.

reason in writing, a statement that expands a claim by offering evidence to support it. The reason may be a statement of fact or another claim. In Toulmin argument, a *reason* is attached to a *claim* by a *warrant,* a statement that establishes the logical connection between claim and supporting reason.

rebuttal an answer that challenges or refutes a specific claim or charge. Rebuttals may also be offered by writers who anticipate objections to the claims or evidence they offer.

rebuttal, conditions of in Toulmin argument, potential objections to an argument. Writers need to anticipate such conditions in shaping their arguments.

reversed structures a figure of speech, referred to more formally as "chaismus," that involves the inversion of clauses, as in *What is good in your writing is not original; what is original is not good.*

rhetoric the art of persuasion. Western rhetoric originated in ancient Greece as a discipline to prepare citizens for arguing cases in court.

rhetorical questions questions posed to raise an issue or create an effect rather than to get a response: *You may well wonder, "What's in a name?"*

ridicule humor, usually mean-spirited, directed at a particular target.

Rogerian argument an approach to argumentation that is based on the principle, articulated by psychotherapist Carl Rogers, that audiences respond best when they do not feel threatened. Rogerian argument stresses trust and urges those who disagree to find common ground.

satire a form of humor in which a writer uses wit to expose—and possibly correct—human failings.

scare tactic a fallacy of argument in which an issue is presented in terms of exaggerated threats or dangers.

scheme a figure of speech that involves a special arrangement of words, such as inversion.

sentimental appeal a fallacy of argument in which an appeal is based on excessive emotion.

simile a comparison that uses *like* or *as: My love is like a red, red rose* or *I wandered lonely as a cloud.*

slippery slope a fallacy of argument in which it is suggested that a relatively inconsequential action or choice today will have serious adverse consequences in the future.

species in a definition, the particular features that distinguish one member of a *genus* from another: *Baseball is a sport* (genus) *played on a diamond by teams of nine players* (species).

stasis theory in classical rhetoric, a method for coming up with appropriate arguments by determining the nature of a given situation: *a question of fact; of definition; of quality;* or *of policy.*

sufficient condition in a definition, an element or set of elements adequate to define a term. A sufficient condition in defining God, for example, might be "supreme being" or "first cause." No other conditions are necessary, though many might be made. (See also *accidental condition* and *essential condition.*)

sufficient reason a cause that alone is enough to produce a particular effect; for example, a particular level of smoke in the air will set off a smoke alarm. (See also *immediate reason* and *necessary reason.*)

syllogism in formal logic, a structure of deductive logic in which correctly formed major and minor premises lead to a necessary conclusion:

Major premise	All human beings are mortal.
Minor premise	Socrates is a human being.
Conclusion	Socrates is mortal.

thesis a sentence that succinctly states a writer's main point.

Toulmin argument a method of informal logic first described by Stephen Toulmin in *The Uses of Argument* (1958). Toulmin argument describes the key components of an argument as the *claim, reason, warrant, backing,* and *grounds.*

trope a figure of speech that involves a change in the usual meaning or signification of words, such as *metaphor, simile,* and *analogy.*

understatement a figure of speech, more formally called "litotes," that makes a weaker statement than a situation seems to call for. It can lead to very powerful as well as to humorous effects.

values, appeal to a strategy in which a writer invokes shared principles and traditions of a society as a reason for accepting a claim.

warrant in Toulmin argument, the statement (expressed or implied) that establishes the logical connection between a claim and its supporting reason.

Claim	Don't eat that mushroom;
Reason	it's poisonous.
Warrant	What is poisonous should not be eaten.

INDEX

faulty causality, 321, 372
feasibility in proposal, 197
Felton, George, 220
field research, 336–37
figurative language, 239–50
    analogy, 243
    anaphora, 246
    anatonomasia, 245
    antithesis, 246
    hyperbole, 244
    inverted word order, 246
    irony, 245
    metaphor, 242
    parallelism, 246
    reversed structures, 247
    rhetorical questions, 245
    simile, 242–43
    understatement, 244–45
films
    APA style in citing, 367
    MLA style in citing, 355, 356
firsthand evidence, 299–302
forensic arguments, 11–12, 373
formal definitions, 112, 373
formal logic, 82
formal presentations, 286–87
Foss, Sonja, 5
Frawley, Jill, 66
free speech, 114
Frost, Robert, 242
FTP (file transfer protocol) site
    APA style in citing, 365
    MLA style in citing, 355
Fulwood, Sam, III, 305
future, arguments about, 12

genus, 112, 373
Gier, Joseph, 170
Gingrich, Newt, 12, 60
Goodman, W. Charisse, 70
gopher site
    APA style in citing, 365
    MLA style in citing, 355

Gordon, Anita, 163
government documents
    APA style in citing, 362
    MLA style in citing, 350
graphics, 283
Graves, Robert, 103
greater or lesser good, arguments
    about, 84
Griffin, Susan, 42
grounds, 99–102, 373

hard evidence, 188
hasty generalization, 320–21, 373
Himes, Chester, 224
Himmelfarb, Gertrude, 85
Hodges, Alan, 103
Hoff, Florence, 40
hooks, bell, 38–39, 51, 242
Hughes, Langston, 240
humor
    abstract, 226
    in character-based arguments, 217
    in emotional arguments, 54–55
    exaggeration in, 220–21
    kinds of, 219–24
    parody in, 84, 218, 223, 228–29
    satire in, 221–23
    signifying, 223–24
humorous arguments, 215–36
    claims in, 227–28
    developing, 224–25
    key features of, 225–26
    proposal in, 228–29
    responses in, 229–30
    topics in, 227
Hurston, Zora Neale, 219
hyperbole, 244, 373
hypotheses in causal arguments,
    168–69, 373

images, emotional power of, 267–68.
    See also visual arguments